COLLINS GUIDE TO

Wild Life in House and Home

Text
HENRI MOURIER
AND
OVE WINDING

Illustrations by
EBBE SUNESEN

Translated and adapted by
GWYNNE VEVERS

Collins
8 Grafton Street, London

Design: Ebbe Sunesen
Photographs: Preben Bang
Filmset by Jolly & Barber Ltd, Rugby, Warwickshire
Printed and bound by Wm. Collins Sons & Co., Ltd., Glasgow

Reprinted in this paperback edition 1986

How to use this book

On finding an animal track or sign in the house, e.g. droppings, holes in woodwork or a gnawed carpet, the list of contents should guide the reader to the section of the book where such tracks and signs are described. The illustrations will help in the identification of the animal concerned.

On finding an actual animal in the house the reader should turn first to the key on p. 12. This and the following keys will lead him to the colour plates and he can then compare his specimen with the animal types depicted. Naturally one could turn first to the plates and look through them without consulting the keys.

The plates indicate the pages where a more detailed description of the animal is given, and the index will refer to other places in the book where the animal is mentioned.

In various places throughout the book the reader will find special sections that deal with the prevention and control of attacks by pests and other animals which in one way or another affect the life of man in his home.

ISBN 0 00 219367 1

Contents

Foreword

In writing this book the aim has been to produce a practical handbook which gives a comprehensive account of the animals which can be met indoors in Europe, with particular attention to the tracks and signs they leave and the damage they sometimes do. The use of the book does not require any previous knowledge of zoology, and the identifications are based entirely on characters which can be seen with the naked eye or with an ordinary good lens.

The book has been written not only for the private house owner, but should be equally useful to all those who in their daily life have to deal with problems involving injurious animals in house, shop, store and factory. By no means all the animals encountered indoors are in any way injurious, so the book should also appeal to all those who have a general interest in biology.

The book was originally planned in collaboration with Preben Dahlstrøm who before he died had produced the keys on pages 12–17 and the colour plates on pages 18 and 19.

The book's photographer and its two authors are associated with the Danish State Pest Laboratory, and they are much indebted to Hans Wickmand, its Director from 1948 to 1975.

Introduction

If one looks back on the history of man which, so far as is known, has covered a period of perhaps a million years, it will be apparent that for some 99 per cent of this time he has been a hunter and gatherer of food. That is, he has collected edible fruits and vegetation, larvae and other small invertebrate animals. At an early period in his history man also learnt to hunt larger animals with increasingly improved weapons and methods. The provision of food for the family or group depended upon what the surrounding countryside had to offer, and there was no knowledge on how to store foodstuffs in any quantity.

True pests of stored goods were therefore unknown to these ancestors, who must however have had problems with blowfly maggots attacking their game and other pests destroying their hides and skins.

Nor would they have been spared by the true parasites. Lice must have infested their hair and bed bugs and fleas must have multiplied, generation after generation, over thousands of years. Sleep must have been disturbed by mosquitoes, with their ceaseless buzzing, and also by the numerous small invertebrates which lived in their dwellings. These would include swarms of flies and other insects which would be attracted by domestic refuse.

About 10,000 years ago there came a significant change. Man began to plant and harvest crops and to keep domestic animals. This new life form brought many advantages, for it provided a more secure existence and the soil could feed far more people when it was used in this way. But it also brought problems. Animals which had hitherto fed on scattered wild grass seeds now had the opportunity, when their food plants were sown in whole fields, to multiply as never before. Food specialists among the invertebrates, which had previously lived in winter on stores they collected during summer and autumn, could now enter and exploit the enormous food stores collected by man.

As man started to establish permanent dwellings, these provided excellent living quarters for many animal species, whether in the house itself or in the outhouses used by the domestic animals. There was also woodwork to gnaw and textiles and furs to eat.

The buildings provided new hunting grounds for animals such as spiders, and also places for nesting and spending the winter for many animals which had previously used hollow trees and rock crevices. Throughout the ages these man-made facilities increased, and even today, with all our technical aids, we are far from being alone in our houses and stores.

Collecting honey;
wall painting c. *5000 B.P.*

HOUSES AS ANIMAL HABITATS

In addition to a favourable climate an animal must have the right food and plenty of places to hide or shelter in if it is to thrive. The average house certainly has plenty of hiding-places, but it does not always fulfil the other requirements. It would be wrong to suppose that the comfortable warmth of our houses throughout the year would be ideal for many invertebrates, for this is far from being the case.

The climate in our houses is very different from the summer climate outdoors in temperate latitudes. Room temperatures may be about the same as on a warm summer's day, but the air is sometimes bone-dry, giving a desert-like climate. This is something that we ourselves may sometimes find uncomfortable, but for most invertebrates it can be catastrophic.

As a result, very few of the animals found indoors are also found outdoors. This, of course, does not apply to the many small invertebrate animals such as moths which come in through windows and doors at night, being attracted by the light. These soon die unless they can find their way out.

Most of the 'house animals' come originally from other parts of the world. Curiously enough, only a few of them are found living in the wild, and so it is not always possible to say exactly where they originally came from, but most of them probably originated in tropical or subtropical regions. Animals with such specialized habits have probably never been numerous in the wild, and may have only become successful on entering a man-made habitat. Some of the species concerned have been associated with human habitations for thousands of years, and during this long period of time, which for insects would involve thousands of generations, they have had plenty of opportunity to evolve new types, with habits and forms that differ considerably from the original ancestral forms.

The insect and other invertebrate pests that live indoors must not therefore be regarded as casual visitors, but rather as highly specialized residents. They are relatively free from competitors and predators, and they usually have a plentiful supply of suitable food.

ANIMAL NAMES AND SYSTEMATICS

In using a book of this type it is essential to understand the method of naming animals. The scientific study known as systematics is concerned with naming animals and plants, and with arranging them in groups which indicate their relationships with one another.

Modern systematics is based on the work of the Swedish naturalist Carl von Linné (1707–1778), also known as Linnaeus. He gave all the then known plants and animals a Latin name and arranged them in groups according to their physical appearance. He chose Latin because at that time this was the international language of science.

The principles of nomenclature established by Linnaeus are still in use today. The Latin or scientific name of an animal or plant consists of two parts, the first denoting the genus (plural genera), the second the species. In the present book it is necessary to use the scientific names because many of the animals mentioned do not have common English names, and when these do exist they are often not standard throughout the country. For example, the song thrush is known in Scotland as a mavis.

In 1859 a book was published which has had a profound effect on man's understanding of the world about him.

Carl von Linné (1707–1778)

Charles Darwin (1809–1882)

This was *The Origin of Species*, by the English scientist Charles Darwin (1809–1882), who put forward the theory of natural selection, which seeks to explain how all existing species have evolved from species which have existed in past ages. Since Darwin's time systematics has become more than a means of naming animals and plants; it has in many cases shown their relationships by grouping together those which are thought to have evolved from a common ancestor. The animal kingdom has been divided into some 14 major groups, known as phyla (singular phylum). Only a few of these have representatives occurring indoors, namely: worms, molluscs, arthropods and vertebrates. The worms are represented in houses only by earthworms, see p. 195. The molluscs, a group that includes snails and bivalves, are not normally found in houses, except for certain slugs that occur in cellars (see p. 164). The vertebrates or animals with a vertebral column include fishes, amphibians, reptiles, birds and mammals, including of course man.

Arthropods are animals with jointed legs. The group contains the crustaceans, scorpions, millipedes, centipedes, mites, spiders and last but not least the insects. About one million animal species have been described and more than three-quarters of these are arthropods. It is not surprising, therefore, that most of the animals found in houses belong among the arthropods.

ARTHROPOD STRUCTURE

As the name implies arthropod limbs are divided into joints; the body too is segmented. The most striking feature, however, is that, in contrast to the vertebrates, arthropods have an external skeleton. Their skin is modified to form a firm exoskeleton, which serves as a protection and also for the attachment of muscles.

The *crustaceans* are primarily aquatic animals and they breathe by means of gills. The body is divided into head, thorax and abdomen. The head has three pairs of jaw-like mouthparts and two pairs of antennae. The only crustaceans that concern us here are the wood-lice or slaters, known zoologically as the Isopoda.

The body of a *scorpion* has a front part or cephalothorax with four pairs of limbs and an abdomen without limbs. The last abdominal segment forms a kind of tail which ends in a sting. They have two pairs of mouthparts, of which one pair is in the forms of pincers.

False scorpions are broadly speaking built on the same plan as the true scorpions, but they lack the tail and sting.

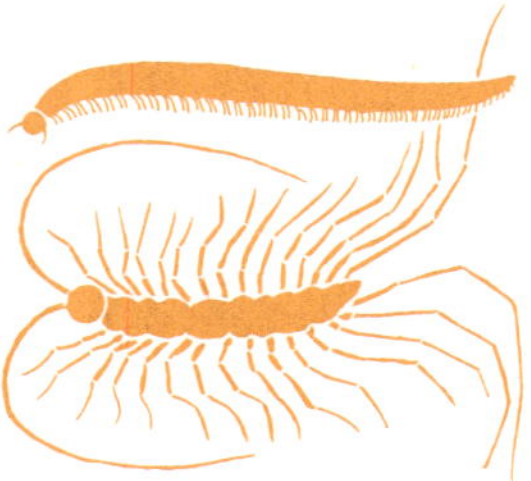

Millipedes and *centipedes* have a distinct head but the thorax and abdomen are united. The body consists of numerous segments, and each of these has one pair of legs, or in the true millipedes two pairs.

Spiders have a body consisting of two parts, which are almost the same size. The front part is formed from the modified head and thorax, and carries the eyes, mouthparts and four pairs of limbs. The rear part or abdomen has no limbs, apart from the spinnerets which are actually modified limbs.

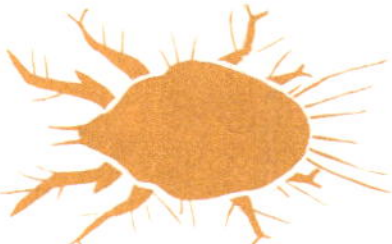

Mites also have four pairs of legs, but the head, thorax and abdomen are fused to form a body showing no apparent segmentation.

Harvestmen also have an apparently unsegmented body, but are much larger than the mites, and the four pairs of legs are extremely long in relation to the body.

Insects are the dominant group within the arthropods. The body is in three parts: head, thorax and abdomen. The head carries the mouthparts, eyes and antennae. The thorax has three segments, each with a pair of legs, and in most insects there is a pair of wings on each of the two foremost thoracic segments. The remaining twelve segments form the abdomen, which contains the main organs such as the alimentary canal and the gonads.

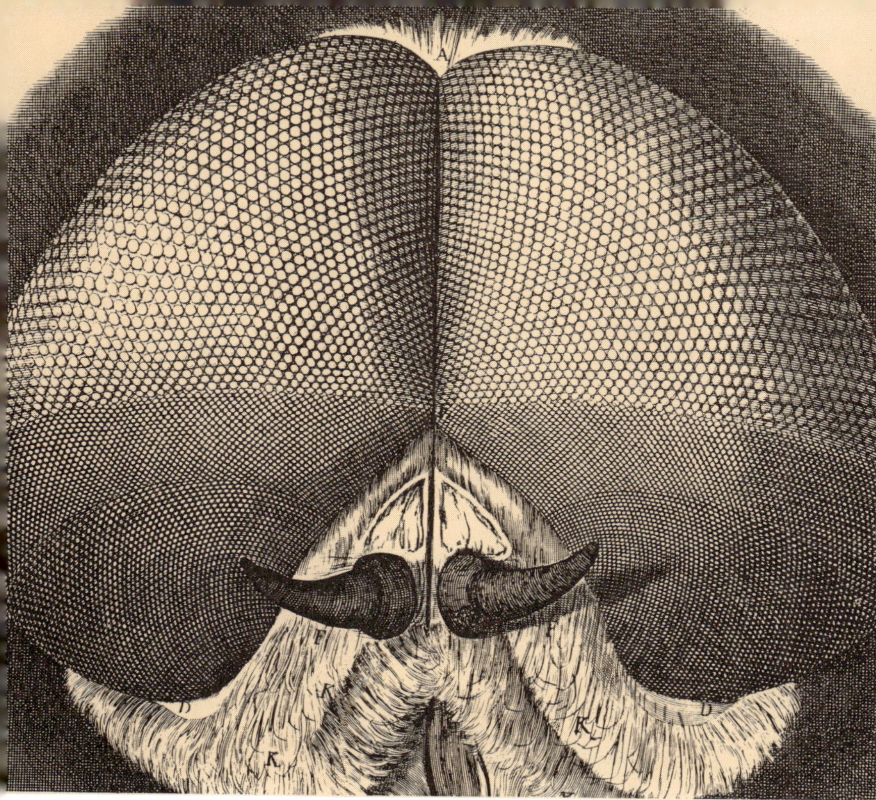

Compound eye of a fly. Copper engraving from Robert Hooke: Micrographia, *1665*

ARTHROPOD SENSES AND BEHAVIOUR

An animal's existence depends upon its ability to avoid being eaten by predators, to find food and to be able to find other members of its species. The animal must, therefore, have sense organs which can receive information about what is happening around it, and it must have a nervous system which can transmit this information to organs capable of giving an appropriate response. With their hard exoskeleton, insects and other arthropods appear somewhat stiff, and one might wonder how much they actually perceive. In fact they receive a great amount of information about what is going on around them and in general they have the same kinds of senses as man and the other vertebrates: touch, hearing, vision, sense of heat and cold, and the chemical senses of taste and smell. It would be wrong, however, to think that they perceive the outside world in the same way as we do.

In the arthropods, the sense of *touch* is associated with various types of hair. When a hair is touched it stimulates a sensory cell which then sends a message to the central nervous system.
Hearing may be associated with hairs which are moved by sound waves, but there are also some insects which have developed true tympanic organs, as for example in the crickets.

Such organs resemble part of a vertebrate ear in having a thin membrane which is made to vibrate by sound waves. *Vision* in the insects is served by the large lateral compound eyes, which are often made up of thousands of individual eyelets or ommatidia.

Taste and *smell* are extremely well developed in many insects. They are associated with certain specialized sensory hairs, which are situated on many parts of the body but particularly on the mouthparts and antennae.

The perception of *heat* and *cold* is not localized in special sense organs, but arthropods are probably made aware of the temperature in the first place by its effect on their internal body processes.

The arthropods are therefore very well provided with senses, which are often extremely sensitive. Bluebottles, for example, can smell meat at a distance of several kilometres and find their way to it with unfailing accuracy.

The behaviour of invertebrates often appears to be extremely rational but there is no evidence that they can actually think about what they are doing.

If their normal activity appears to be rational, this is because they have innate behaviour patterns which are in certain situations released by a given set of stimuli. Animals, such as insects and other arthropods, which live such a short time, are in fact better served by effective, inbuilt reactions than by having a well-developed capacity to learn, for they simply do not have the time to gain experience and to learn from it.

WHERE DO INVERTEBRATES COME FROM?

For a long time it was thought that small invertebrate animals appeared spontaneously, from dirt and dust, and indeed even that small vertebrates, such as mice, came from woollen textiles. It was only in 1650 that the Italian physician Francesco Redi finally showed that maggots are the larvae of flies. He placed meat and fish heads in two containers, tied a cover over one of them, and left the other uncovered. After some days there were maggots in the open container, which had been visited by bluebottles, but none in the closed container. This was a very simple experiment, but it demonstrated an extremely important biological principle, namely that even the smallest animals do not arise spontaneously but are always produced by an individual of the same species. There is good reason to mention this principle, for many people still have a deep-rooted feeling that animals, such as lice and fleas, can arise from dirt. This is not right, although it is true to say that they may be more difficult to get rid of where the standard of hygiene is low.

Man with flea. 16th-century woodcut.

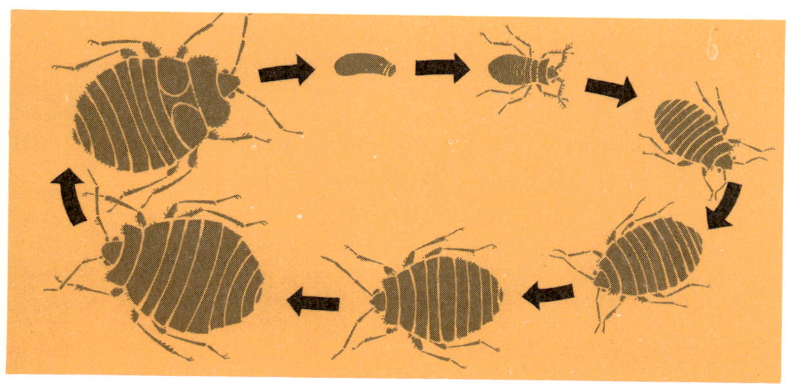

ARTHROPOD DEVELOPMENT

Most arthropods lay eggs, but there are a few that produce live young. One of the disadvantages of having an external skeleton is that growth cannot proceed gradually, and so during their life arthropods have to moult a number of times, becoming a little larger each time. Among the insects development is associated with the process known as metamorphosis, which can take place in two different ways. In some insects, such as bed bugs and cockroaches, the newly hatched young look like miniature versions of the adults. They go through a number of stages, separated by a series of moults. This is known as incomplete metamorphosis. Other insects, such as flies, beetles and butterflies, have complete metamorphosis, in which the young stages show no resemblance at all to the adults. Here a special immobile stage, the pupa, occurs between the larva and the adult. When the adult insect emerges from the pupal stage it ceases to grow, so there is no truth in the idea that, for example, small flies can become large flies.

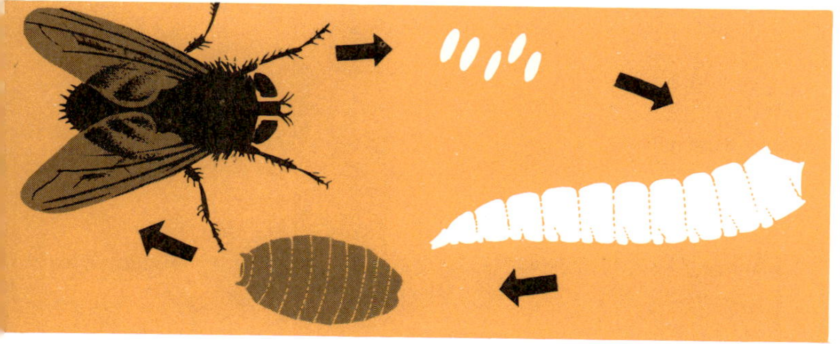

Keys

Start with the figures on the left hand side of the key. The bracket alongside each of these figures encloses 2–4 choices. Select the most suitable alternative. Your choice leads either to a new figure or directly to a species or an animal group. The keys are based entirely on external characters, which can be seen with the naked eye or with the help of a lens giving a magnification of *c*. 5 times.

Naturally one may make a mistake and must then start again. It is a good idea to use the plates as an aid when using the keys.

In view of the nature of the material these keys are naturally very approximate. It is no use taking them out into the fields or woodland, for they have been designed exclusively for the identification of animals commonly found indoors.

Key to the Main Groups

1
- Without legs ... **2**
- With three pairs of legs. Often with wings ... **insects,** key II, p. 13
  - N.B. Newly hatched mites also have three pairs of legs, but they are extremely small, under 1 mm, see Plate 3, p. 20
- With four pairs of legs ... **spiders,** mites, scorpions etc., key I, p. 13
- With more than four pairs of legs ... **3**

2
- It may be a slug ... **slugs,** see p. 18
- It may be a worm ... **worms,** see p. 18
- It may be a maggot-like insect larva ... **insect larvae,** key III, p. 1

3
- With three pairs of true legs, and prolegs on abdomen ... **certain insect larvae,** key III, p. 1
- With 7 pairs of legs ... **woodlice,** see p. 1
- With many legs, more than 14 pairs ...

4
- Flat animals, legs protruding laterally ... **centipedes,** see p. 1
- Cylindrical animals, legs attached ventrally ... **millipedes,** see p. 1

KEY I, animals with 4 pairs of legs; spiders, mites, scorpions etc.

1 Abdomen with distinct joints **2**
Abdomen without distinct joints **4**

2 Abdomen elongated, forming tail with sting .... **scorpions,** see Plate 2, p. 19
Abdomen not ending in a tail **3**

3 Small animals (less than 5 mm), with claws .... **false scorpions,** see Plate 2, p. 19
Larger animals with very long legs .... **harvestmen,** see Plate 2, p. 19

4 Body clearly divided into two parts .... **spiders,** see Plate 2, p. 19
Very small animals with undivided body .... **mites,** see Plate 3, p. 20

KEY II, animals with 3 pairs of legs; insects

1 Wings well developed **2**
N.B. Front wings may be developed as 'shields' which cover the flight wings when these are not in use
Wings lacking **9**

2 Wings small, with hairy fringes. Small animals, less than 2 mm .... **thrips,** Plate 5, p. 22
All the wings transparent, possibly with a few hairs.. **3**
Front pair of wings not transparent **5**

3 With a single pair of transparent wings .... **flies,** see Plates 13, 14, 15, pp. 30–32

With 2 pairs of transparent wings 4

4 Front pair of wings larger than back pair .... **wasps, bees, chalcids, ichneumons, 'flying ants',** Plates 11–13, pp. 28–30

Wings all about the same size, transparent or smoke-coloured .... **winged termites,** Plate 3, p. 20

Wings all about the same size, greenish .... **lacewings,** Plate 5, p. 22

5 Wings densely covered with scales, which are easily rubbed off .... **butterflies and moths,** Plates 6, 7, pp. 23, 24

Front pair of wings as shields which are parchment-like, leathery or hard 6

6 Front wings short, covering only front part of abdomen 7

Front wings covering whole of abdomen, or nearly so 8

7 Abdomen in a pair of forceps .... **earwigs,** Plate 3, p. 20

Abdomen not ending in forceps .... **staphylinid beetles,** Plate 8, p. 25

Front part of front wings leathery, rear part clear and transparent .... **true bugs,** Plate 5, p. 22

8 Front wings (tegmina) leathery with distinct veins. Antennae long, whip-like .... **cockroaches** or **crickets,** Plates 3, 4, pp. 20, 21

Front wings (elytra) forming hard shields, without distinct veins. Antennae normally short, never whip-like .... **beetles,** Plates 9–11, pp. 26–28

Elongated, worm-like .... **certain insect larvae,** key III, p. 16

9 Elongated or more plump, with dense hairs .... **certain insect larvae,** key III, p. 16

Not worm-like, and without hairs **10**

With three long segmented 'tails'

0 at hind end .... **silverfish,** Plate 3, p. 20

With a 'wasp waist' .... **ants,** Plate 13, p. 30

Without long 'tails' and without a 'wasp waist' **11**

Large animals, i.e. the adults are larger than an ordinary black garden ant **12**

1 About the size of a black ant, but pale .... **termites,** Plate 3, p. 20

Smaller than an ordinary black ant **14**

2 With biting mouthparts, and very long whip-like antennae .... **cockroaches,** Plate 4, p. 21

With sucking proboscis, folded in beneath head **13**

13 Body outline almost circular .... **bed bugs,** Plate 5, p. 22

Body outline oval, always covered with dust .... **fly bug** (nymphs), Plate 5, p. 22

14 Dark, shiny, hard (almost impossible to squash) .... **fleas,** Plate 15, p. 32

Paler and softer (easily squashed) **15**

15 Sluggish, living as parasites on man and animals .... **lice,** Plate 4, p. 21

Active, free-living **16**

16 With a forked springing organ at rear end........................ **springtails,** Plate 3, p. 20

Without a springing organ .... **booklice,** Plate 4, p. 21

KEY III, insect larvae

1 With prolegs on the abdomen .... **mealworms** or **caterpillars,** Plate 16, pp. 104–105

Without prolegs **2**

2 With powerful, functional legs **3**

Without legs, or with small rudimentary legs **4**

3 With dense hairs. The rear end with a tuft of hairs .... **dermestid larvae,** Plate 16, pp. 104–105

With scattered hairs, or naked ....**certain beetle larvae,** Plate 16, pp. 104–5

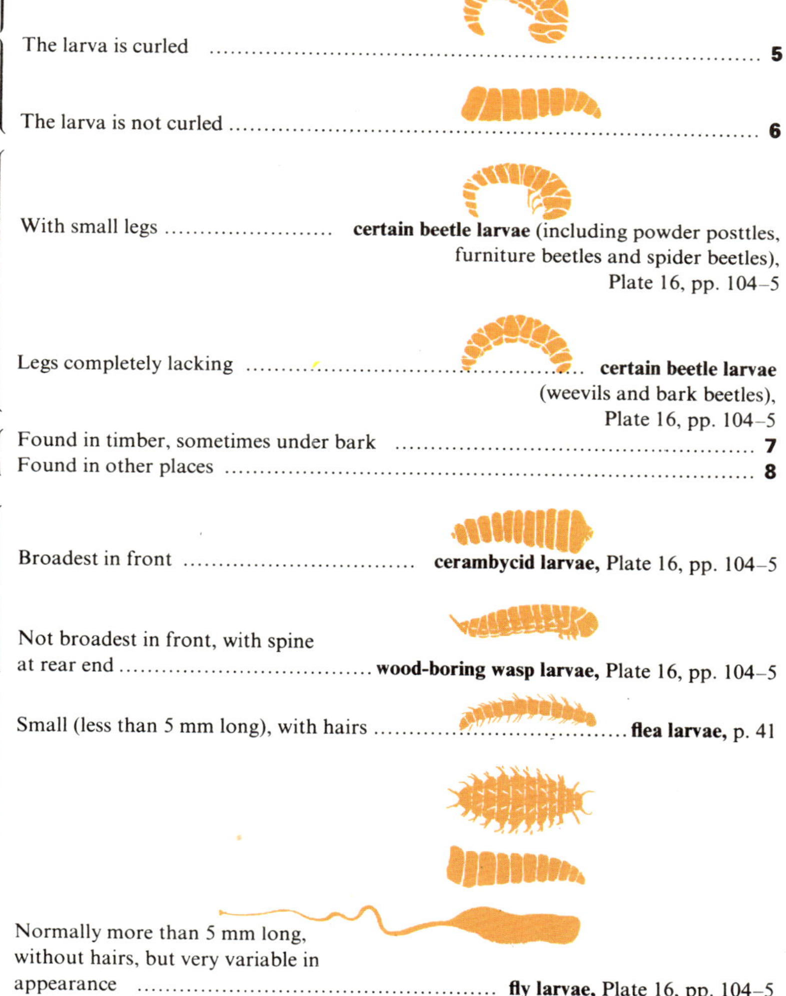

4 The larva is curled **5**

The larva is not curled **6**

With small legs .... **certain beetle larvae** (including powder posttles, furniture beetles and spider beetles),
5 Plate 16, pp. 104–5

Legs completely lacking .... **certain beetle larvae** (weevils and bark beetles), Plate 16, pp. 104–5

6 Found in timber, sometimes under bark **7**
Found in other places **8**

Broadest in front .... **cerambycid larvae,** Plate 16, pp. 104–5

Not broadest in front, with spine at rear end .... **wood-boring wasp larvae,** Plate 16, pp. 104–5

Small (less than 5 mm long), with hairs .... **flea larvae,** p. 41

Normally more than 5 mm long, without hairs, but very variable in appearance .... **fly larvae,** Plate 16, pp. 104–5

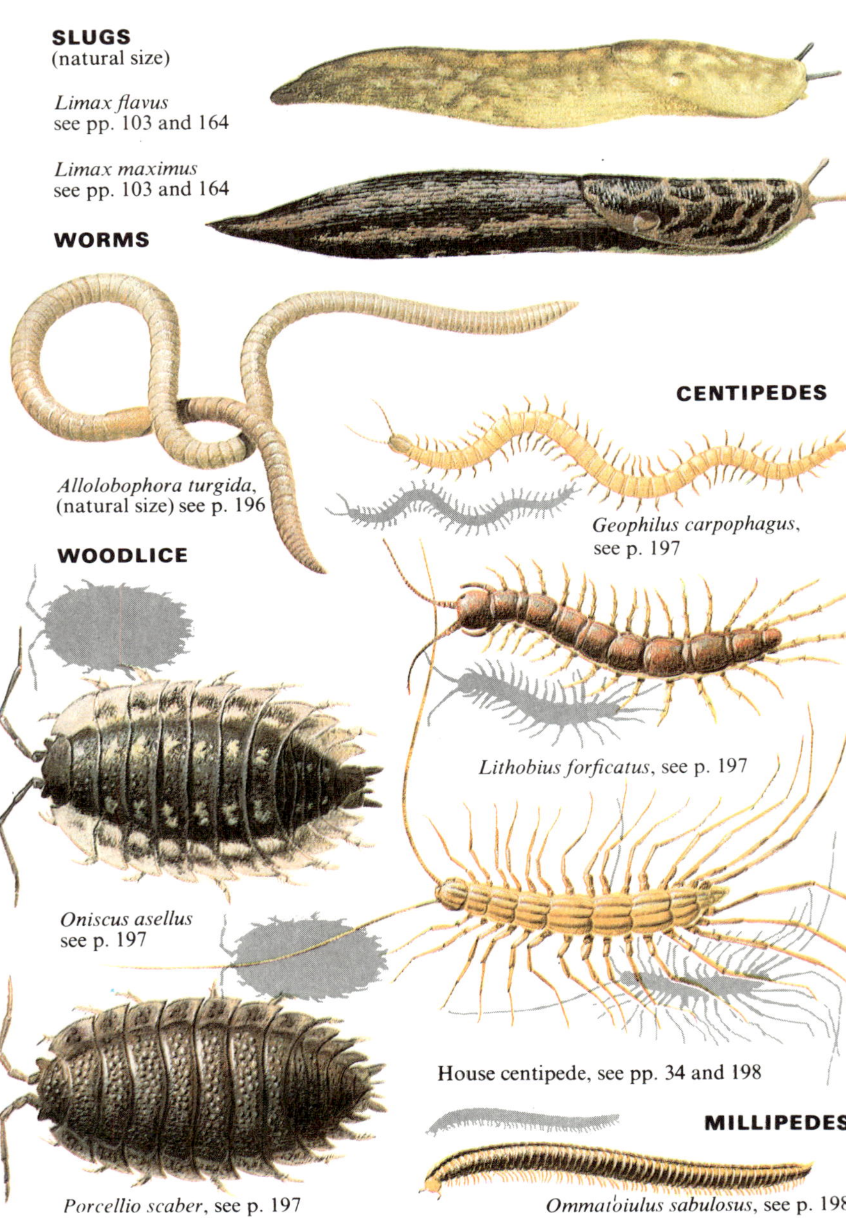

Grey outlines show the animals' natural size

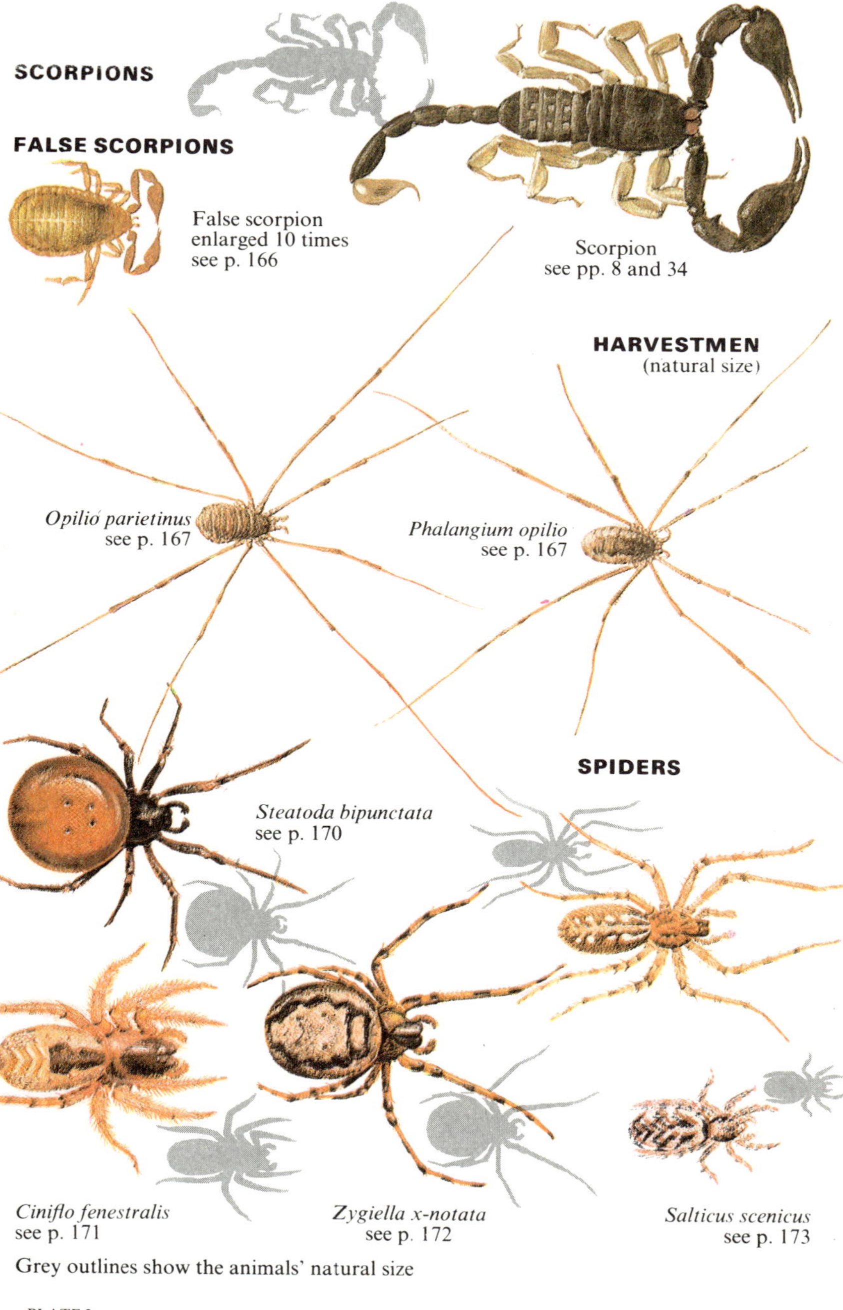

Grey outlines show the animals' natural size

MITES

All mites enlarged 10–20 times

Pigeon tick, see p. 36

Brown dog tick, see p. 37

Castor bean tick, see p. 36

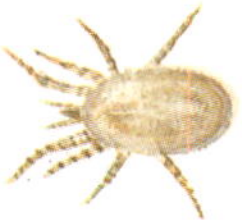

Red poultry mite see p. 35

Bed mite see p. 35

Common house mite see p. 100

Flour mite see pp. 57 and 212

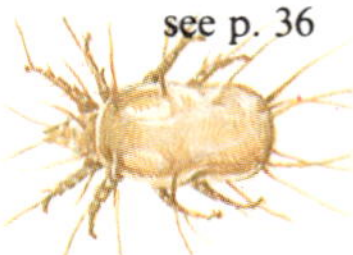

Cheese mite see p. 58

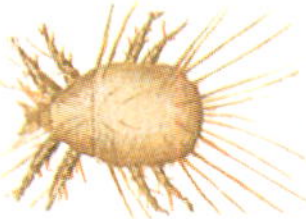

Tyrophagus longior see p. 58

Prune mite see pp. 35 and 59

Bryobia praetiosa see p. 198

Gamasid mite see p. 199

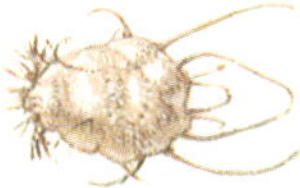

Itch mite see p. 35

INSECTS (grey outlines show the animals' natural size)

Thysanurans

Silverfish, see pp. 59 and 100

Firebrat, see p. 59

Springtails

see pp. 38 and 199

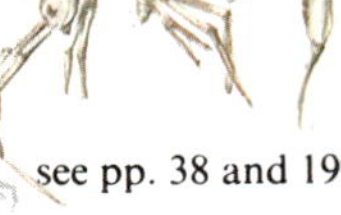

see pp. 38 and 19

Common earwig see p. 200

Crickets

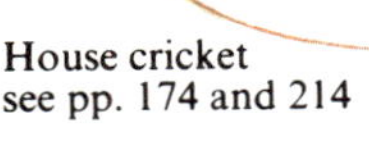

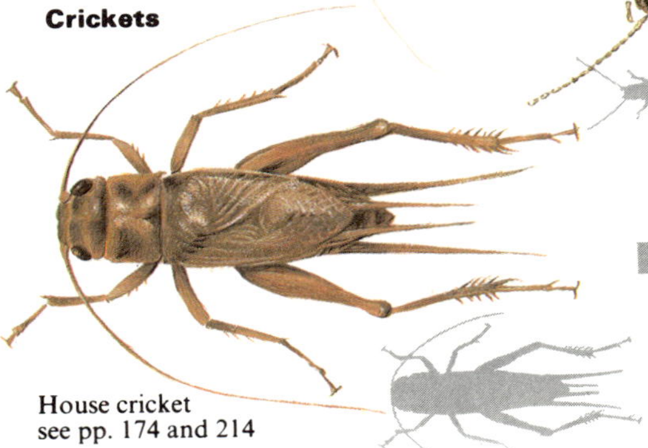

House cricket see pp. 174 and 214

TERMITES

Reticulotermes flavipes see p. 149

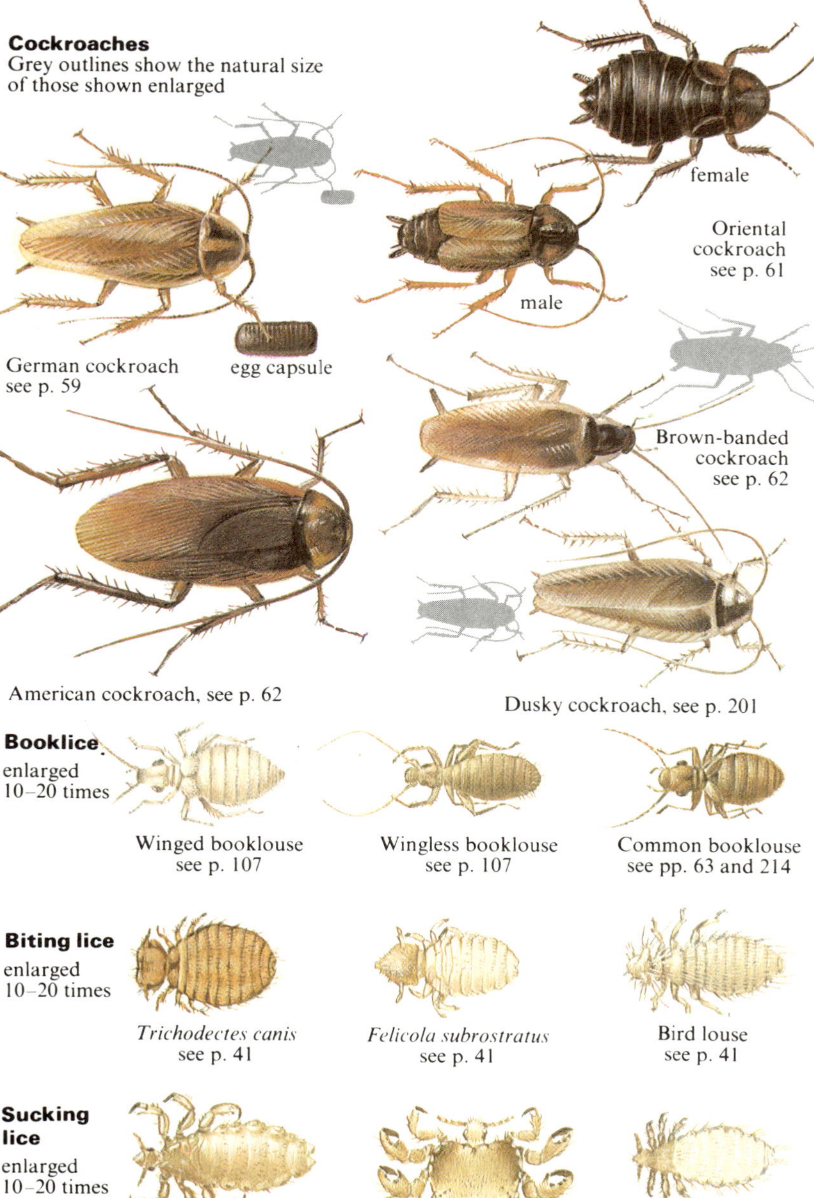
Cockroaches
Grey outlines show the natural size of those shown enlarged
female
male
Oriental cockroach see p. 61
German cockroach see p. 59
egg capsule
Brown-banded cockroach see p. 62
American cockroach, see p. 62
Dusky cockroach, see p. 201
Booklice
enlarged 10–20 times
Winged booklouse see p. 107
Wingless booklouse see p. 107
Common booklouse see pp. 63 and 214
Biting lice
enlarged 10–20 times
Trichodectes canis see p. 41
Felicola subrostratus see p. 41
Bird louse see p. 41
Sucking lice
enlarged 10–20 times
Head louse, see p. 39
Crab louse, see p. 40
Dog louse see p. 41

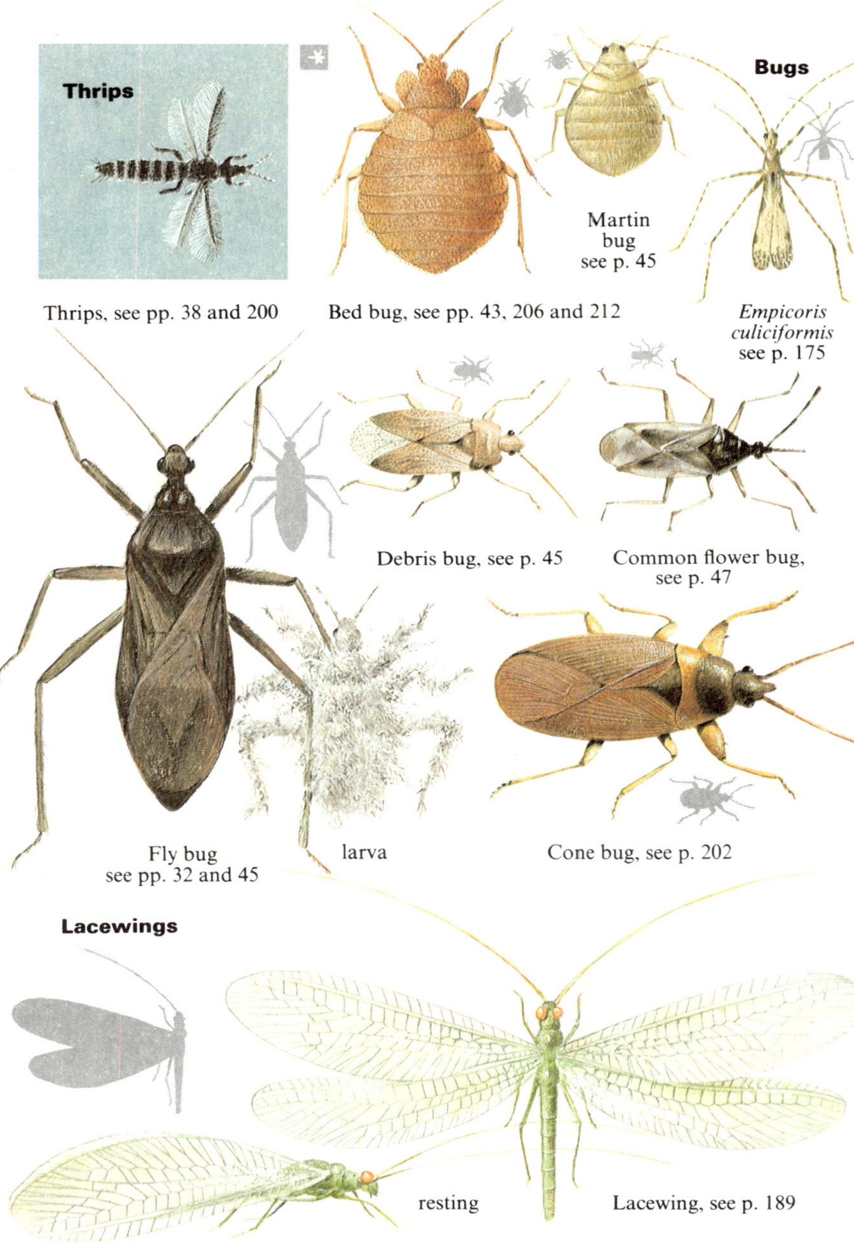

Grey outlines show the animals' natural size

Grey outlines show the natural size of the animals and their larvae

Aphomia sociella
see pp. 109 and 181

Caradrina clavipalpis, see p. 159

Grey outlines show natural size

Larvae, see pp. 104–5

Goat moth
see pp. 117 and 147

Large white pupa
see p. 193

Goat moth larva

Small tortoiseshell, see p. 192

Peacock, see p. 192

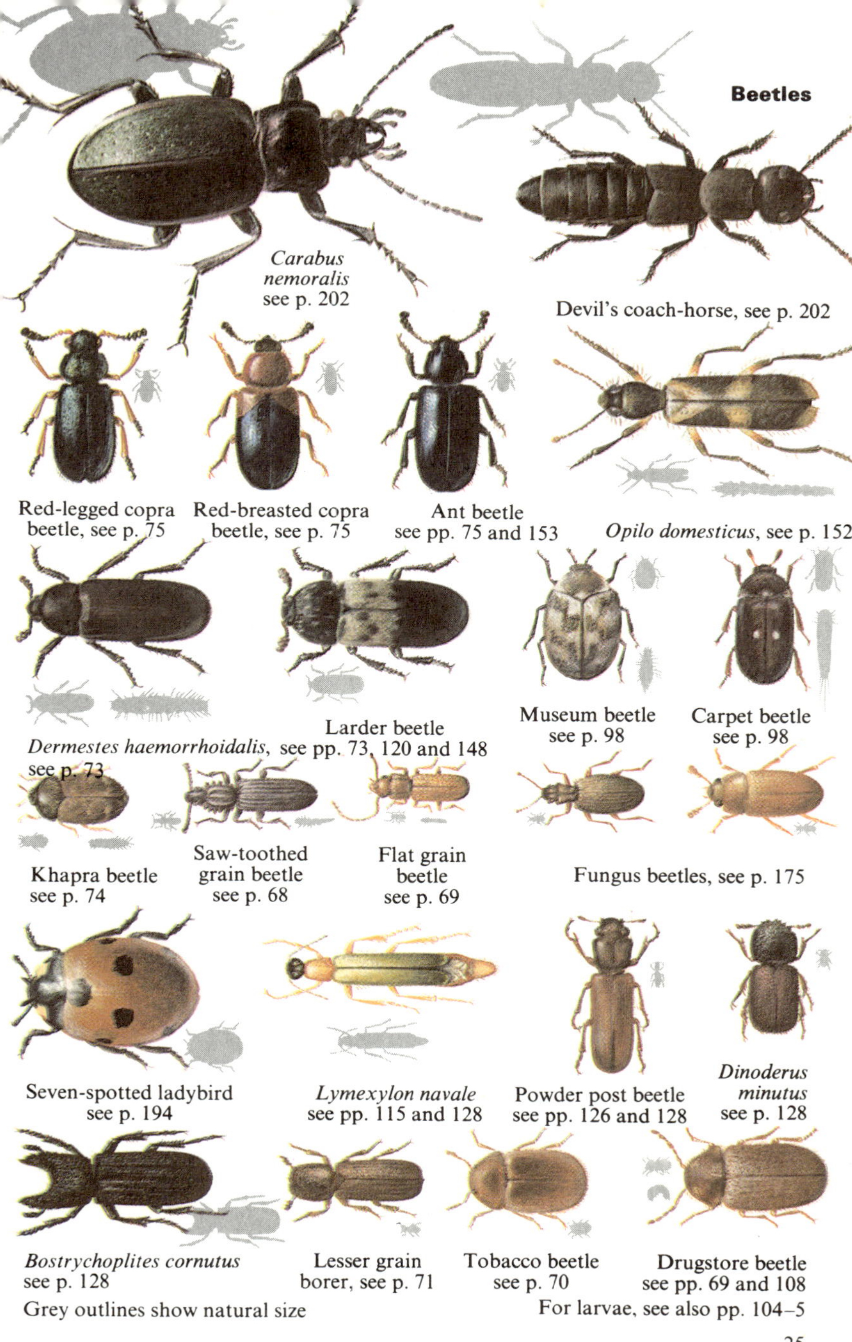

Carabus nemoralis see p. 202

Devil's coach-horse, see p. 202

Red-legged copra beetle, see p. 75

Red-breasted copra beetle, see p. 75

Ant beetle see pp. 75 and 153

Opilo domesticus, see p. 152

Dermestes haemorrhoidalis, see p. 73

Larder beetle see pp. 73, 120 and 148

Museum beetle see p. 98

Carpet beetle see p. 98

Khapra beetle see p. 74

Saw-toothed grain beetle see p. 68

Flat grain beetle see p. 69

Fungus beetles, see p. 175

Seven-spotted ladybird see p. 194

Lymexylon navale see pp. 115 and 128

Powder post beetle see pp. 126 and 128

Dinoderus minutus see p. 128

Bostrychoplites cornutus see p. 128

Lesser grain borer, see p. 71

Tobacco beetle see p. 70

Drugstore beetle see pp. 69 and 108

Grey outlines show natural size

For larvae, see also pp. 104–5

Common furniture beetle
see pp. 114 and 121

Fan-bearing wood-borer
see pp. 115 and 121

Ernobius mollis
see pp. 114, 122 and 162

Dendrobium pertinax
see pp. 114 and 123

Death-watch beetle
see pp. 115 and 125

Cis boleti
see p. 203

Spider beetle
Sphaericus gibbioides
see p. 75

Spider beetle
Gibbium psylloides
see p. 76

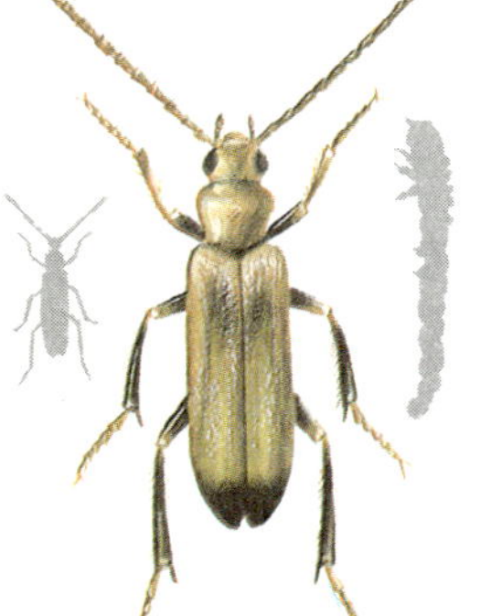

Wharfborer
see pp. 117 and 141

male

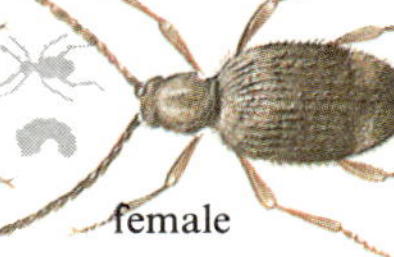

female

White-marked spider beetle, see p. 76

Golden spider beetle
see p. 76

Australian spider beetle
see pp. 76, 120 and 148

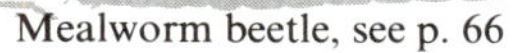

Mealworm beetle, see p. 66

Cadelle beetle
see p. 68

Flour beetle
see p. 67

Tribolium destructor, see pp. 67 and 212

Grey outlines show natural size of beetles and larvae

For larvae see also pp. 104–5

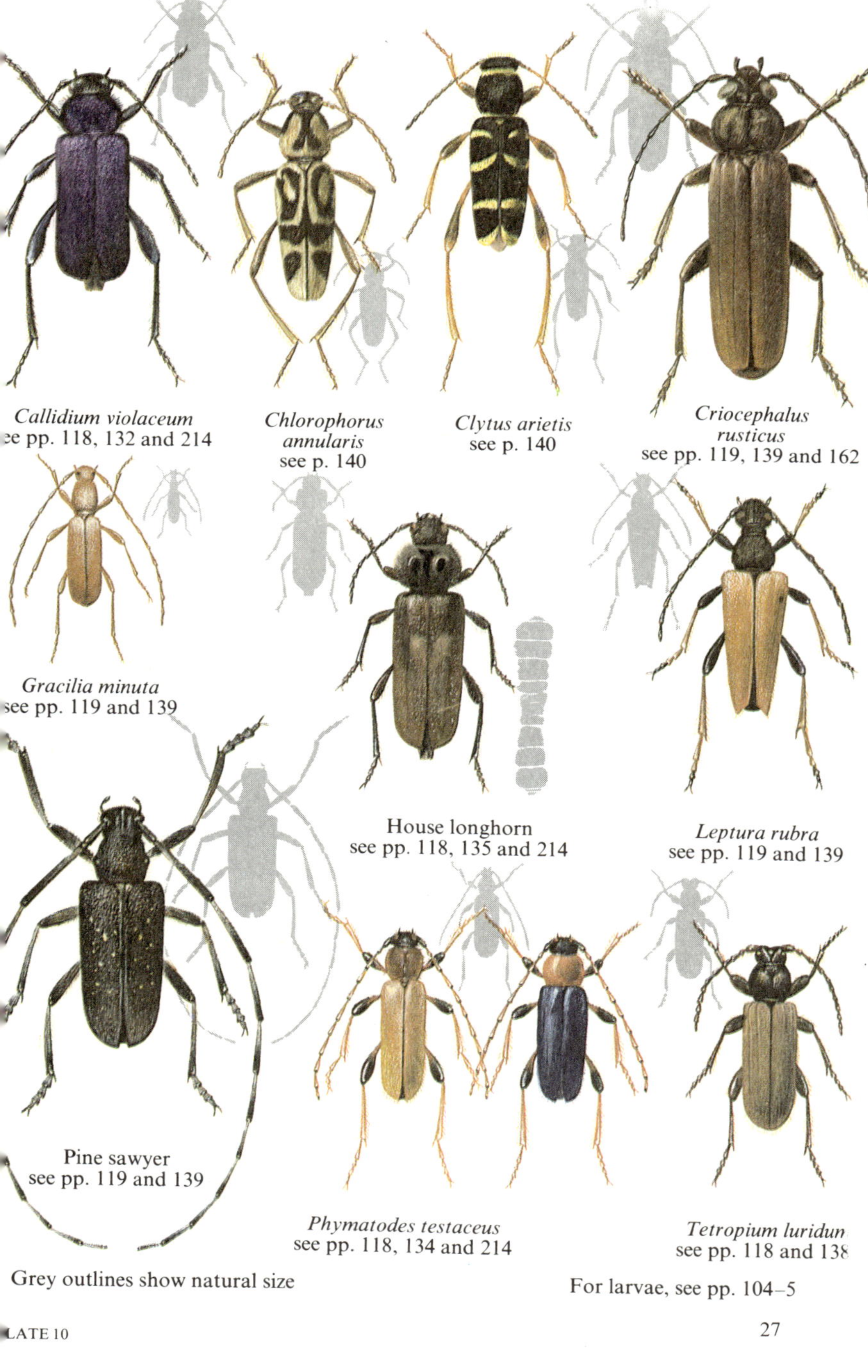

Callidium violaceum
ee pp. 118, 132 and 214

Chlorophorus annularis
see p. 140

Clytus arietis
see p. 140

Criocephalus rusticus
see pp. 119, 139 and 162

Gracilia minuta
ee pp. 119 and 139

House longhorn
see pp. 118, 135 and 214

Leptura rubra
see pp. 119 and 139

Pine sawyer
see pp. 119 and 139

Phymatodes testaceus
see pp. 118, 134 and 214

Tetropium luridun
see pp. 118 and 13

Grey outlines show natural size

For larvae, see pp. 104–5

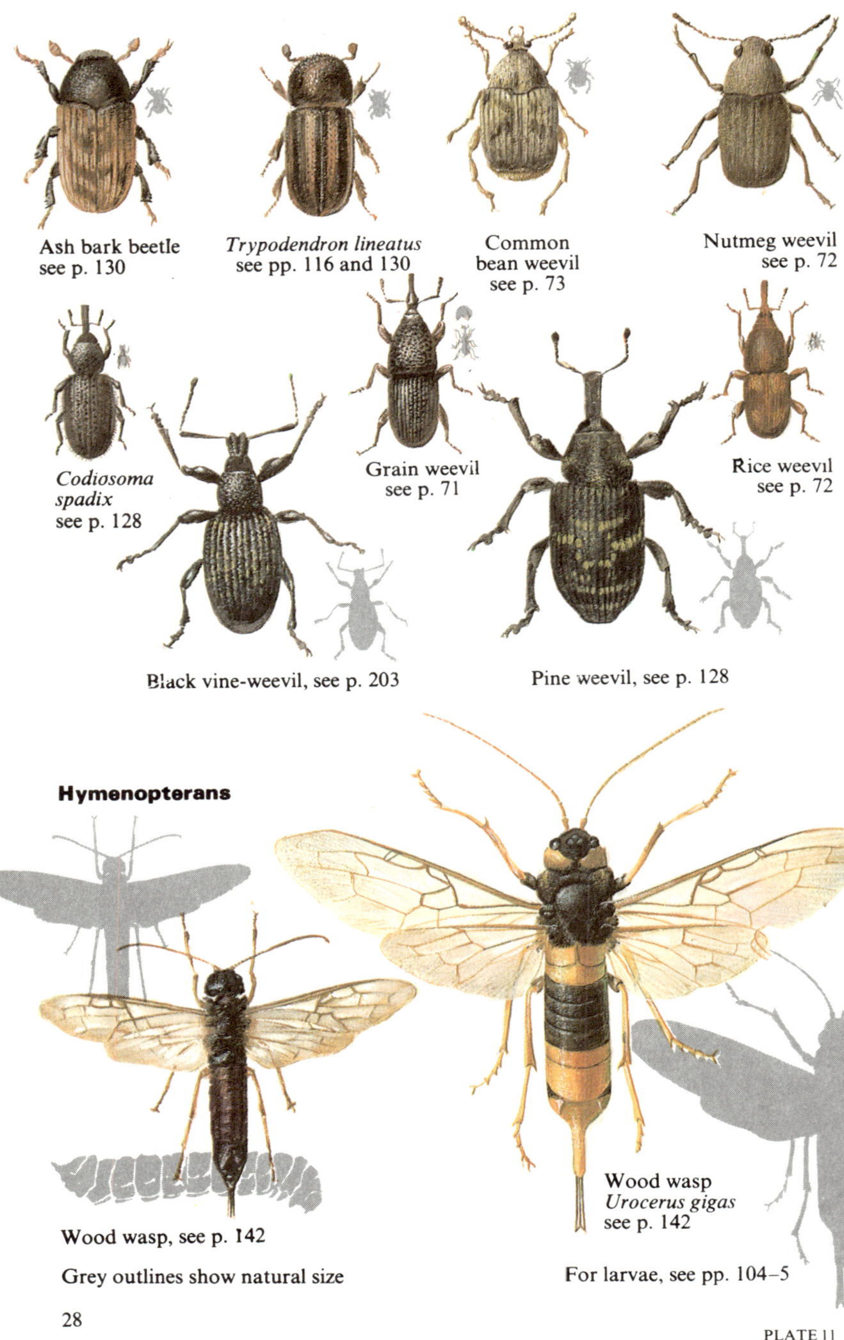
Ash bark beetle
see p. 130
Trypodendron lineatus
see pp. 116 and 130
Common
bean weevil
see p. 73
Nutmeg weevil
see p. 72
Codiosoma
spadix
see p. 128
Grain weevil
see p. 71
Rice weevil
see p. 72
Black vine-weevil, see p. 203
Pine weevil, see p. 128
Hymenopterans
Wood wasp, see p. 142
Wood wasp
Urocerus gigas
see p. 142
Grey outlines show natural size
For larvae, see pp. 104–5

Hornet
see pp. 50 and 176
German wasp
see pp. 50 and 176
Honey bee
see p. 178
Mason bee
see p. 181
Common wasp
see pp. 50 and 176
Bumble bee
Bombus hypnorum
see p. 179
Bumble bee
Bombus lapidarius
see p. 179
Patchwork leafcutter
see p. 180
Davies's colletes
see p. 157
Chalcid
see pp. 114 and 152
Ichneumon (*Ophion* sp.)
see p. 51

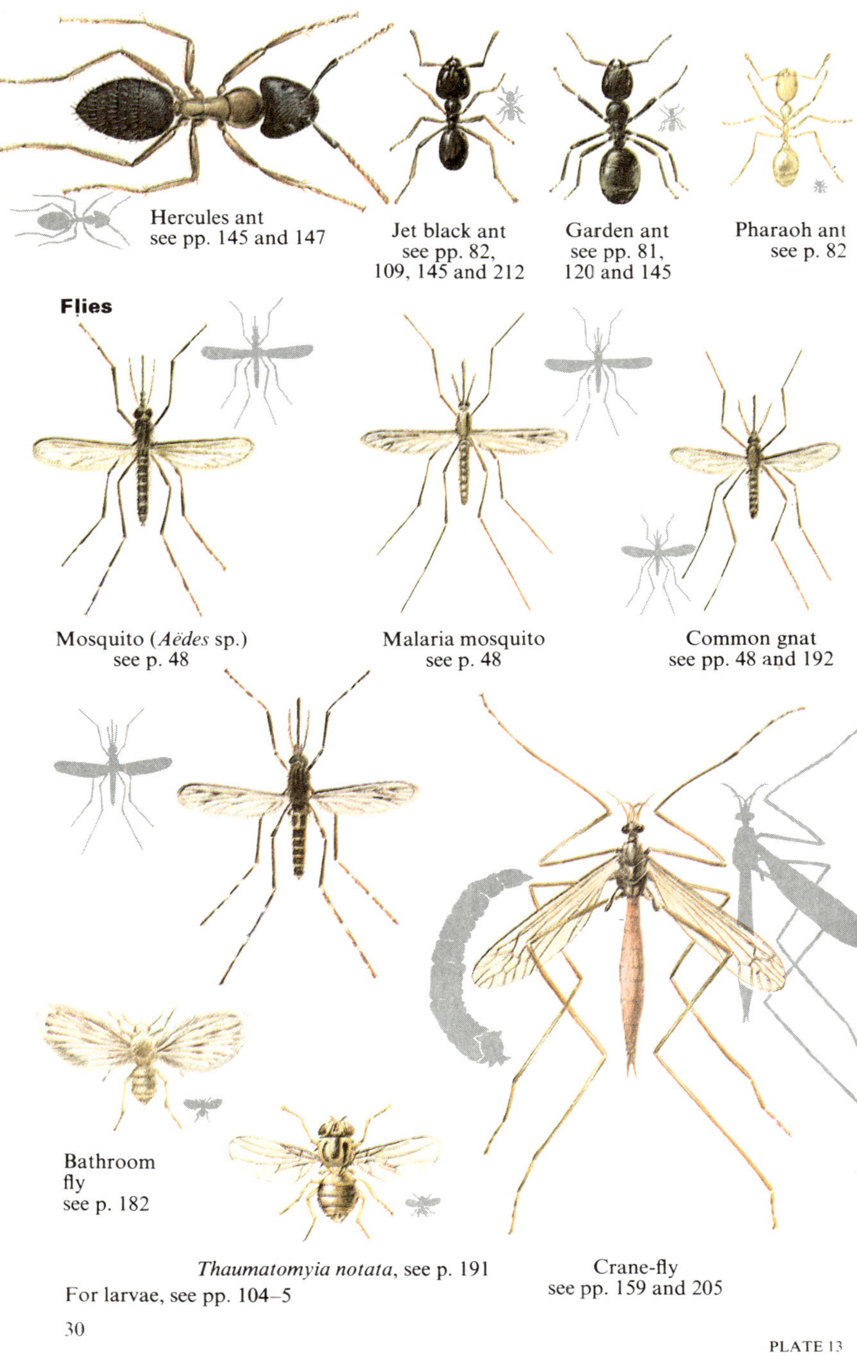

Hercules ant
see pp. 145 and 147

Jet black ant
see pp. 82, 109, 145 and 212

Garden ant
see pp. 81, 120 and 145

Pharaoh ant
see p. 82

Flies

Mosquito (*Aëdes* sp.)
see p. 48

Malaria mosquito
see p. 48

Common gnat
see pp. 48 and 192

Bathroom fly
see p. 182

Thaumatomyia notata, see p. 191

Crane-fly
see pp. 159 and 205

For larvae, see pp. 104–5

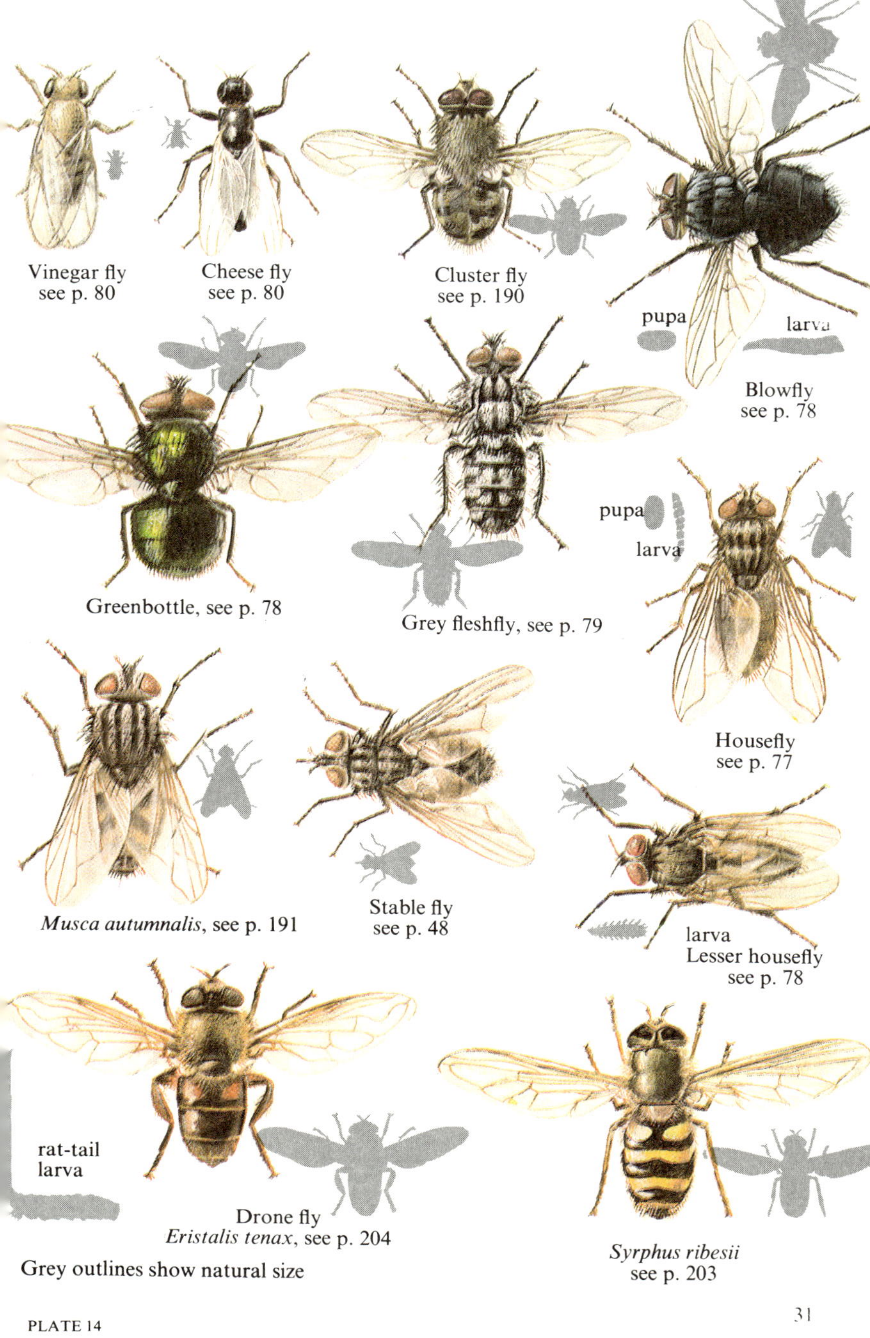

Grey outlines show natural size

Forest fly, *Crataerina pallida*, see p. 49

Forest fly, *Stenepteryx hirundinis*, see p. 49

Fleas

Cat flea
see p. 42

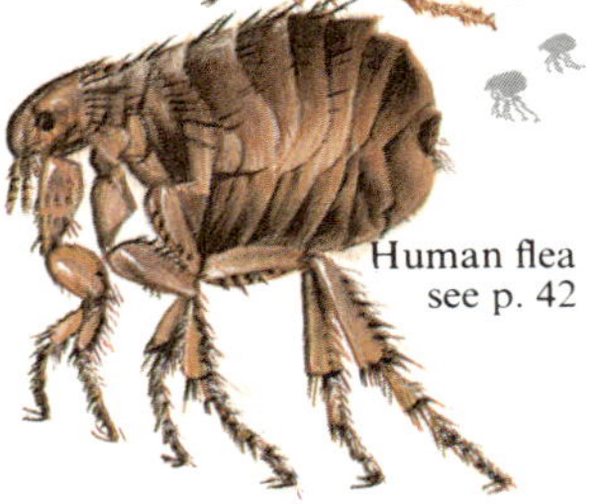

Human flea
see p. 42

Fly bug sucking body contents of a larder beetle larva

Animals that Bite, Sting and Irritate

Parasitism is very common in the animal kingdom. It has been estimated that about a quarter of the existing animal species live in or on the remaining three-quarters.

The words bite and sting are often used indiscriminately, but it is best to say that an animal bites when it uses its mouth, even when this is modified to form a sucking proboscis, and that it stings with a special organ, the sting, which is normally situated at the rear end.

When one animal bites another, it does so to obtain food, either by sucking blood as a mosquito does, or by killing the prey and consuming the contents of its body, as is done by the predacious fly bug *Reduvius personatus* among others. On the other hand, animals with a sting use this as a weapon, either for attack or defence, as for example in the hornet.

For an animal that sucks blood it is normally in its own interest that it should do so with as little disturbance as possible. The sucking proboscis is normally a delicate structure consisting of two tubes, one very thin down which saliva passes and the other a little larger through which the blood mixed with saliva is sucked up. The saliva may contain substances which prevent the blood coagulating and it may also contain substances that act as a local anaesthetic. The inflammation and itching that follow a bite are probably due to the foreign proteins in the saliva intro-

Gnat pushing its proboscis into a finger

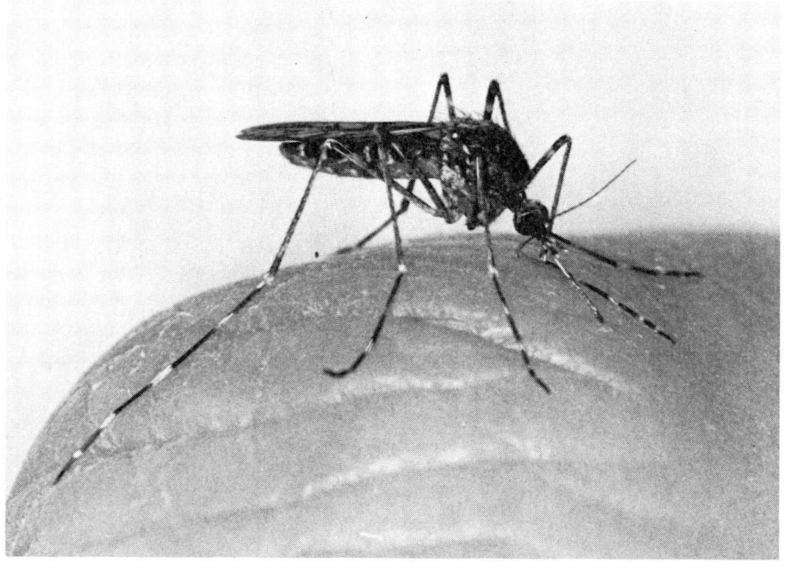

duced by the biting animal. Humans react very differently to bites, some swelling to an alarming extent, while others scarcely react at all.

The position is very different in animals that sting their prey or sting in self-defence. Here the victim is usually paralysed or rendered incapable of resistance. In such cases the sting usually has associated glands which produce a venom, that is, a substance which even in very small amounts can kill or paralyse other animals or cause them pain.

In view of the fact that people react so differently to bites and stings it is almost impossible to identify immediately the causative organism. There is also a possibility that bites may be confused with pimples or other reactions due to hypersensitivity. In many cases, it is possible that other factors may help to identify the cause, as for example the position of the bite (see p. 52). It is also as well to note the time of the attack, whether domestic animals might be involved, and whether there have been other opportunities for parasites to enter the house (see p. 53).

Scorpions, Order Scorpiones
(Page 19)

Scorpions are animals of the tropics and subtropics and some species, such as *Euscorpius italicus*, occur in Southern Europe. They shun the light and hide during the day under rocks or loose bark; some species hide in crevices in houses.

Scorpions produce live young which are at first tended by the mother, and in fact they are carried round on her back for the first couple of weeks. Scorpions feed on insects and spiders which they seize with their claws (known technically as palps). In some cases they kill the prey with venom injected by the sting, although this organ is primarily defensive.

The scorpions found in Europe are normally not dangerous to man, the action of their venom being roughly the same as that of a hornet. Medical help should, however, be sought if a child is stung.

Many stories associated with scorpions are pure fantasy, as for example the idea that they will cooperate with each other by hanging from the ceiling in a long chain in order to reach and sting a human being. They played an important part in the religion of the ancient Egyptians, and are mentioned in several places in the Bible.

House centipede,
Scutigera coleoptrata
(Page 18)

This centipede comes from the Mediterranean countries where it is often found indoors. It has been recorded a few times in northern Europe.

Like other centipedes this is a predator which kills its prey by using the foremost limbs which are modified to form a pair of poison claws.

In contrast to the small centipedes found in the garden, this species can, when molested, bite in areas where the skin is thin. The bite can be seen and it may result in swelling, but it is not serious.

Mites and ticks, Order Acari

In Europe it is only the itch mite which can be regarded as an important parasite of man, but other mites may occasionally cause trouble. Some can suck blood, while others are responsible for hypersensitive reactions.

Itch mite, *Sarcoptes scabiei*
(Page 20)

This mite lives actually in the skin, burrowing tunnels in the upper horny layer, rather like a mole. It is only $\frac{1}{3}$ mm long and is very seldom seen, but its presence is betrayed by the inflamed and eczema-like condition it causes (see p. 52).

The eggs are laid in the burrows made by the female and it takes a good two weeks for the young to reach the adult stage. Infection is usually by females with eggs being transferred from one person to another by direct contact.

Bed mites, Genus *Dermatophagoides*
(Page 20)

These mites feed on the scales which are continually falling from our skin. They prefer a high humidity (*c.* 80%) and temperature (*c.* 25° C), and so are particularly common in beds. Surprisingly enough it is only quite recently that the presence of these mites has been observed. The discovery was made during an investigation of the causes of asthma. It had long been known that some patients react violently to house dust, but it was not clear what substances caused the attacks. It has now been shown that these mites are widespread wherever man lives, and that it is the dust containing them that causes the more acute attacks of asthma in sensitive patients. It is not only the mites themselves but also their cast skins and faeces which produce the symptoms, and as these are easily disturbed during dusting and bed-making, people can inhale them in large numbers.

Apart from sprays it has been found that the best method to get rid of these mites is frequent and thorough vacuum-cleaning of mattresses, etc. Fortunately, these mites are completely harmless to most people.

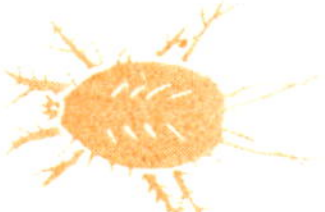

Prune mite, *Carpoglyphus lactis*
(Page 20)

Many of the mites occurring in foodstuffs can cause eczema in those likely to come in contact with them.

This mite, which thrives particularly in dried fruit, can cause the condition known as 'grocer's itch' in those who work with mite-ridden goods in stores and warehouses.

Red poultry mite,
Dermanyssus gallinae
(Page 20)

When filled with blood this mite is a beautiful red colour. Gradually as the blood is digested the mite becomes a little smaller and the colour changes to grey or blackish, and if it has fasted for a long period it is almost white.

The poultry mite lives in henhouses, in dovecotes and similar places, where it remains hidden in crevices during the day. At night it emerges to suck blood.

The female lays up to 10 eggs at a time in the hiding-places. She may repeat this process several times, but must have a blood meal between each egg-laying session. In the summer the development from the egg to the adult takes 8–10 days.

The adults can survive for 4–5 months without blood.

When one of these mites is found indoors it will nearly always have come from birds and usually from a bird's nest. When the young birds have flown the hungry mites start to wander. Their bite causes itching and as they often occur in large numbers they can be very unpleasant. The infected nest should be removed and the surrounding area sprayed or treated with a suitable powder.

Pigeon tick, *Argas reflexus*
(Page 20)

This is a bird parasite which may occasionally occur in the house. It is much larger than the red poultry mite and has a leathery, oval, red-brown body. The mouthparts are situated on the underside of the body and are not normally seen.

Pigeon ticks, which occur particularly in dovecotes, have similar habits to poultry mites, but they can survive without food for a longer period. There have been cases where pigeon ticks have appeared 2–3 years after the birds have gone. They may sometimes bite humans.

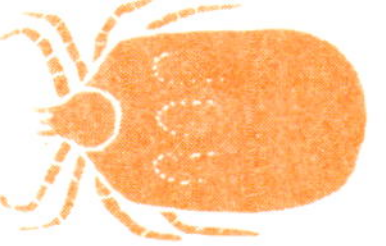

Castor bean tick, *Ixodes ricinus*
(Page 20)

The adult male is *c.* 2 mm long, the female twice this length, but these measurements only apply to individuals which have not recently fed. The red-brown, leathery skin of the abdomen can stretch to an incredible extent.

This species is very common in some areas, but not in others. This is because it requires fairly critical environmental conditions. It is, for instance, sensitive to desiccation and is therefore found mainly

Ticks may feed on many different mammals and birds. Here a couple of large female ticks feed on a mouse.

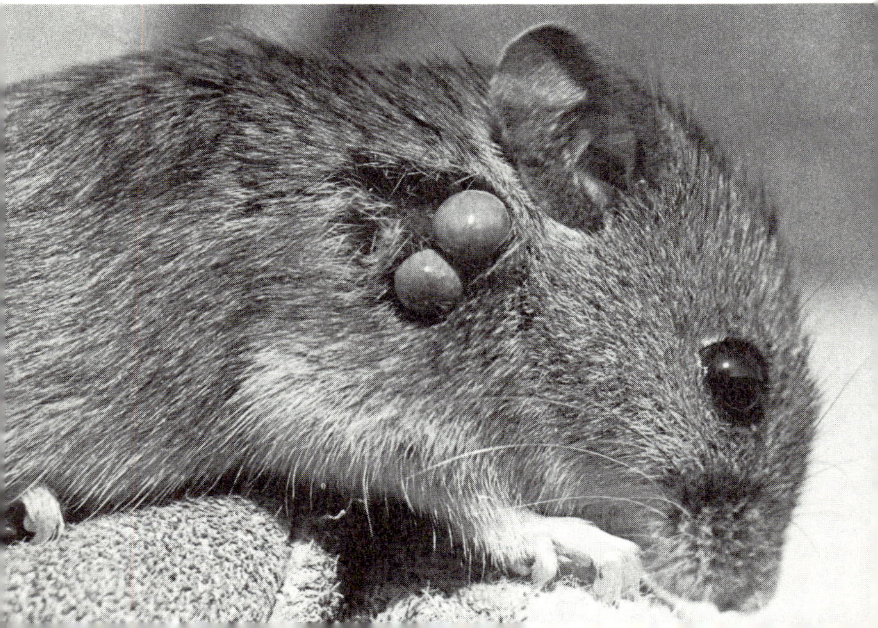

in damp undergrowth and other dense vegetation.

A hungry tick will move up to the tip of a grass stem or out on to a leaf and wait there until an animal passes by. The castor bean tick is not fastidious as regards the animal from which it sucks blood. It may use mammals of any size, even man, and also birds and reptiles. When an animal passes by and touches it the tick grips it firmly.

It wanders about on the host until it has found a suitable, preferably thin-skinned site and then inserts its mouthparts which are serrated and elongated to form a sucking channel.

Neither the piercing of the skin nor the sucking of blood is perceived at the time, but after a period the site starts to itch.

The tick remains on its host for 5–6 days and then releases its grip and falls to the ground, where it seeks shelter and digests its meal. During the course of its life a tick has to find a host on three occasions, twice when young, and once as an adult before it can lay eggs. A female tick may lay over 2,000 eggs, but these do not survive indoors where the environment is too dry.

When living on its host a tick is very firmly anchored and is not easily removed with forceps. It is, however, essential to remove the whole animal, otherwise inflammation may occur. If anaesthetised with ether the tick will release its grip and can then be removed. Alternatively it can be smeared with a little fat and after about fifteen minutes it can be picked off.

Brown dog tick, *Rhipicephalus sanguineus* (Page 20)

This tick comes originally from Africa but is now widely distributed throughout the

Unlike the castor bean tick the brown dog tick sometimes lays its eggs indoors

tropical and subtropical areas of the world. In Europe it is common in the Mediterranean countries.

It occurs mainly on dogs and rarely on man. Like the previous species it has to have three separate blood meals before it becomes sexually mature, and under favourable conditions development from egg to adult takes about 65 days at a temperature of 25–30°C.

In temperate areas the dog tick is completely dependent upon warm buildings during the cold part of the year. As it originally evolved in very dry climates, it is able, unlike the castor bean tick, to live and breed in centrally heated houses with a dry climate.

Fully fed female dog ticks are scarcely one centimetre long when they leave the host, and this most often happens in the dog's bed. Even in this condition they are surprisingly mobile and while searching for a suitable site for egg-laying they have a tendency to wander upwards.

The 2,000–4,000 red-brown eggs are attached in large or small clumps in a sheltered position, as for example small cavities in panelling, along piping or behind cupboards and pictures.

To control these ticks it is essential to treat both the dog and the surrounding areas at the same time.

Thrips, Order Thysanoptera
(Page 22)

On warm summer days the tiny insects known as thrips may occur in enormous numbers and even enter houses. They have a tendency to creep in under clothing, or into ears, mouths and eyes, and they tickle as they move around on the skin.

Thrips feed by sucking plant juices, but occasionally they may insert their mouthparts into human skin, in some cases causing a rash and itching. They can jump by striking the abdomen against the substrate and so are sometimes confused with fleas.

Springtails, Order Collembola
(Page 20)

Like thrips the springtails can also jump. They do not bite humans but may cause irritation if there are large numbers crawling around on the skin.

Sucking lice, Order Anoplura
(Page 21)

The members of this small insect group show many adaptations for their specialized parasitic life. They are wingless, have much reduced eyes and their mouthparts are adapted for biting and sucking. The skin of a louse is leathery and greyish, and the abdomen becomes much distended when full of blood. Each leg ends in a claw which is adapted for gripping hairs.

Lice feed exclusively on blood and as they have to feed twice a day if they are to remain in good condition they can only survive for a few days in the absence of a host. A louse that is really hungry may be so greedy when it does again find a host that it feeds until it almost bursts.

Lice are completely dependent upon the special microclimate found near the surface of the skin. If the temperature changes as, for example, when the host has a fever, they will move away, and in former times it was regarded as a very bad sign when lice left their host. Lice also move off very quickly from a cold, dead person and this naturally increases the risk of spreading infection during epidemics (see p. 39).

A female louse lays about 10 eggs per day during its month of life. The eggs are quite large and yellowish-white and so firmly attached that it is almost impossible to remove them. After about a week the egg is ready to hatch and the young louse inside inflates itself with air,

Beggar family infested with lice. 17th-century woodcut.

The body louse lays its eggs mainly in the seams of underclothing

pushes off the top of the egg and crawls out. The newly hatched louse starts to feed immediately and after about 8 days it is ready to mate and lay eggs. A population of lice that is left undisturbed can therefore increase at a fast rate.

Lice are by no means a new problem, most mammals harbour their own special species and there is no doubt that our primate ancestors also harboured them. It is, in fact, probable that the louse now found on modern man is the same or closely related to the species that infested early man.

In most periods of history lice have been regarded as something that one lived with, and the job of delousing one another was an important part of family life.

Two types of louse are adapted for living on man: the human louse and the crab louse.

The human louse occurs in two forms, the body louse and the head louse, and these are very similar to one another. In fact they can only be distinguished with certainty by their habits.

Body louse, *Pediculus humanus* var. *corporis* (Page 21)

Found only on the body and in clothing, the body louse lays its eggs in the seams and similar sheltered places. It is somewhat hardier than the head louse and at 23° C it can live for 4 days without access to blood.

The best conditions for the spread of these lice are when humans are living close together in primitive conditions. They do not thrive among people who maintain a good standard of hygiene with frequent changing and washing of clothes.

Body lice are important as vectors of typhus fever, trench fever and louse-borne relapsing fever. In populations where these diseases do not occur, the only effect of louse bites is the resultant annoying itch.

Head louse, *Pediculus humanus* var. *capitis* (Page 21)

The head louse attaches its eggs firmly to hairs close to the scalp. The eggs are extremely tenacious and can only be removed from the hair by using a fine comb and much effort. Even frequent washing of the hair may not be sufficient to remove them.

The empty eggshells remain on the hair

Hatched and unhatched eggs of the head louse

and move outwards as it grows. Under a lens they can be distinguished from unhatched eggs, because they are more transparent and they lack a lid.

As already mentioned, lice require a blood meal twice a day, and at ordinary room temperatures a head louse can only survive a couple of days when not living on a human.

Head lice do not transmit diseases. They can be controlled by special preparations, but these do not usually kill the eggs, so treatment has to be repeated several times at intervals of 4–5 days.

Delousing. 16th-century woodcut.

Crab louse, *Phthirius pubis*
(Page 21)

A crab louse is almost as broad as it is long. Its 'claws' are extraordinarily well developed and together with the shape of the body give it a crab-like appearance. Its preferred habitat is among the body hairs and particularly among the pubic hairs.

The large claws are well adapted for gripping these very strong hairs. Crab lice can also occur in the armpits, in beards and sometimes on eyelids and eyebrows, and indeed they have even been found among the very fine hair on the heads of infants.

A pair of crab lice climbing on a body hair, with a firmly attached egg between them

A female crab louse lays about 25 eggs, each firmly fixed to its own hair. The development from egg to adult takes about three weeks.

Crab lice are sedentary. Having found a suitable place a louse will seize the host's hair, bore into the skin with its mouthparts and suck blood several times in succession, with only short intervals. It will die within about a day if removed from its host. There is no doubt that crab lice are mostly transmitted from one human to another during copulation. There are, however, records of small children carrying crab lice, so they can be transmitted by other means.

Dog louse, *Linognathus setosus*
(Page 21)
Although very similar to the human louse there is little chance of a human becoming infested with dog lice. Like their relatives these parasites are very much tied

to their own specific host. They mostly live on the back, flanks and at the root of the tail of dogs. In addition to the irritation that they cause these lice are also intermediate hosts for one of the dog's intestinal worms. The infection takes place when the dog swallows infected lice as it scratches itself.

Biting lice, Order Mallophaga
(Page 21)

These insects are somewhat similar in appearance to the true lice, but the head is

broader, they usually have two claws on each leg, and they do not suck blood. They feed by gnawing fur and feathers and also scraps of skins. They do not affect man.

Biting lice attach their eggs firmly to feathers or fur and the whole development from egg to adult takes only a couple of weeks. They are so dependent upon the warm, damp climate under feathers or among fur that they only survive for a few hours after the host animal dies.

Dogs and cats each have their own species of biting louse known respectively as *Trichodectes canis* and *Felicola subrostratus*. Apparently these cause irritation, for animals carrying them scratch continuously.

Cage birds may also become infested with feather lice, and these cause a lowering in condition. In the wild many birds attempt to rid themselves of lice by taking dust baths, but this is not really practicable in the case of cage birds, which should be treated with a suitable insecticide.

Fleas, Order Siphonaptera
(Page 32)

Fleas are extremely well adapted for their special way of life. The hard, tough, chitinous exoskeleton makes it almost impossible to squash them and the tall, thin body allows them to move about very rapidly among hairs or feathers. If all else fails, a flea can jump up to about 30 cm. This may not sound much, but it is more than 200 times the flea's own body length and is comparable to a man being able to jump about 350 m.

Each individual flea species is more or less dependent upon its own host species, but in many cases it can also suck the blood of other species. Of the 50–60 different species of flea found in Europe, about half occasionally bite humans, but only one species – the human flea – is able to breed on a diet of human blood only.

Flea eggs are smooth, oval and greyish-white. They are about $\frac{1}{4}$ mm long, so they can be seen by the naked eye. Unlike louse eggs, they are not attached to hairs but are dropped on the ground and are therefore usually found in the lair or nest of the host. At room temperature they hatch in about 10 days.

The larvae feed on various types of organic matter, including the blood-

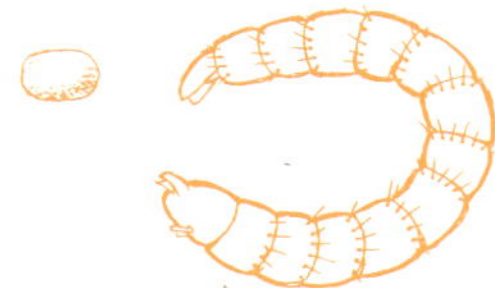

Flea egg and larva

containing faeces of the adult fleas. They are white, blind and worm-like and they have a row of bristles on each segment. The duration of development depends largely upon the temperature and may vary from 8 to 150 days.

When fully grown the larva pupates in a cocoon spun from a salivary secretion. The cocoons are normally covered with dust and are therefore difficult to discern. The pupal stage may vary from one week to several months.

The adult fleas may remain in the cocoons for a long time – even for years – waiting until an animal comes near them. Emergence from the cocoons is stimulated by vibration. If an infested house has stood empty for a long time the hungry fleas will start to emerge as soon as the new occupants move in.

Lady wearing a flea cravat. Painting by F. M. Parmigianino, c. *1536. National Gallery, Naples.*

Human flea, *Pulex irritans*
(Page 32)

The human flea has become a rather rare insect, but in former times it was the constant companion of men of all classes. At one time the Chinese and others used flea traps made of ivory or bamboo which were gently warmed and placed between the sheets before they went to bed, the idea being that the fleas would crawl in and could then be easily killed. In the 14th-16th centuries ladies wore fur collars, known now as flea cravats, which were supposed to catch fleas, which could then be shaken out.

Nowadays when one acquires a human flea it is usually as a result of a visit to a pigsty. The human flea also thrives on pigs. There is little risk of this flea multiplying in the home. Modern houses are much too clean and in particular too dry for the larvae to survive.

Cat flea, *Ctenocephalides felis*
Dog flea, *Ctenocephalides canis*
(Page 22)

Cat and dog fleas are very similar in appearance and both species can live on both dogs and cats. Humans are mainly attacked by cat fleas.

A cat or a dog may have a light infection of fleas without the human inhabitants of the house noticing, but if the domestic animals are carrying large numbers of fleas, there is naturally a greater likelihood that the humans will be attacked. A heavy infestation may occur if the cat or dog is removed from the house, for then the fleas left behind have no choice but to move to the humans.

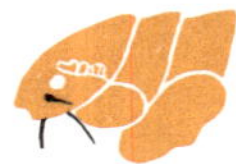

Human flea

Cat flea

Dog flea

Bird flea

In such cases one may comfort oneself with the fact that cat and dog fleas cannot breed without their principal host, and so the infestation will die out on its own. On the other hand, they can live for months on a diet of human blood, so it needs an unusual amount of patience to wait until the fleas die of old age.

Fleas can be removed from domestic animals, either by washing or by treating them with an insecticide, but it is just as important to deal with the places where the larvae are developing, by vacuum-cleaning and then spraying with an insecticide.

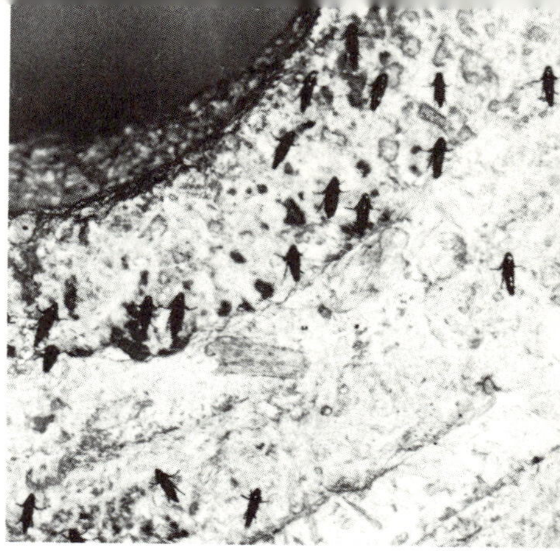

Enticed out by a warm spring, bird fleas sit around the entrance of a nest box, waiting for a 'bite'

A bedroom infested with lice and fleas, 16th-century woodcut

Bird fleas, genus *Ceratophyllus*

These insects spend the winter in their pupal cocoons in birds' nests. They emerge in the warmth of the spring sun and if they do not quickly find a bird to suck blood from, they start to move about. In such circumstances they may well enter houses, but one may also acquire them when gardening in the vicinity of infected nesting boxes or nests. Bird fleas can, of course, multiply enormously in hen houses.

Fortunately, bird fleas only live for a short time indoors, and they can only breed in birds' nests. It is a good idea to clean out nesting boxes very thoroughly in the early spring.

True bugs, Order Hemiptera

Bugs are insects which, among other features, have powerful, piercing mouthparts. The majority of the species live outdoors and suck the juices of plants, but there are a few which are predatory or parasitic, and of these one has become adapted for living indoors.

Bed bug, *Cimex lectularius*
(Page 22)

Unlike most other bugs, the bed bug is wingless. When it has not recently fed the

Bed bug sucking

body is paper-thin, and almost red-brown.

So far as is known bed bugs came originally from Asia, but they have now spread to all parts of the world. They were well known in ancient times in the Mediterranean area. As they require a warm, dry climate they did not spread to northern regions until buildings started to be heated more or less efficiently, but when this did happen they soon became very abundant. They are now less common and are largely kept under control by modern insecticides.

Bed bugs only search for blood donors when they are actually hungry. In the intervals between meals they spend their time in suitable hiding-places in the vicinity of the bed. These may be crevices in timber, joints in the bed, beneath loose carpeting, and behind pictures and wallpaper. When hungry, bed bugs come out from their retreat and start to search. Their senses are not capable of guiding them to a distant blood donor, but at distances of 5–10 cm they will be attracted by the body warmth of the victim.

Bed bugs can crawl up a wall and can also walk upside down on rough ceilings, but if they are not skilled they often fall down. This is the basis of stories that bed bugs, having observed that their victim had placed the legs of the bed in dishes of water, crawled up the wall and along the ceiling and let themselves fall on to the poor sleeping victim. However, the bed bug is not as crafty as this.

In the course of about 10 minutes an adult bed bug can suck up to 7 times its own weight in blood. It then retreats to its hiding-place, where it digests, mates and lays eggs until it is hungry again.

The eggs are laid in the hiding place, where they are attached to the substrate. A female lays a total of 200 eggs, 4–5 per day, but the actual number depends upon the temperature and other external factors. They do not lay at all at temperatures below 10 C.

Young bed bugs are like small versions of the adults. They moult 5 times during their development and at each stage they require a new meal of blood.

Bed bugs can be controlled by thorough treatment of their hiding places with an insecticide.

Some of the vertebrates which we more or less voluntarily share our homes with are also attacked by other bugs which live in the vicinity of their nests or sleeping quarters. These resemble the common bed

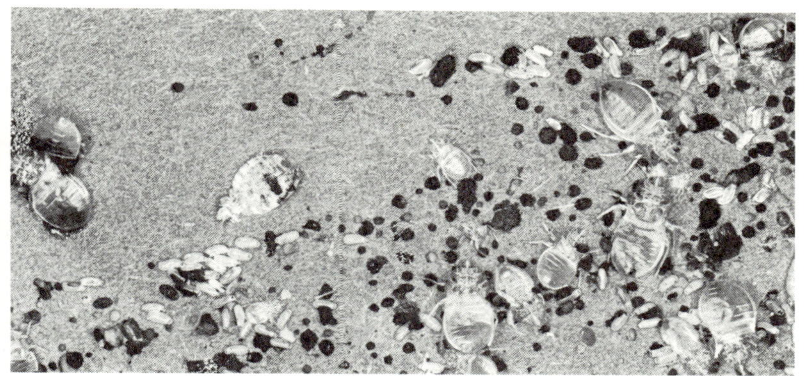

Underside of a carpet with bed bugs, empty casts and faeces

bug very closely. Sometimes they move about and enter houses, and in rare cases they may attack humans:

Bat bug, *Cimex pipistrelli*
This species may occur in lofts where bats roost.

Pigeon bug, *Cimex columbarius*
Possibly only a subspecies of the common bed bug, and sometimes known as *C. lectularius columbarius*. It occurs in dovecots and in lofts where feral pigeons roost. It is very voracious but fortunately not very common.

Martin bug, *Oeciacus hirundinis*
(Page 22)

This relatively small species is found in the nests of house martins and swallows, and sometimes in those of house sparrows and woodpeckers. It may occasionally be found in a house, particularly after young house martins have left the nest.

Debris bug, *Lyctocoris campestris*
(Page 22)

This bug also comes from birds' nests where it lives as a predator on the numerous small invertebrates, such as moth larvae, which feed on the debris that accumulates in the nests. Like the martin bug it may occasionally find its way into the house and may sometimes attack people when they are asleep.

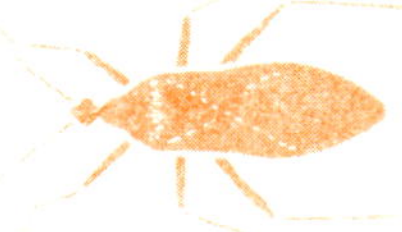

Fly bug, *Reduvius personatus*
(Page 22 and Page 32)

The larvae of this bug produce a sticky, oily substance, to which dust and debris adhere, so that they become well camouflaged.

The adults, on the other hand, are glossy brownish or dull black. They have well developed wings and fly well. The rostrum or proboscis is very short and powerful and when not in use is folded back beneath the body. The female lays up to about 200 very large, brown eggs which are deposited singly and at random.

A well-camouflaged fly bug larva moves out to hunt

Development is slow and at ordinary room temperature may take a year from the hatching of the egg to the adult insect.

Fly bugs are predators that suck the body fluids of other insects. They are often found in lofts, outhouses and similar places where there are usually other insects of various kinds. They avoid the light and spend the day hidden in crevices. Specimens found in houses are usually strays from their normal habitat, but exceptionally they may be hunting bed bugs.

An adult fly bug on a curtain

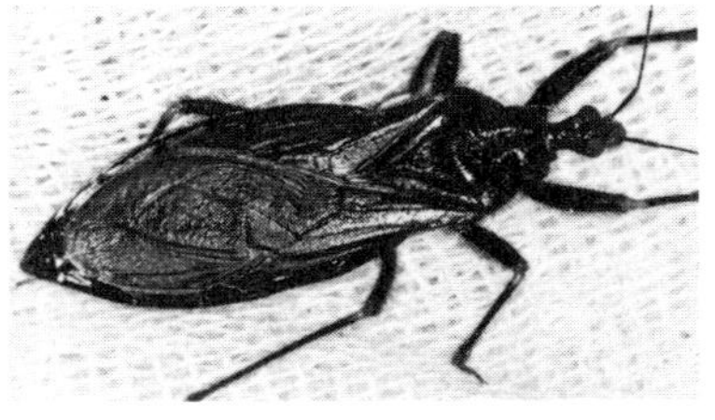

There have been a few records of fly bugs biting sleeping humans, and they may also bite in self defence when picked up.

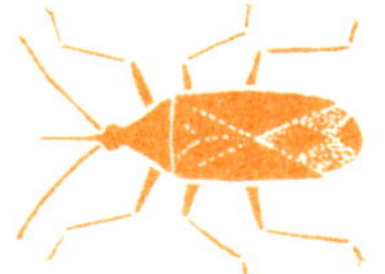

Common flower bug,
Anthocoris nemorum
(Page 22)

These are common bugs normally seen outdoors on trees and bushes, where they live by seizing aphids, mites and other small invertebrates, from which they suck the body fluids. They are often seen when one is picking fruit or they may be taken indoors on cut flowers.

The proboscis is long and thin and the insect often bites humans. In many cases the bite is quite painful but normally there are no after-effects.

Gnats and **mosquitoes,**
(Page 30) Family Culicidae

These insects usually spend their whole lives outdoors, but some enter houses in autumn to spend the winter (see p. 191). They may also come in through open windows during summer and if this causes a serious problem, as it does in the tropics, it may be necessary to fit mosquito netting or at least to treat the curtains with an insect deterrent. As a rule the female must have a blood meal before she can lay eggs, and after mating she will go in search of a mammal, human or otherwise, or a bird. Gnats and mosquitoes are most active around sunset or in the early morning, when the air is usually still and humid. They spend the greater part of the day resting in dense undergrowth.

When the female has had an opportunity to engorge with blood, her eggs start to ripen and she then searches for a suitable place in which to lay them. Mosquitoes in the genus *Aedes* lay their eggs in damp hollows which become filled with water in spring, whereas the malaria

A mosquito with a full load of blood

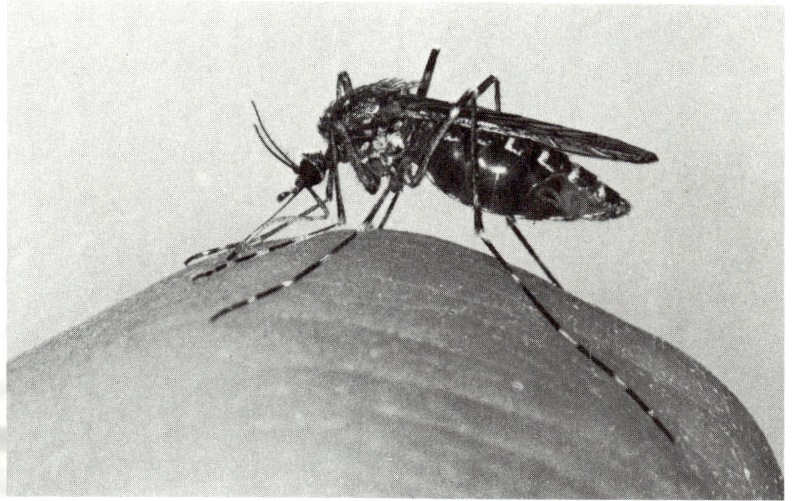

mosquito and the gnats lay their eggs directly on the surface of the water.

In all these insects the larval and pupal stages are spent in the water.

Mosquitoes of the genus *Aëdes*
(Page 30)

These insects breed mainly in pools and ditches of the kind that fill up with water in the spring months, but dry up later in the year. They have only one generation in the year, which flies in May, normally at the same time as the beech comes into leaf. Some species live in or near to woodland. Others frequent areas of coastal salt-marsh, breeding in brackish pools, and these may have several generations in the course of the summer.

Malaria mosquito,
Anopheles maculipennis
(Page 30)

This is the malaria mosquito of parts of Europe, including Britain. The larvae live in ponds and lakes with fairly dense vegetation. The indigenous malaria of Britain, commonly known as ague, was transmitted by this insect, and it still occurred in certain coastal districts until about the end of the nineteenth century.

Theobaldia annulata
(Page 30)

This is one of two species of mosquito that often occur indoors. It breeds in small bodies of water, and the larva can tolerate water that is somewhat polluted. In fact the larval stages are frequently found in garden ponds, water storage tanks and even in rain butts and blocked gutters. There are several generations in the course of the summer and in autumn the mated females may enter cellars and outhouses to spend the winter.

Common gnat, *Culex pipiens*
(Page 30)

This small mosquito does not usually bite humans, but evidently prefers the blood of birds. Its habits are more or less the same as those of the preceding species, and specimens may also be found spending the winter in damp cellars, often in quite large numbers.

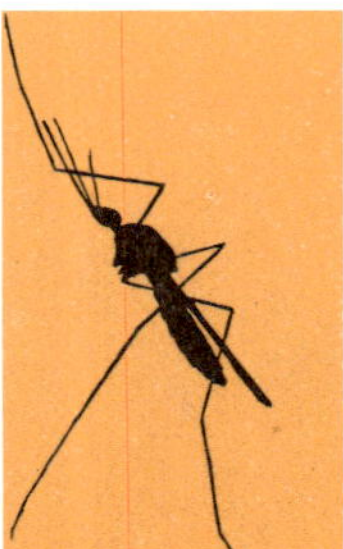

When perched a malaria mosquito (left) can be distinguished from gnats or culicines by the body posture

Stable or **Biting housefly,**
Stomoxys calcitrans
(Page 31)

In late summer one often hears people saying that the flies have started to bite. This is not because the ordinary houseflies have suddenly changed their habits. It refers to the activities of the stable fly, which

Forest fly clinging to an arm. These flies rarely bite humans, but they look unpleasant. They can cling very efficiently to the skin with their claws, and are extremely tough.

is very similar in appearance to the housefly. It can, however, be distinguished by its prominent proboscis, which is hard and pointed and well adapted for piercing skin, unlike the soft suctorial proboscis with broad tips of a housefly.

Stable flies appear in cowsheds and similar places, where the larvae live in and on manure. The adults prefer the blood of cattle and pigs and very rarely attack humans, although they are sometimes found in houses.

Forest flies, Family Hippoboscidae (Page 32)

The insects in this family have an unattractive, flat body and a crab-like gait and they cling to their victims with powerful claws. At first sight they do not look very much like flies. They are specialized for living on mammals or birds, where they crawl around in the fur or among the feathers and suck blood. The proboscis is somewhat like that of a stable fly.

The larvae develop within the female's body and pupate immediately they are released by the female.

Two of the species which live on birds may wander into houses from the nests. These are *Crataerina pallida* and *Stenepteryx hirundinis*, which occur on swifts, martins and swallows.

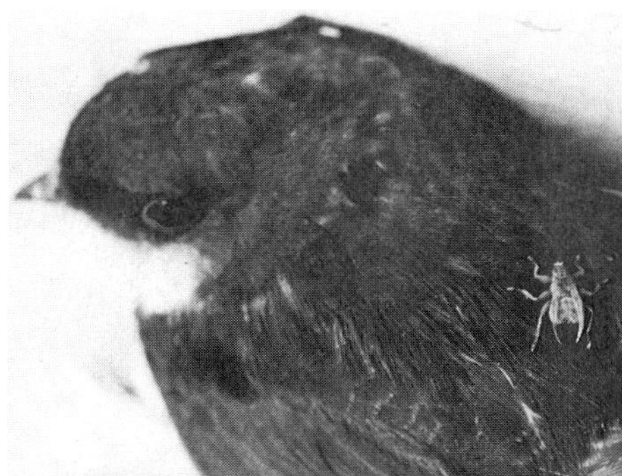

A forest fly on a young house martin

Wasps and hornets

(Page 29)

A wasp uses its sting for killing prey, but it can also use it very effectively as a defensive weapon. The sting has associated glands which produce a venom.

A hornet sting can be very painful, but is normally not dangerous, as the amount of venom injected is very small. In some cases, however, people do become ill after being stung by a hornet. This is due either to the venom being injected directly into a blood vessel or to the victim being hypersensitive to one or more of the substances contained in the venom. A sting in the mouth or on the neck can be serious, as the mucus epithelium may become very swollen, making it difficult for the victim to breathe. An ordinary uncomplicated sting can be treated with ammonia or alcohol or with a cold poultice, followed by an antihistamine ointment. If the victim becomes pale and feels unwell with giddiness and nausea it is advisable to seek medical advice immediately.

Care should be taken when collecting fallen fruit, as it may contain a wasp

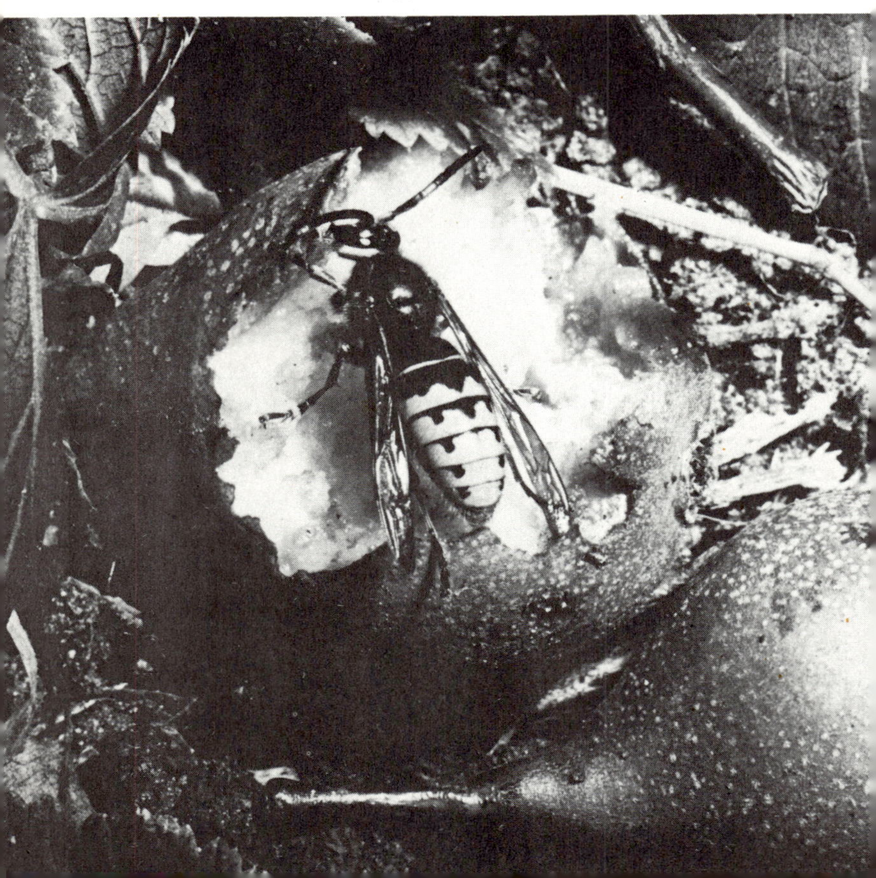

Although honey-bees are normally good-tempered, they should be treated with respect

Bees
(Page 29)

Solitary bees (p. 180), honey bees and bumblebees (p. 179) can all sting.

The sting of a small solitary bee is normally very mild, but a bumblebee sting may be very painful. On the other hand, it is very unusual for bumblebees to sting and in fact they have to be very severely provoked before they will do so. Honeybees will attack and sting if their hive is threatened, or of course if they are picked up.

Chalcids
(Page 29)

These small hymenopterans belong to a group with a very large number of species. Their larvae live as parasites in other insect species. The female inserts an egg into the victim with the help of her ovipositor, and in some cases this organ can also be used as a defensive weapon. The small dark parasitic forms which are common in houses (see p. 150) will normally not sting humans. There are, however, species which can give a mild, but irritating, sting.

Ichneumons of the genus *Ophion*
(Page 29)

These insects lay eggs in moth larvae. The adults often enter houses at night, being attracted by the lights. They have a powerful ovipositor which may be long or quite short, according to the species.

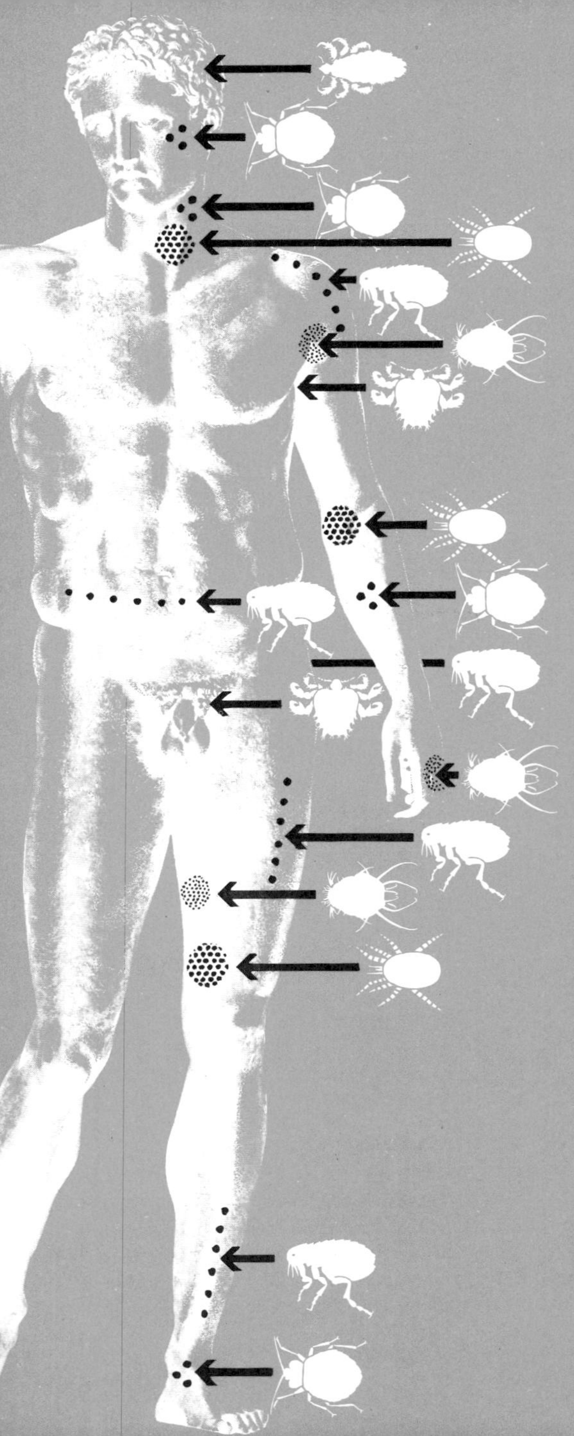

Bites and itching on the scalp are usually due to head lice (p. 39).

Bites, at night, on the face, neck, arms and feet, i.e. on those parts of the body which normally stick out from the bedclothes, may be due to bed bugs (p. 43): but of course they may be gnat or mosquito bites (p. 48).

Tiny itching 'dots', mainly on arms, legs and neck, are caused by red poultry mites (p. 35).

Red spots, usually very irritating, particularly in the armpits, on the inside of the thighs and between the fingers may be due to itch mite (p. 35).

Bites in series or groups, on the stomach or back, under a trouser belt, or under any restriction, are usually flea bites (p. 42).

Bites and itching around the genitals (or in the armpits) are normally due to crab lice (p. 40). Characteristic blue spots may appear due to discoloration of the skin caused by the crab louse's salivary secretions.

Bites, at night, on thighs or shoulders will often be flea bites. Fleas like to crawl in beneath the body, and bite where it is in contact with the bedclothes.

Bites on the legs will usually be made by fleas, which sit on the ground and jump directly on to the legs (p. 42).

Where do the biting and irritating organisms come from?

From outside, through windows and doors	Gnats, mosquitoes (p. 48) Stable flies (p. 48) Thrips (pp. 38 and 200)
From birds' nests or nesting boxes	Bird fleas (p. 43) Poultry mites (p. 35) Pigeon ticks (p. 36) Martin bugs (p. 45) Forest flies (p. 49)
From dog or cat, or from their quarters	Fleas (p. 42) Certain mites
From other humans	Itch mite (p. 35) Head lice (p. 39) Body lice (p. 39) Crab lice (p. 40) Human fleas (p. 42)
From foodstuffs	Certain mites (p. 35)
When travelling (in hotel rooms)	Bed bugs (p. 43) Fleas (p. 42)
From second-hand furniture or paintings	Bed bugs (p. 43)
From public lavatories	Crab lice (p. 40)
At home, after being in garden or woodland	Animal fleas (p. 42) Ticks (p. 36) Flower bugs (p. 47)

Illustration from a flea circus poster

PREVENTION OF BITES AND STINGS

The chances of being attacked by animals that bite or sting are really quite high. It is not possible to provide complete security against such attacks, but certain precautions can be taken, as for example by not bringing old birds' nests into the house.

If one is bitten the first thing to do is to identify the species involved, and to trace where it came from. If this is not possible, the position of the bite (see p. 52) and an analysis of possible sources of attack will often provide useful clues.

Protection by nets

If the animals involved come into the house from outside, for example mosquitoes and gnats, nets fixed over the windows and doors will be effective. In the absence of nets, ordinary curtains will provide a certain amount of protection, especially if they have been treated with some kind of deterrent.

Deterrent substances

There are several substances that deter insects and mites and these can either be sprayed on to the skin and clothes or used as an ointment. The best of them remain effective for about 4 hours. They are mainly for use outdoors and do not really provide a solution to the problem indoors.

The insecticide pyrethrin also acts as a deterrent and can, for example, be sprayed on to shoes and socks if one has to enter a flea-infested house. Pyrethrin is also included in some of the fumigants which may prove very effective in keeping mosquitoes away.

Insecticides

Certain insecticides, obtainable from the chemist, can be used directly on the skin or in the hair, and these are effective against mites and lice. Other pests, such as fleas, ticks and bed bugs, only attack from time to time, and so it is not sufficient just to treat oneself, but better to treat their hiding-places and surrounding areas with an insecticidal spray or powder.

INVERTEBRATES AND HYGIENE

Some of the insects, mites and other arthropods occurring indoors may have a direct or indirect influence on our health and well-being. In other words, they may become a hygiene problem.

Invertebrates carrying disease or causing annoyance

Some blood-sucking and stinging arthropods may cause pain by their attacks on the skin (see p. 33). Others may increase sensitivity, as mites do, for example, in the case of asthma (see p. 35). In rare cases the presence of certain invertebrates in foodstuffs may constitute a danger to health, as for instance when there are fly larvae in meat or large numbers of mites in cereal products. In addition, the mere presence of completely harmless animals has a depressing effect on certain people. There are several transitional stages from general malaise to a state of anxiety neurosis, sometimes with hallucinations, in which the patient believes that he or she is being persecuted by these small animals.

Invertebrates and the spread of disease

There are two principal ways in which pathogenic micro-organisms can be transmitted by invertebrates. In some cases a disease may be completely dependent upon certain species of insect or mite and can be transmitted only by them. Well-known examples are yellow fever and sleeping sickness, which do not occur in temperate regions, and malaria, which has, in practical terms, been exterminated in Europe. In these diseases the micro-organisms have to pass through part of their developmental cycle in the gut of the insect before they can be transmitted to a

human at the next session of blood sucking. In other diseases, such as typhus, which is transmitted by head lice, and plague, which is transmitted by rat fleas, the infective organisms arrive on the skin in the faeces of the insect and reach the host's blood stream by way of small skin abrasions caused, for example, by scratching.

In other cases transmission is more a matter of chance, as for example when insects such as houseflies, blowflies, cockroaches and Pharaoh ants pick up pathogenic micro-organisms from carrion, offal and dunghills and pass them elsewhere.

There is always a chance that intestinal and other infections may be transmitted when insects land on foodstuffs which are not to be subsequently cooked or washed, and particularly if the micro-organisms have an opportunity to breed for a day or two.

It is very difficult to estimate the extent to which dissemination by insects plays a part comparable to other methods of transmission, e.g. directly through the air and by contact. However, invertebrates must in all cases be regarded as undesirable wherever there is a demand for strict hygiene, as in laboratories, in hospitals and in any establishment where food is produced or processed.

Animals in Foodstuffs

Ever since our ancestors found out how to keep foodstuffs in reserve for bad times, insects and rodents have taken their toll of such stores. The remains of pests of stored products (e.g. flour beetles) have been found in graves from 2,500 B.C., and drugstore beetles, spider beetles and tobacco beetles were found in the grave of Tutankhamun.

Animal pests of stored products are still with us. Indeed it has been estimated that about 15 per cent of all stored foodstuffs never reach human mouths, but end up in the bodies of insects or rodents.

It is possible to distinguish between two types of pest that attack stored products. First, there are those that only visit foodstuffs when they are hungry, but which otherwise live and breed in cracks and crevices and similar hiding-places. These include cockroaches, silverfish and ants. Secondly, there are animals which lay their eggs in or on a foodstuff and in fact spend their whole life in it.

Animals which only visit foodstuffs when they are hungry are very catholic in their choice of food and they may also make do with odd fragments, but many of those that live directly in their food are more fastidious.

Mites, Order Acari
(Page 20)

Mites of various kinds can thrive in foodstuffs which are kept a little too damp. These are tiny animals which look like specks of dust when seen by the naked eye, but when examined more closely, under a lens, they can be seen to move, albeit slowly.

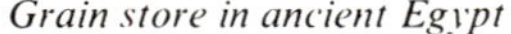

Grain store in ancient Egypt

In former times the kitchen provided a wonderful environment for many invertebrates

Flour mite, *Acarus siro*
(Page 20)

This is the commonest species of mite in foodstuffs; it has reddish legs. Flour mites can live in almost any kind of flour or in fodder and, not least important, in stores of seed and corn. They are also to be found on old cheese. A single female can lay up to 500 eggs during its life.

After hatching the life cycle consists of a larval stage, two so-called nymphal stages, and the adult stage, which at 25° C is reached in three weeks. These mites can go through their life cycle at a temperature as low as 4° C, but they do require adequate humidity, and will not thrive if the relative humidity is less than 65 per cent.

Flour mites are able to survive periods with unfavourable conditions. After the second nymphal stage they may pass into what is known as a hypopus stage, in which they are almost immobile and very resistant to desiccation. In the hypopus stage they can also be transported, e.g. by flies.

If there is any doubt as to whether flour is infested with mites it is only necessary to spread a little of it out on the table and leave it for a quarter of an hour. If mites are present the surface of the flour will become uneven, as the mites start to wander about.

Mite-infested foodstuffs acquire a characteristic sweetish, sickly smell, and a taste which renders them unsuitable for human consumption. Heavily infested

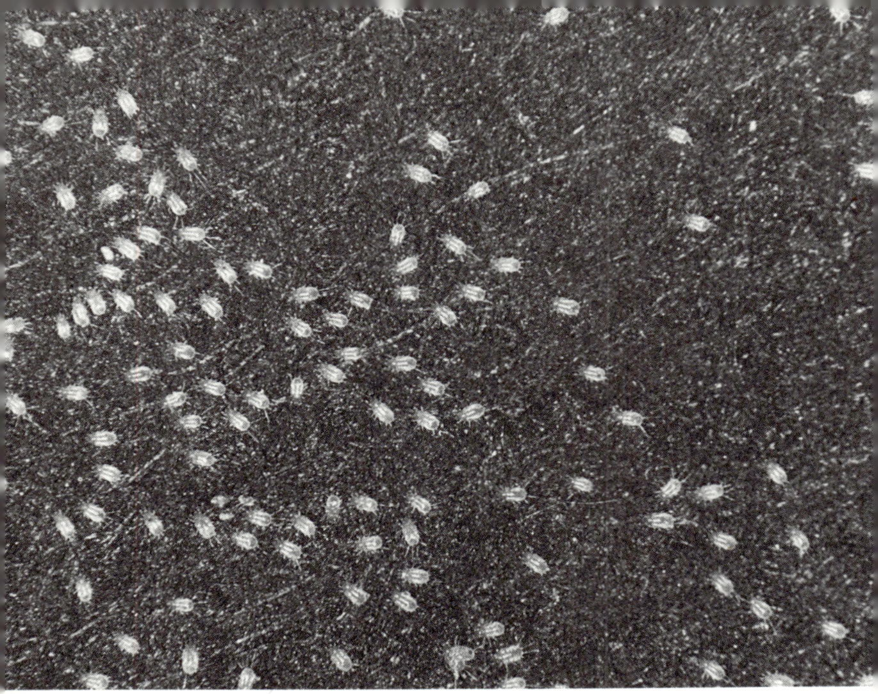

When flour mites are numerous, they resemble reddish specks of moving dust

products are definitely injurious and should be discarded.

The only effective method of controlling mites is to ensure that the foodstuff in question is stored as dry and as cool as possible.

Tyrophagus longior
(Page 20)

This mite is very similar to the preceding species and thrives in the same kind of place. It feeds mainly on moulds which grow on damp goods, but seldom becomes a serious pest.

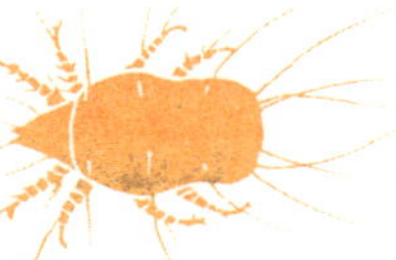

Cheese mite, *Tyrophagus casei*
(Page 20)

Cheese mites can also live in corn, flour, etc., but they are best known for their occurrence in cheese, in which they gnaw small holes. A ripe, mite-infested cheese will be more or less covered with a grey powder, which consists of the mites themselves and their moulted skins and faeces. Cheese mites can live at low temperatures but not in the refrigerator. For many cheeses the presence of mites is highly undesirable, but there are certain types in which a culture of cheese mites is introduced. Cheese can be protected by a thin layer of paraffin wax.

Prune mite, *Carpoglyphus lactis*
(Page 20)

This is very similar to the flour mite and it also has pinkish legs, but it can be distinguished, amongst other things, by the fact that its body is not divided into two by a transverse line. These mites live mainly in dried fruit, and sometimes in jam.

People who work with mite-infested goods may suffer from an eczema-like condition because they become sensitive to the mites and to their moulted skins and faeces.

Prune mites are particularly likely to produce this type of condition, often known as grocer's itch, but flour mites may also be responsible.

Order Thysanura

These are primitive insects, and the few living species are thought to be the descendants of a group which was very numerous about two hundred million years ago.

Two species may be encountered indoors.

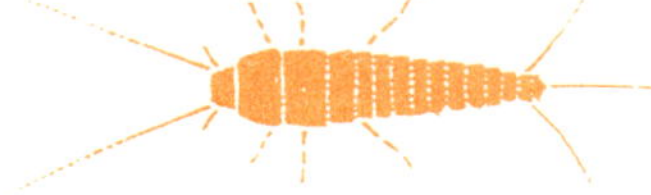

Silverfish, *Lepisma saccharina*
(Page 20)

The common silverfish frequently occurs in kitchens and comes out at night to feed on crumbs and odd scraps of food. It is capable of digesting cellulose and so can derive nutriment from paper. It is described in greater detail on p. 106 together with other pests that attack paper.

Firebrat, *Thermobia domestica*
(Page 20)

As its popular and scientific names suggest, this is an insect that likes warmth. In fact it thrives best at a temperature around 37° C, and is therefore frequently found in bakeries and restaurant kitchens. Unlike the common silverfish it can survive under very dry conditions.

Cockroaches, Sub-order Blattodea
(Page 21)

Cockroaches are also regarded as primitive insects, and fossil species known from the Carboniferous period some 250 million years ago are very like those known today. There are about 3,500 different species of cockroach, and the vast majority of these live in the open and almost never come in contact with man. A few small species are native to northern Europe (see p. 201), but the majority are tropical. The cockroaches found indoors in temperate regions have been introduced from the tropics during the last 200 years, and most of them are completely dependent upon heated buildings.

German cockroach,
Blattella germanica
(Page 21)

This is by far the commonest species of cockroach in Europe.

For most people the idea of having cockroaches on the kitchen table is intensely unpleasant, but for those with an eye for such things these are elegant insects.

Both sexes have very well-developed wings, which cover the whole of the abdomen, but these are used not for active flying, but for gliding when they jump, for instance, from the table to the floor.

The female lays her eggs in a special brown capsule which is divided into 30–40 small compartments, each containing a single egg. In the German cockroach the female carries this egg capsule protruding from her genital aperture until the small, wingless young are ready to hatch out. At room temperature the full development to the adult stage takes about 6 months.

Cockroaches are practically speaking omnivorous. They are active at night, spending the hours of light hidden in crevices, particularly near warm places, such as ovens or radiators.

They are very gregarious, and a substance produced in the alimentary canal and passed out with the faeces may serve to attract and keep them together. During the mating period cockroaches are also motivated by scent. The females produce a scent which the males perceive by way of special sense organs on their antennae.

In many parts of northern Europe cockroaches occur in bakeries and restaurants, and also in hospitals, canteens, food factories and many private kitchens. Normally cockroaches cause no real damage. It has been suggested that they transmit disease but this has not been directly proved (see also p. 55). On the other hand, there is a need to be watchful, for several species of pathogenic bacteria have been isolated from cockroaches caught at random. These insects may also destroy foodstuffs, partly by gnawing them, but mainly by fouling, and by tainting them with their unpleasant smell. Cockroaches also cause damage by gnawing paper, leather and textiles.

German cockroaches, adults and nymphs of various sizes on the wall of a bakery. The numerous spots of faeces show that this is one of their regular haunts.

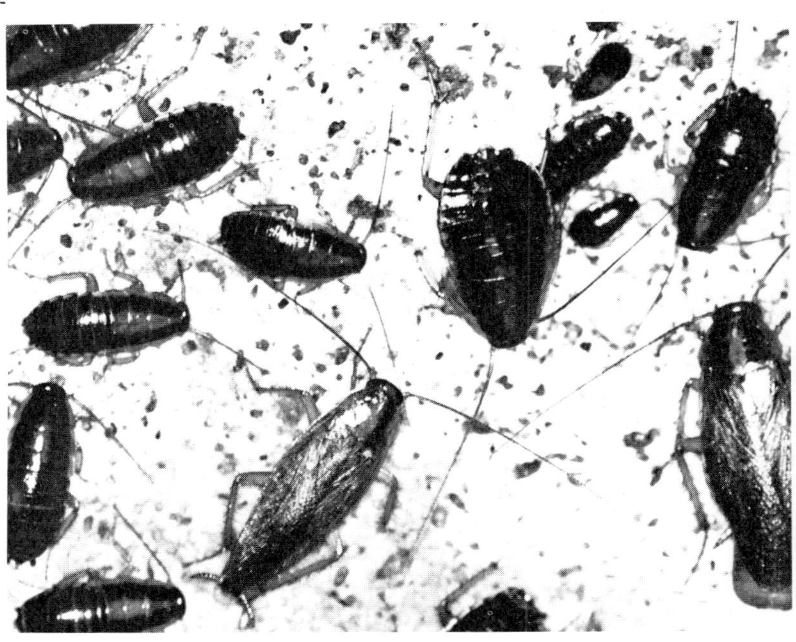

Nymphs and adults of the oriental cockroach

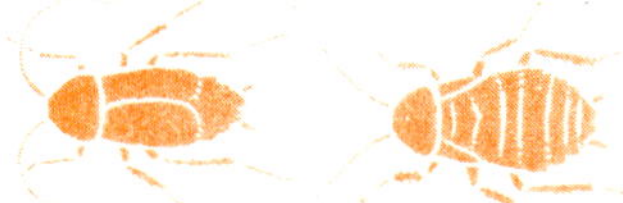

Oriental or **common cockroach,**
Blatta orientalis
(Page 21)

This species is found in the same kind of place as the German cockroach, but usually at an even higher temperature, and it is not so common. The wings are well-developed in the male, but they are reduced to short stumps in the female.

The egg capsule contains about 15 eggs, and the female only carries it for a few days. She then deposits it in a dark, sheltered place and after about two months it splits open and the small nymphs crawl out.

Nymphs of the oriental cockroach just hatched from their egg capsule and still pale

Baking oven with cockroaches. Woodcut 1550.

American cockroach,
Periplaneta americana
(Page 21)

A species introduced into Europe with food cargoes. Both sexes have wings which are longer than the body. They thrive in warm places with a high humidity, such as greenhouses and conservatories, but will not tolerate cold or dryness.

Brown-banded cockroach,
Supella supellectilium
(Page 21)

There are several other species of tropical cockroach which may suddenly appear in a warehouse or greengrocer's shop, having been introduced with goods from warmer regions, but most of them quickly die in northern Europe. The brown-banded cockroach, which is now common in central Europe, has been recorded as breeding in south Devon and more recently in London. It now has a cosmopolitan distribution but probably originated in Africa.

Egg capsules of:

German cockroach

Oriental cockroach

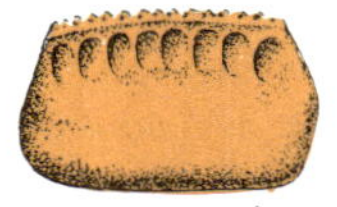

American cockroach

Brown-banded cockroa

Booklice, Order Psocoptera
(Page 21)

These insects are not related to the true lice. They prefer damp places, such as cellars, damp outside walls, or outhouses, and they may be found in new houses before the walls are dry. They cannot tolerate dryness.

A female booklouse can lay a couple of hundred eggs, and under favourable conditions development to sexual maturity takes about a month, so it is not surprising that booklice often occur in very large numbers. In kitchens and stores they mainly attack flour, cereals and other goods containing starch, and they have a fantastic ability to get into packets that are not tightly sealed. They are in no way dangerous to health, but may cause commercial losses if they become established in grocery stores.

Small moths, 'Microlepidoptera'
(Page 23)

Although one does not generally associate moths with foodstuffs there are in fact some species which are adapted to exploit foods, and some of them are among the most serious pests in stores and factories.

Mill or **flour moth,**
Ephestia kuehniella
(Page 23)

This moth came originally from India. It was first found in Europe in about 1877 in some American wheat. Nowadays there are few concerns dealing with flour and cereals which do not suffer from time to time from the depredations of this moth. It may also become a menace in private households.

The adult moths fly about at dusk, and the females each lay up to about 300 eggs in the flour. When the eggs hatch the larvae start to feed immediately. All the time they are spinning a sticky silken thread, which causes the meal to hang together in large clumps. It also acquires an unpleasant smell and a grey-brown colour due to the faeces.

The fully grown larvae move up to the

When flour contains silk it is a sure indication of a flour moth infestation

surface of the flour and wander off to find a nearby crevice in which they can pupate. The pupa, which is *c.* 7 mm long, is completely enclosed in a thick, white silken cocoon.

The adult moths emerge from the hiding places after 2-3 weeks.

Mill moth larvae prefer wheat flour, but will also feed on all sorts of grains, cereals, seeds, macaroni, dried fruits, cocoa, nuts and almonds.

In mills the silken threads may cause a blockage of piping, funnels and sieves, so that the process has to be stopped for a thorough cleansing and possibly gassing.

In the house it will normally be sufficient to discard the tainted goods, but it is as well to remember that larvae ready to pupate will have hidden themselves nearby, and may make their presence known a few weeks later.

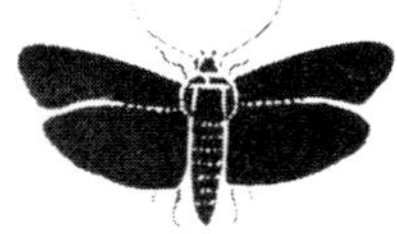

Warehouse or **cocoa moth,**
Ephestia elutella
(Pages 23 and 104)

This species is closely related to the meal moth but its taste is more in the way of nuts, almonds, cocoa beans and dried fruit. It is therefore a serious problem in the chocolate industry. The moths nearly always reach a factory with the raw materials. In addition, the remains of cocoa beans and other materials may be seats of infection, and the machinery itself may harbour pockets of suitable food for these moths. If the moths appear in the factory there is always a risk that they may have laid eggs on the finished goods, and so one may have the problem of 'worms' in the chocolate. The infection may also, of course, take place in a store or shop.

The larvae cannot penetrate hermetically sealed packages, but if there is the slightest gap the female moth, attracted by scent, will lay eggs nearby and the newly hatched larvae will crawl in and start to feed.

This moth can also eat tobacco. Remarkably enough it can tolerate nicotine and, together with the tobacco beetle, it is one of the most serious pests in the tobacco industry.

When a cocoa moth is seen in a private house or the larvae are observed climbing up a wall it will almost always be because a packet of raisins or nuts has been left open over a long period.

Dried currant moth,
Ephestia cautella

This is very similar to the preceding species and it has the same habits. Also known as *Cadra cautella.*

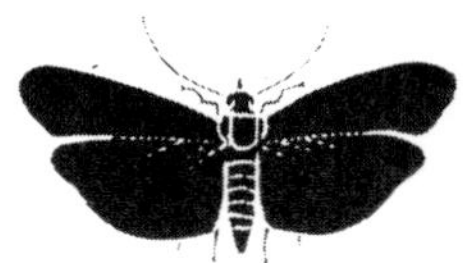

Indian meal moth,
Plodia interpunctella
(Pages 23 and 104)

This is a particularly serious pest in stores of food in warm regions of the world. It mainly attacks dried fruit, nuts and almonds, and the larvae are also found in chocolate, and sometimes in cereal products. Under the most favourable conditions (at 25° C) development from egg to adult takes only 35 days. As in the other moths that attack foodstuffs the

'Worms' in chocolate are the larvae of various moths. They actually prefer nuts and almonds to chocolate.

Larvae of the Indian meal moth on a prune

larvae leave the material they have been feeding on and move off, often upwards, in search of sheltered places in which to pupate. In the house the larvae may be found in packets of nuts or almonds.

Brown house moth,
Hofmannophila pseudospretella
(Pages 23 and 105)

The larva of this moth is sometimes to be found in grain warehouses or among foodstuffs, but it is primarily a pest of textiles (p. 96).

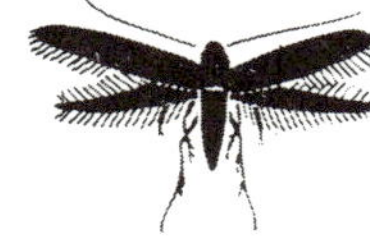

Wine moth, *Oinophila v-flavum*
(Page 23)

This is not really a pest of foodstuffs, but somewhat of a specialist, for it is often found in wine cellars where the larvae gnaw holes in the corks. They thrive particularly in damp cellars, feeding on the mould growing on the walls and on the wine corks, and what is worse they can live in mouldy corks. The debris produced by their activities can be seen hanging from the corks, often covered with wine that has seeped out of the bottle.

Signs left by larvae of the wine moth; the debris and faeces have been removed

Beetles, Order Coleoptera

This is by far the largest of the insect groups, so it is not surprising that it has numerous representatives that attack foodstuffs. Normally it is the adult beetles that are first observed, but it is the larvae that do the damage and they must be found and dealt with.

Mealworm beetle, *Tenebrio molitor*
(Pages 26 and 104)

This beetle is best known from its larvae, known as mealworms, which are a favourite food for cage birds and vivarium animals. Mealworms are particularly associated with corn or flour, but sometimes they can also be found in sparrows' nests where they feed on the birds' droppings. Most of them overwinter as larvae, change into beetles during the following summer and die in the autumn. In former times mealworms were very common in bakeries, mills and grain warehouses, but nowadays they are no longer important as a pest. The adult beetles seen usually come from birds' nests in the neighbourhood. On warm summer evenings they often fly in through the windows, attracted by the light. They normally do no harm in the living rooms of a house, and as they take so long to develop they do not become a problem in the kitchen.

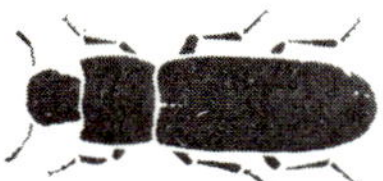

Tribolium destructor
(Pages 26 and 104)

This species is like a small edition of the mealworm beetle, and its larvae look like small mealworms. It probably came originally from tropical Africa and has been distributed with goods to many parts of the world. It is now common and well established in Europe.

The beetle secretes a substance with a smell resembling lysol, which clings to the goods that it infests.

During its life the female beetle can lay about 1000 eggs, usually in flour or grain, or in foodstuffs such as bread, biscuits, spaghetti or bird seed. In a normally heated kitchen the development from egg to adult beetle takes about 3 months. The adults have an incredible wanderlust and so they may be found far from the kitchen.

The beetle itself can live for more than 3 years, and can survive for months without food.

Flour beetle, *Tribolium confusum*
(Page 26)

This beetle is like a slightly smaller and paler edition of the preceding species. It is found mainly in flour and cereal products, but it also attacks a variety of other foodstuffs, such as beans, dried fruit, spices and chocolate. It is particularly in-

Flour beetles and larvae in flour

jurious in warehouses and in factories making starch products, but is not uncommon in private households. Flour infested by the larvae has a greyish colour and a tendency to go mouldy.

This is a prolific species. The female lays several hundred eggs and can find her way even into tightly closed packets of food. On the other hand, these beetles require a high temperature, preferably about 30° C, and will not develop or breed at temperatures below 18° C.

Rust-red flour beetle,
Tribolium castaneum

This is very like the preceding species, but is a little smaller and darker. It has similar habits, but requires even more warmth, and in an unheated warehouse will probably die during the winter in northern Europe.

Cadelle beetle,
Tenebroides mauritanicus
(Pages 26 and 104)

Originally an African species, this beetle has now spread to almost all parts of the world. It is found particularly in grain warehouses, silos and mills. The larvae live hidden away, feeding on corn and flour, but also live to a certain extent as predators on other insects. The species is probably not very common in Europe but may be a serious pest in flour mills because it destroys the sieves by biting holes in them. Development is rather slow, so this species should never become a problem in private households.

Saw-toothed grain beetle,
Oryzaephilus surinamensis
(Pages 25 and 104)

This is another beetle from the tropics. It has a series of serrations on each side of the thorax. It can live in grain stores and silos and feeds on all types of dried food products, mostly those containing starch, such as flour, bread and cereal products, but also in dried fruits and nuts. In recent years it appears to have become quite common in private houses in Europe.

These beetles can live for 3 years, and during the course of her life the female may lay about 400 eggs. They like a high temperature and development is most rapid at 32° C, taking only 25 days from egg-laying to the emergence of the adult beetle from the pupal stage. Breeding ceases if the temperature falls below 18° C. The beetle itself is very active and

The merchant grain beetle can find its way into tightly closed packages and into unopened walnuts

A walnut kernel attacked by merchant grain beetles

Saw-toothed grain beetles on a piece of crispbread. These small beetles have become very common in wholesale grocery stores and in kitchens.

can penetrate cracks and crevices, while the small, freshly hatched larvae can find their way even into tightly closed packets of food.

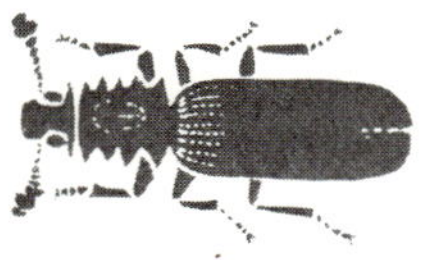

Merchant grain beetle,
Oryzaephilus mercator

Very similar in appearance to the preceding species, and difficult to distinguish. The present species is not so commonly seen, and seems to like even higher temperatures. It prefers vegetable foods that contain oil, so it is mainly found in imported nuts, almonds and copra.

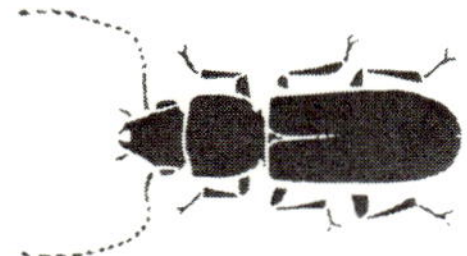

Flat grain beetle,
Cryptolestes ferrugineus
(Pages 25 and 104)

This is a pest found mainly in grain warehouses, but it may also occur in private houses. It is not normally a very serious pest, but if the temperature and humidity are sufficiently high it can do quite a lot of damage, partly because the larvae eat the seed germ and partly because they may occur in very large numbers, up to 4000 beetles per kilogram of grain.

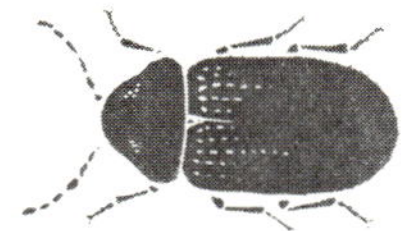

Biscuit or **drugstore beetle,**
Stegobium paniceum
(Pages 25 and 104)

This is actually a member of the furniture beetle family which has become adapted to a diet of starch-containing foods, and the round exit-holes made by the larvae of this beetle are exactly like the holes in timber made by furniture beetles. The species has become distributed to all parts of the world. In fact, these beetles must have been spread by ships in former times, and the old habit of banging ship's biscuits on the table before eating them perhaps

Drugstore beetle larvae, like those of wood-boring beetles, live inside their food and only emerge as adults

served to drive out the biscuit beetle larvae. The female lays her eggs either in the food itself or in crevices nearby. The small larvae, only ½ mm long, hatch out in about 2 weeks and are very active. They can live a whole week without food and they are very clever at entering packages which are not tightly closed. When they have found a food that suits them they gnaw their way in and feed very rapidly, and become so fat and lethargic that they are quite helpless if they should accidentally fall out.

The larvae prefer hard, dried products such as crispbread, pasta and dog biscuits. They can also live in dried vegetables, nuts and spices.

The adult beetles fly well and as they are attracted by light they are sometimes found on window frames, often far from the place where they developed. At a temperature of 22° C, development from egg to adult takes 2–3 months.

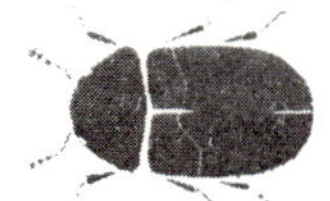

Tobacco beetle,
Lasioderma serricorne
(Page 25)

This is also related to the furniture beetles and it is very similar to the biscuit beetle, from which it can be distinguished by its serrated antennae. It is primarily a tropical and subtropical beetle which requires plenty of warmth. Egg-laying ceases below 21° C, and all movement ceases at temperatures below 18° C. The beetles are often carried with goods to temperate regions, where they can survive in heated buildings.

The larvae, which can tolerate nicotine, live both in raw tobacco and in finished tobacco products, and are a very serious and costly pest of the tobacco industry. They also have a very varied diet, for they are found in many other products, such as rice, dried fish, spices and dates. As in the case of the preceding species the newly hatched larvae are extremely active and can live for a week without food. The adult beetles fly extremely well.

It is sad to open a box of cigars only to find that tobacco beetles have been there first

A pair of grain weevils emerging from the barley ears in which they have spent their larval life

Lesser grain borer,
Rhizopertha dominica
(Page 25)

This species belongs to the family Bostrychidae, a group of tropical beetles which includes several wood-boring species (p. 128). It can be a very serious pest of stored rice and grain in warm regions (see p. 93).

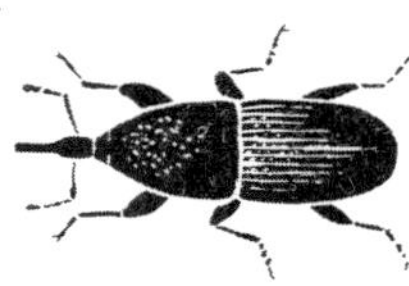

Grain weevil, *Sitophilus granarius*
(Pages 28 and 104)

This is the commonest pest in stored grain. It cannot fly but is a tireless walker. When egg-laying the female gnaws a small depression in a grain of cereal, lays an egg in it and then covers the hole with a secretion that is the same colour as the cereal. She only lays 2–3 eggs a day but she lives a long time, at any rate until she has produced 200–300 eggs.

Grain weevils prefer wheat, rye and maize, but in default of these they may lay eggs in hard starch-containing products such as dry biscuits and pasta.

The small larva has no limbs and cannot leave the grain. As it eats and grows the grain becomes a hollow husk by the time the larva is fully grown. It then pupates inside the husk and about a week later it emerges as a fully developed beetle (see

p. 93). At 26° C the whole development takes a month.

When found in a house in the country this beetle has usually come from the remains of a store of grain, but if this is not the case it will nearly always have originated in a packet of bird seed. Because of its rather specialized requirements this beetle is unlikely to become established in a private house.

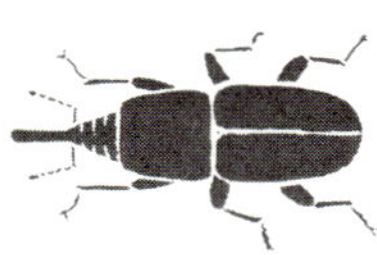

Rice weevil, *Sitophilus oryzae*
(Page 28)

This beetle is a little smaller than the grain weevil, and can be recognized by the four reddish spots on the elytra, which cover a pair of functional wings. This is one of the most serious pests of cereal crops in the tropics and subtropics. It is often brought to northern Europe and is not uncommonly found in kitchen cupboards, usually in a packet of rice (see p. 93). As in the grain weevil it lays an egg in a small groove which it has gnawed in a rice grain. The larva lives and feeds in the grain. This beetle does not attack other foodstuffs, and as it requires warmth it does not survive the winter in unheated stores.

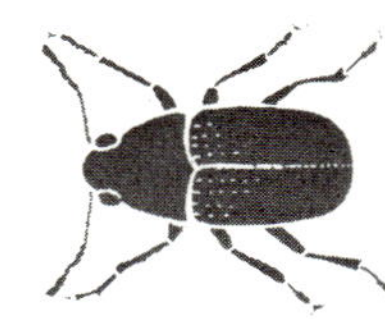

Nutmeg or **coffee weevil,**
Araeocerus fasciculatus
(Page 28)

This beetle lacks the well-developed snout of the curculionid weevils. It is widespread in tropical and subtropical regions and is often brought to Europe in goods. It is now found quite commonly in Britain, mainly as a pest in cocoa beans, nutmegs and coffee beans. It has

Grain and rice weevils destroy large quantities of cereals in warehouses and silos. Here rice weevils are crawling about on wheat, with a good coating of flour.

on occasions caused serious trouble to coffee exporters in south-east Asia. It requires warmth and a high humidity, so in temperate regions it will die off in winter unless the infested goods are stored in well-heated places.

Common bean weevil,
Acanthoscelides obtectus
(Page 28)

This beetle mainly attacks haricot beans, but it may also occur in other related crops. It can lay eggs in fresh beans in the fields or in dried stored beans.

The female lays several eggs in each bean. When the larvae are fully grown they gnaw their way out towards the surface of the bean and pupate, leaving a thin shell between themselves and the outside world. When the adult beetles are ready to emerge they only have to break through the circular 'windows' to be free (see p. 93).

Hide and **bacon beetles,**
Family Dermestidae
(Page 25)

The members of this beetle family live principally on the dried remains of plants and animals. Many species live on for example cartilage and scraps of dried meat, and some can utilize hair and feathers (see p. 98). This way of life will, of course, bring them into conflict with human interests, for they frequently attack dried foodstuffs.

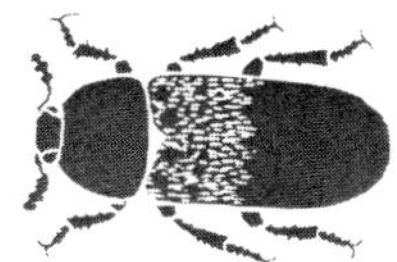

Larder beetle, *Dermestes lardarius*
(Page 25)

In former times this was a serious pest in private houses, for it attacked smoked hams and sausages hanging from the ceiling and also dried fish. Nowadays when most meat products are kept in a refrigerator or a deep freeze it is no longer a serious pest in private households. It sometimes multiplies rapidly in dried cat and dog foods, and may be very destructive in factories working with dried fish or hides.

The larvae are fully grown about a month after hatching and many then move away to find a suitable place for pupation. They sometimes gnaw tunnels in timber (p. 148) or plaster, but also into many other materials, and when this happens in a store they can cause a lot of damage to goods not otherwise attacked by insects.

The adult beetles fly very well, so if found in a house they may have come from far away. Sometimes the source of infection may be food remains left in odd corners of the kitchen, but more often it will be a pigeon's nest or a dead mouse under the floor boards.

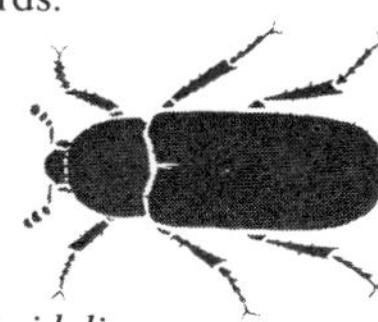

Dermestes haemorrhoidalis
(Pages 25 and 104)

This is a close relative of the preceding species which also lives on dried animal remains. Larvae ready to pupate have the same habit of gnawing their way into all kinds of materials.

This is a recent addition to the European fauna, but it appears to have become quite common, particularly in large towns. The adult beetles fly very well and so an odd one may appear in any house. In general, they can do no damage in a normal household, but they may multiply if the remains of food and other kitchen waste are left lying around for months. In many cases the beetles come from a pigeon's nest.

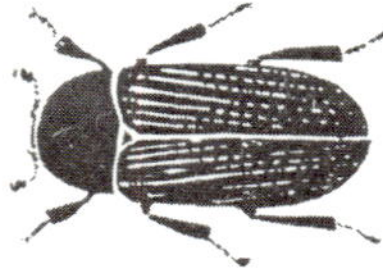

Dermestes frischi
(Page 25)

In addition to the two preceding species, other very similar dermestid beetles are

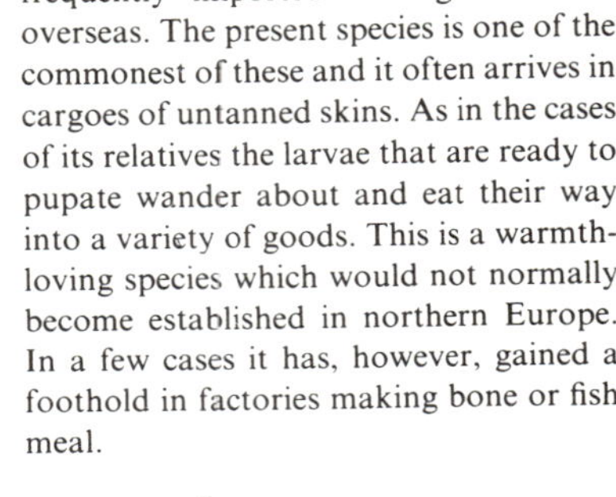

frequently imported with goods from overseas. The present species is one of the commonest of these and it often arrives in cargoes of untanned skins. As in the cases of its relatives the larvae that are ready to pupate wander about and eat their way into a variety of goods. This is a warmth-loving species which would not normally become established in northern Europe. In a few cases it has, however, gained a foothold in factories making bone or fish meal.

Khapra beetle, *Trogoderma granarium*
(Pages 25 and 104)

Khapra beetles came originally from India. They often congregate in large

Bacon beetles and their larvae on salami

numbers in the cracks and crevices of walls in warehouses. Unlike the preceding dermestids this beetle feeds mainly on plant material. It has now spread to almost all tropical and subtropical regions, and those areas where it has not appeared have very stringent quarantine regulations to prevent its introduction. For it is regarded as one of the most serious pests, particularly in grain and foodstuff stores.

The khapra beetle is sometimes brought to temperate regions but as it requires a temperature of at least 24° C for breeding there is little risk of it becoming established.

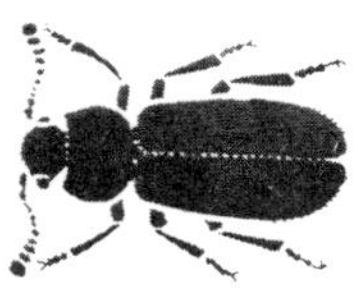

Red-legged copra beetle,
Necrobia rufipes
(Page 25)

This beetle has spread to most parts of the world owing to the trade in copra (dried coconut). Apart from copra it also eats carrion and like the larder beetle it will thrive in parts that are too dry for other carrion-eaters. It can also live on museum specimens, and has been found, for example, in Egyptian mummies. In factories and warehouses it attacks concentrated fodder, fish and bone meal, milk and egg powder, and will occasionally even cause damage to pharmaceutical products.

At a temperature of 22° C, development from the egg to the adult beetle takes about a month. In temperate regions it only produces a single generation in the year.

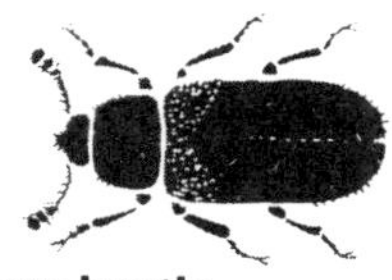

Red-breasted copra beetle,
Necrobia ruficollis
(Page 25)

This species can be found on dried carrion where it feeds partly on scraps of meat and partly as a predator on the other invertebrates infesting the carrion. It sometimes occurs outdoors in temperate regions, but is mainly seen in factories making meat and bone meal.

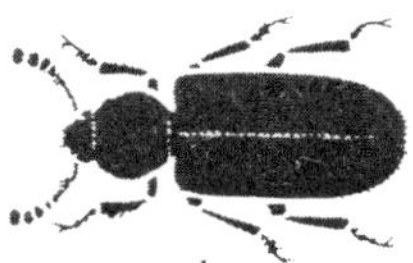

Ant beetle, *Corynetes coeruleus*
(Page 25)

This beetle is similar to the copra beetles, but is a uniform iridescent green. The larvae feed on dried carrion and may also eat smoked meat products. In roof spaces suffering attack by wood-boring beetles it lives as a predator (p. 121), its larvae hunting the wood-boring larvae like a mole hunting earthworms.

Spider beetles, Family Ptinidae
(Page 26)

These beetles have a certain resemblance to spiders, for they have very long legs and a marked constriction between the thorax and the arched abdomen.

Many of the species are practically speaking omnivorous. The newly hatched larvae are very active, but once they reach a source of food they soon become fat and almost immobile. They can spin a kind of silk and often sit sheltered in loosely spun cocoons. The fully grown larvae sometimes leave the material they have been living in, even biting through very tough packaging. They then spin a whitish cocoon and pupate.

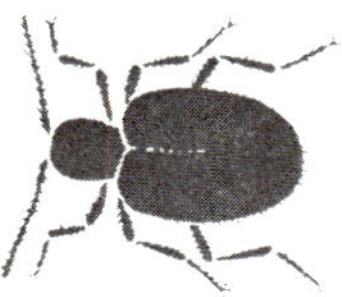

Australian spider beetle,
Ptinus tectus
(Page 26)

This species arrived in Europe from Australia as recently as 1900, but it is now common more or less everywhere.

The female can lay up to 1000 eggs, and the larvae will live in all kinds of dried plant products, such as grain, flour and spices. They may also breed in birds' nests and in desiccated carrion. In lofts and warehouses they can make do with the remains of insects and rat or mouse faeces that collect in corners. In factories producing foodstuffs or bone meal this beetle can be a very serious pest, and it also destroys insect collections and stuffed animals. At room temperature development from egg to adult takes 3–4 months. Unlike its larva the adult may gnaw textiles (p. 99).

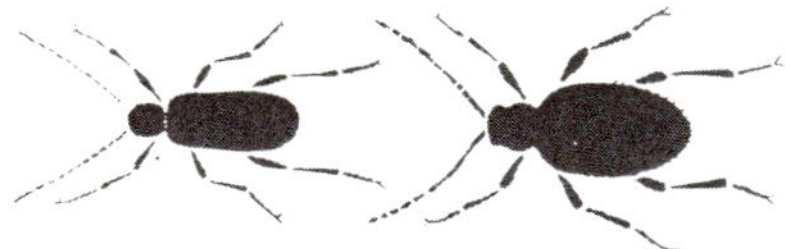

White-marked spider beetle,
Ptinus fur
(Pages 26 and 104)

Nowadays this European beetle is not so common as the Australian species just described. It eats the same kinds of food, including offal, but it is never a serious pest, partly because the female lays only about 50 eggs. This beetle is found both indoors and out in the open in Britain

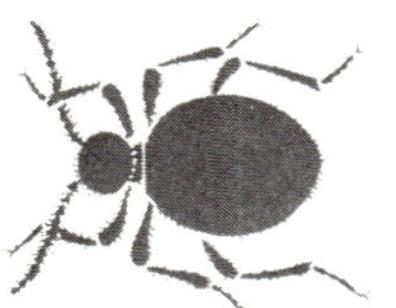

Golden spider beetle,
Niptus hololeucus
(Page 26)
In this beetle the body is closely beset with yellow hairs. It can feed on almost anything and when it appears in a house the source of infection may be dead chicks in a bird's nest or little collections of seeds in the loft. Now and again this beetle has been recorded as a pest of textiles.

Spider beetle, *Gibbium psylloides*
(Page 26)

A less active spider beetle, which crawls around slowly on its long legs. It may attack cereals and cereal products in, for example, India, where it is sometimes a pest. In Europe it is occasionally found in imported goods.

Spider beetles (Gibbium psylloides) *look like small shiny glass beads. Here they are in saffron.*

A single fly on the breakfast table may be tolerated, but there are rather too many here

Flies, Order Diptera
(Page 31)

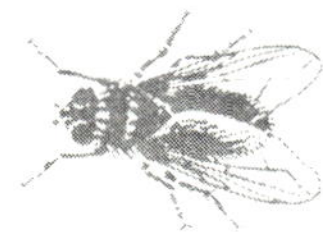

Housefly, *Musca domestica*
(Pages 31 and 104)

This is by far the commonest fly found in houses, and although it may occur in any room it is mainly found near to foodstuffs.

It has been suggested that this fly came originally from Africa, but nowadays it has followed man to all corners of the earth. In northern Europe it probably did not become established before man kept domestic animals indoors during the winter, a practice which did not start until about the beginning of the Iron Age, *c.* 400 B.C.

Housefly larvae live in manure, but they can also develop in kitchen waste and similar materials. A single female lays about 200 eggs and under favourable conditions, at a temperature around 30° C the whole development from egg-laying to adult fly takes only 7 days.

Houseflies are believed to have come to northern Europe when cattle farming started. The two pupae on the left are from an Iron Age cowshed, those on the right from a modern dunghill

A housefly feeding from a tablecloth and at the same time cleaning its wings

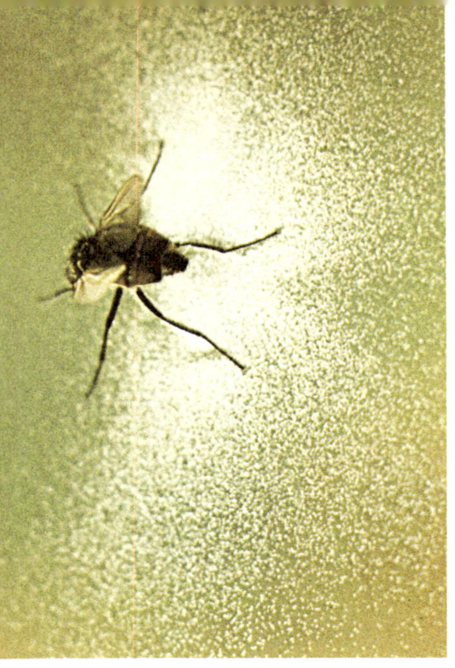

A housefly killed by fungus. Many flies are attacked by this fungal infection, particularly in the autumn. The inflated fly adheres to the substrate, here a window-pane, and is surrounded by a halo of white powder, the fungal spores.

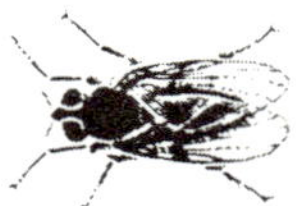

Lesser housefly, *Fannia canicularis*
(Pages 31 and 104)

This is the fly, common in houses, which circles ceaselessly round lamps and candles. The female lays eggs in very damp rotting material, such as wet manure, at the outflow of the kitchen sink and similar places, and there the characteristic, flat larvae develop (p. 104). This little fly is often very abundant in the vicinity of poultry farms.

Houseflies visit dung, carrion and offal of all kinds and naturally they pick up bacteria and viruses. They can, therefore, act as carriers of diseases (p. 55) and are wholly undesirable from the hygienic viewpoint. In addition, they can be intensely irritating when they occur in swarms, settling on man and animals.

Sometimes various tiny invertebrates can be found hanging on to the legs and body of a housefly. These may be mites of various kinds, which in this way are transported from place to place by the more mobile flies, or they may be false scorpions (p. 66). In all cases these are species which live in or on the manure where the flies develop, and they only release their grip when they come close to more manure, so there is no danger that they will become established indoors.

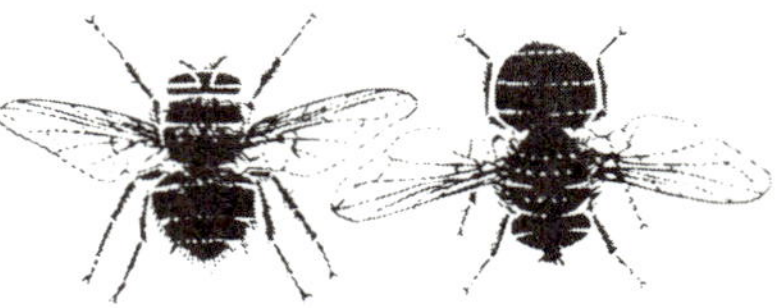

Blowflies, Family Calliphoridae
(Pages 31 and 104)

Long ago, before the months were named after Roman emperors, the month we now call July was called worm month in certain parts of northern Europe. The worms concerned were blowfly larvae or maggots and it reminds us of what a problem it must have been to keep meat fit for human consumption during the summer months. The blowflies most commonly seen in the house are the large bluebottle, *Calliphora erythrocephala* and the slightly smaller, iridescent greenbottles such as *Lucilia sericata.*

Under normal conditions female blowflies lay their eggs on dead animals, the smell of which can attract them from a

Housefly eggs laid on a fish's head

distance of several kilometres. They also lay on other decomposing organic matter and on faeces.

The eggs hatch in less than a day and the larvae immediately bore straight down into the food. They grow very rapidly and will be full size in about a week, and they will then normally leave the carrion. If the larvae have no opportunity to bury themselves in the ground they will crawl around until they find a suitable place in which to pupate.

Blowfly larvae found indoors may come from dead nestling birds, or from dead rats or mice. A single dead rat will provide food for 4000 maggots.

The creeping larvae may have an unpleasant appearance, but on the other hand they do remove the objectionable smell of a dead rat which is often far worse. The larvae move away from the light, so they will often pupate behind panelling or under a carpet. After a further 8–10 days the pupae wriggle their way into the light and the adult flies emerge. They are immediately able to fly off, mate and lay eggs.

Like other flies, the various blowflies have been suspected of carrying diseases, and this subject is discussed in more detail on p. 55. The metabolic products of such flies are themselves very undesirable, and meat that has been tainted by them must be very carefully washed before use.

Grey fleshfly, *Sarcophaga carnaria*
(Page 31)

This large grey fly is occasionally seen indoors. Like the true blowflies it lays on dead animals, so all meats and meat products must be kept out of its reach. The eggs hatch just before they are laid so the fleshfly can be said to produce live young.

Vinegar fly, *Drosophila funebris*
(Page 31)

These small yellowish-brown flies can sometimes be seen when a peeled banana or a cut tomato is left on the kitchen table. Vinegar flies frequently settle on bottles with drops of wine, milk or beer on the outside and they also visit jams, ketchup and vinegar.

The female lays eggs directly in such substrates and these hatch after about a day into larvae which move down into the food. They are fully grown after 4–5 days and then pupate.

The flies which emerge from the pupae can start to lay eggs when they are 24 hours old, so when the conditions are suitable the whole life cycle can be completed in 10 days.

In everyday life these small flies can be annoying and for factories making jam or cooking fruit and vegetables they may become a serious economic problem. As a precaution all such foodstuffs should be adequately covered to prevent the flies laying eggs on them.

For many years, species of *Drosophila*, variously known as fruitflies or vinegar flies, have been widely used as experimental animals in biological laboratories, and have been particularly useful in research on genetics.

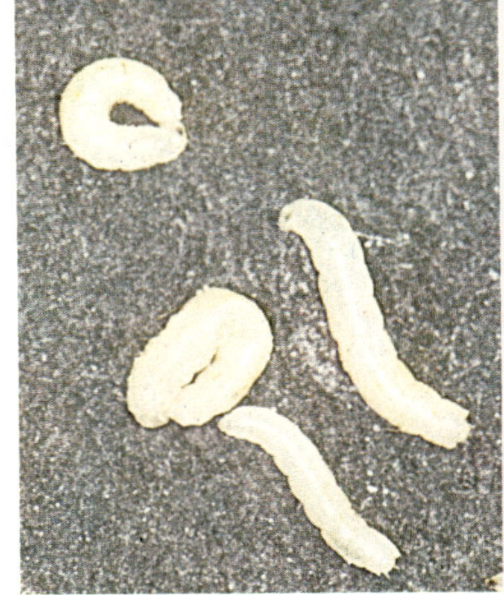

Cheese skippers, the larvae of the cheese fly, can jump about by biting their own tail and then straightening out the body with a bound

Cheese fly, *Piophila casei*
(Page 31)

This fly lays its eggs not only on cheese but also on other milk products, on meat as well as offal and faeces. The larvae, known as cheese skippers, have a fantastic ability to hop. They do this by bending themselves in the middle so that they can grasp the hind part of the body with the mouth-hooks. They then suddenly release their hold and the body is hurled into the air. At one time they were something of a scourge in shops selling cheese and smoked products and also in private houses, but they have now become very rare pests.

Cheese flies on a piece of Emmenthal

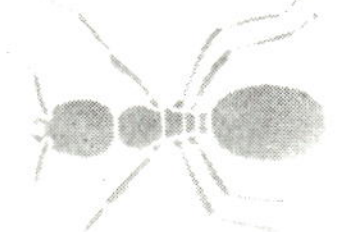

Ants, Superfamily Formicoidea
(Page 30)

Ants can be found more or less everywhere. Something like 3,500 different species have been described, and these are adapted for widely varying conditions. Common to them all, however, is the fact that they are social.

The winged ants frequently seen in the middle of the summer are males and females which come out in swarms for the nuptial flight. The males die soon after mating but each of the mated queens is capable of founding a new colony. The eggs laid by the queen hatch into larvae that develop into worker ants, which fetch food, keep the colony clean and tend the eggs, larvae and pupae.

Small black or **garden ant,**
Acanthomyops niger
(Page 30)

These are the ants most commonly seen on verandas and in the house. They live in the ground, frequently under rocks or flagstones, and they will often penetrate under the house itself, particularly if it has been built directly on the ground. Ants frequently build nests in the insulation layer and from there they penetrate up into the house itself through the cracks which inevitably appear in the cement. Garden ants can also build in mouldering timber (see p. 145). In nature, these ants search for flower nectar and for what is poetically known as honeydew but which is actually a sweet, sticky secretion produced by aphids or greenfly. When garden ants get into the house it will soon be seen that they are particularly attracted to sweet substances, such as drops of jam or scraps of pastry and cake. As soon as one ant has found such a delicacy there will soon, as though by magic, be a whole trail of them.

A pile of debris ejected from their nest in a cellar wall by garden ants

Naturally, of course, there is nothing magical in this. Ants cover a wide area in search of food. When one has found something sweet it can communicate the fact to others by tapping them with its antennae and also by feeding them with some of the contents of its crop. The jet **black ant,** *Acanthomyops fuliginosus*, (Page 30) may also find its way into the kitchen. It makes its nest in timber and is discussed in more detail (p. 145) together with the pests of timber.

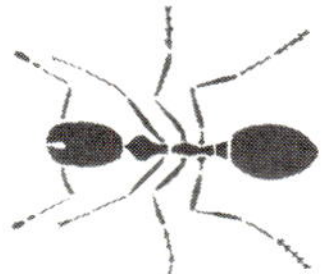

Pharaoh ant, *Monomorium pharaonis* (Page 30)

This small yellowish-red ant gets its popular and specific names from the fact that it was erroneously believed to have been one of the plagues of ancient Egypt.

Pharaoh ants on a piece of loaf sugar

In fact, it came originally from the tropics and reached Europe in the early years of this century. It is completely dependent upon heated houses.

Like the native ants. this tropical species lives in colonies, but in contrast to most other ants there are sometimes several queens in each colony. When a colony has reached a certain size some of the workers and queens leave, taking with them a number of eggs and larvae. The nests are established in sheltered dark places, usually near à source of warmth, for these ants prefer a temperature of 27–30° C. Once a building is infested there will soon be several so-called satellite colonies which live peacefully together. They can be regarded as one large family, consisting sometimes of hundreds of thousands of ants.

Pharaoh ants are almost omnivorous. They usually feed on sweet substances, but they also visit meat products, cheese, dead insects and carrion. They are sometimes found in food stores, shops, canteens and even in private houses. In most cases they do little or no damage but they can be rather annoying. In hospitals where conditions are more or less ideal for them these ants may be dangerous as possible distributors of disease. They can penetrate beneath bandages and find their way into sterile packs.

They are usually spread from place to place by the introduction of materials that contain a colony.

Birds, Class Aves

House sparrow, *Passer domesticus*

This is normally a harmless, quite attractive small bird when it builds in the eaves of a house (p. 183), but in food

Garden ants attracted to a drop of fruit juice

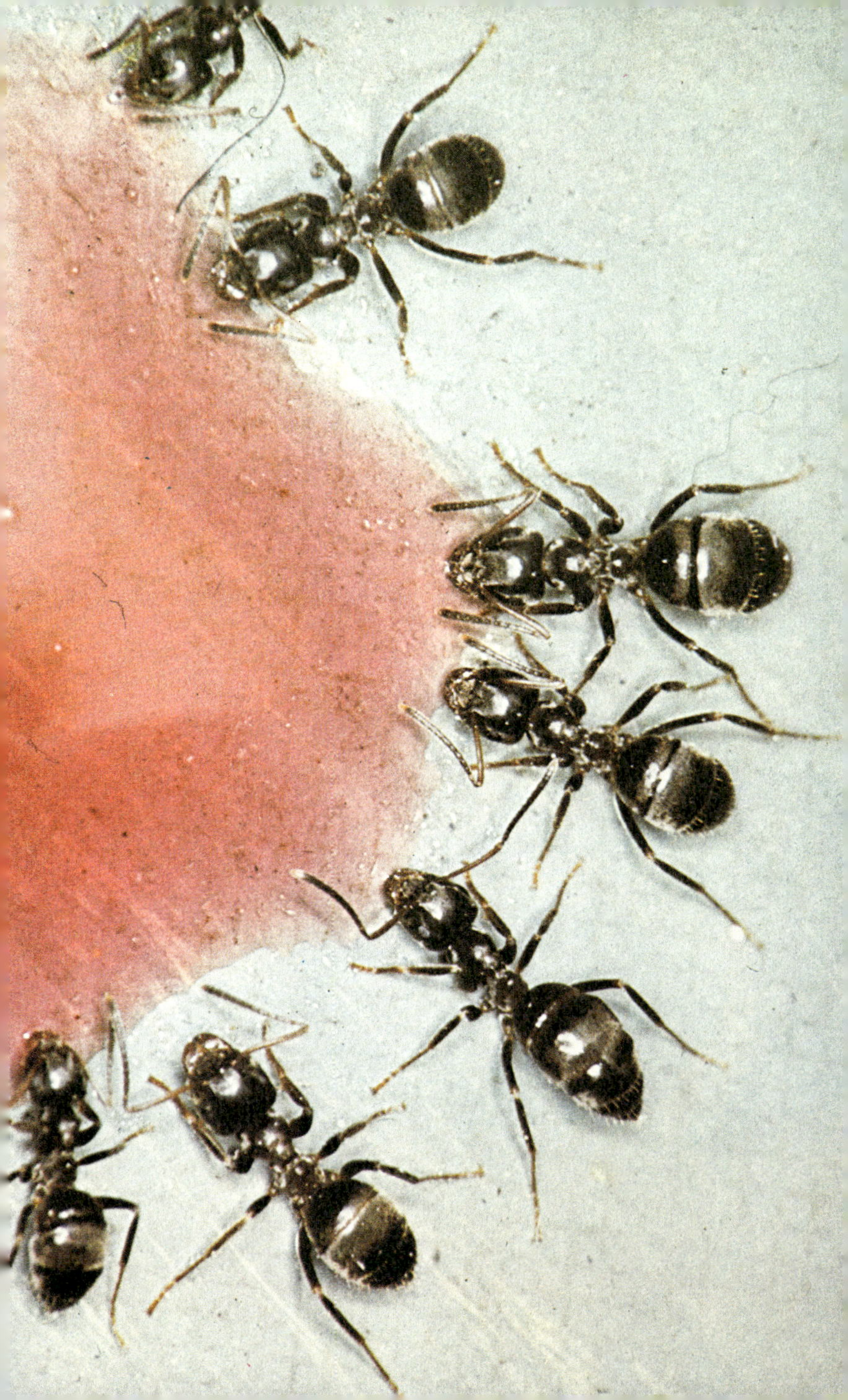

factories and stores it can do a lot of damage, and has been called a winged rat! Sparrows eat foodstuffs, foul them with their droppings and peck holes in packaging materials. They find their way in through any small hole and soon start to build their nests in the building.

The first step in combating sparrows is to destroy their nests and prevent them building again. They should not be poisoned, but they can be trapped and their young should be killed.

In many places it is quite simple to fix sparrow-proof netting over the windows, but if people are going in and out of a building the whole time it is extremely difficult to prevent sparrows from finding their way in.

Rodents, Order Rodentia

The rodents comprise about a third of all the living mammal species, and they include several of man's most serious pests. Their most characteristic structural feature is the dentition. Rodents have two large curved incisors in the upper jaw and two in the lower jaw, and these are separated from the remaining teeth by a toothless gap. The actual gnawing is carried out primarily by the lower incisors, while the upper incisors serve to hold the head in position. The shape and size of the toothmarks provide a clue to the identity of the species which has been at work.

Rodent skull. In adults the total breadth of the upper incisors is 1.5 mm in the house mouse, but c. *3 mm in the rat.*

House mouse, *Mus musculus*

The house mouse came originally from south-western Asia whence it has spread to all parts of the earth, mainly with the help of man. It has an amazing ability to adapt and it now occurs more or less wherever man has settled.

In most areas this mouse is associated with buildings, often moving out into the fields in summer, but almost always retreating indoors in autumn.

In buildings these mice will establish themselves wherever they can find sufficient food and nest material. They live mainly in lofts, under floors and in cavities in masonry, whence they gnaw their way through wooden partitions into kitchens and other places where they can find food.

The nest is always built in a sheltered position, and it consists merely of an irregular mass of any available material, such as cloth, wool or paper.

When conditions are favourable, house mice can breed throughout the year, producing up to ten litters in that period, but more usually no more than five or six. House mice are omnivorous but they prefer seeds, particularly cereals and cereal products, but when these are lacking they will feed on the strangest things, such as soap, wax candles and putty. An adult mouse eats about 3 grams of solid food a day, which corresponds to 70–100 grains of wheat, but they destroy many more because they seldom consume the whole

A house mouse gnawing its way into a loaf of ryebread. There are mouse droppings in front of the loaf.

House mice can cause serious damage in a seed store

grain. In fact the main damage done by mice is to foul goods with urine and excrement and to destroy sacks and other packing by gnawing through them.

They also damage many other things by gnawing them, as for example timber, insulating materials, paper and textiles.

A house mouse nest consists of almost any available material. This one is made mainly of chewed paper.

When opened up this mouse nest had a litter of new-born young, still naked and blind

Mouse-proofing

Naturally it is better if a house can be made proof against mice when it is actually being built. Even the best houses have their weak points where mice can gain entrance, and it is often difficult to find these and render them secure. It is always a good idea to ensure that cellar windows are closed, that window-panes are unbroken, and that doors close tightly.

All cracks and holes in the walls that are more than 7 mm across must be covered with fine-mesh netting; this would include ventilation openings. In prefabricated buildings it is important that the joints between the outer sheets are closed, for quite commonly there is free passage up under the lowermost sheets.

Mice can climb up rough vertical surfaces (timber, bricks, cement etc.) and they can often find their way up into a cavity wall and reach the ventilation space under the roof.

A 20 cm wide band of hard, smooth paint, about 1 metre above the floor, will prevent mice from climbing up, and a bent metal plate with an overhang of only 2 cm will have the same effect. Vertical pipes can be fitted with a metal guard which the mice cannot pass. It should be remembered that creepers and other plants growing up a wall make it easier for mice to ascend.

Mouse eradication

Small caches of poison can be laid outdoors along the base of the walls, where the mice try to find a way in. The poison must be protected from wind and weather, and positioned so that birds and other animals cannot reach it. In fact, it is best to put it in a length of drainpipe, or under a plank laid obliquely against the base of the house.

When mice are already in the house the first thing to do is to try and eradicate them with the help of traps. If poison is used indoors it often happens that dead mice lying in inaccessible places will produce a most unpleasant smell, and they will also provide breeding places for blowflies, larder beetles and other insects.

Spring traps can be baited with a suitable substance such as cheese, bread or a piece of sausage, which must be fixed firmly to the trigger of the trap

Plenty of traps should be used, and they are best positioned at right angles to the wall, with the baited end nearest to the wall, as this is where the mice will pass along. There is no need to scald the traps after use to get rid of the smell.

It may seem strange but in fact mousetraps are in most cases more efficient and more humane than poison

Brown rat, *Rattus norvegicus*

The brown rat, now found in almost all parts of the world, is believed to have originated in eastern Asia, whence it spread partly on foot, partly by ship. It came to Europe relatively late, probably about the beginning of the 18th century, but when it did it spread very rapidly, for this large rodent has a great ability to adapt and it soon drove out the black rat.

The brown rat thrives in all sorts of places, but it is primarily associated with buildings, warehouses and farm buildings, where it prefers the damper parts.

In towns it often frequents drainpipes, feeding on the kitchen waste that passes by, and builds its nest of paper, wadding or similar materials wherever it can find a dry place.

[*below*] *Rats are almost omnivorous. Here one has been gnawing a cake of toilet soap.* [*opposite*] *Brown rats in a barn. They cause great losses of grain and foodstuffs.*

When brown rats invade urban property they will nearly always have come up through a break in the sewers. Brown rats are omnivorous, and will eat any animal or plant food, and they may even become predatory, taking live chickens and ducklings. In many places in the world it has been reckoned that the rats eat more than half the available foodstuffs. The position is not as serious as this in temperate regions but losses can be quite substantial. As in the case of mice most of the damage is due to the rats gnawing through packaging and fouling with urine and faeces. In fact, rat urine and faeces often contain disease germs, which may present a risk to the health of man and his domestic animals.

Under favourable conditions, in grain warehouses and outhouses, brown rats will breed throughout the year and they are extraordinarily prolific. A pair of rats and their offspring can produce about a thousand individuals in the course of a year.

Brown rats live in groups, the individuals within each group recognizing each other by smell. They are shy animals which are mainly active during the hours of darkness. They never willingly move out on to an open area, but will always go along the walls.

Black rat, *Rattus rattus*

This rodent probably originated in south-east Asia, whence it has spread to large areas of the world. It arrived in Europe early in the Middle Ages and became very widespread until it was largely replaced by the brown rat. Black rats were responsible for spreading plague (black death) in Europe during the Middle Ages.

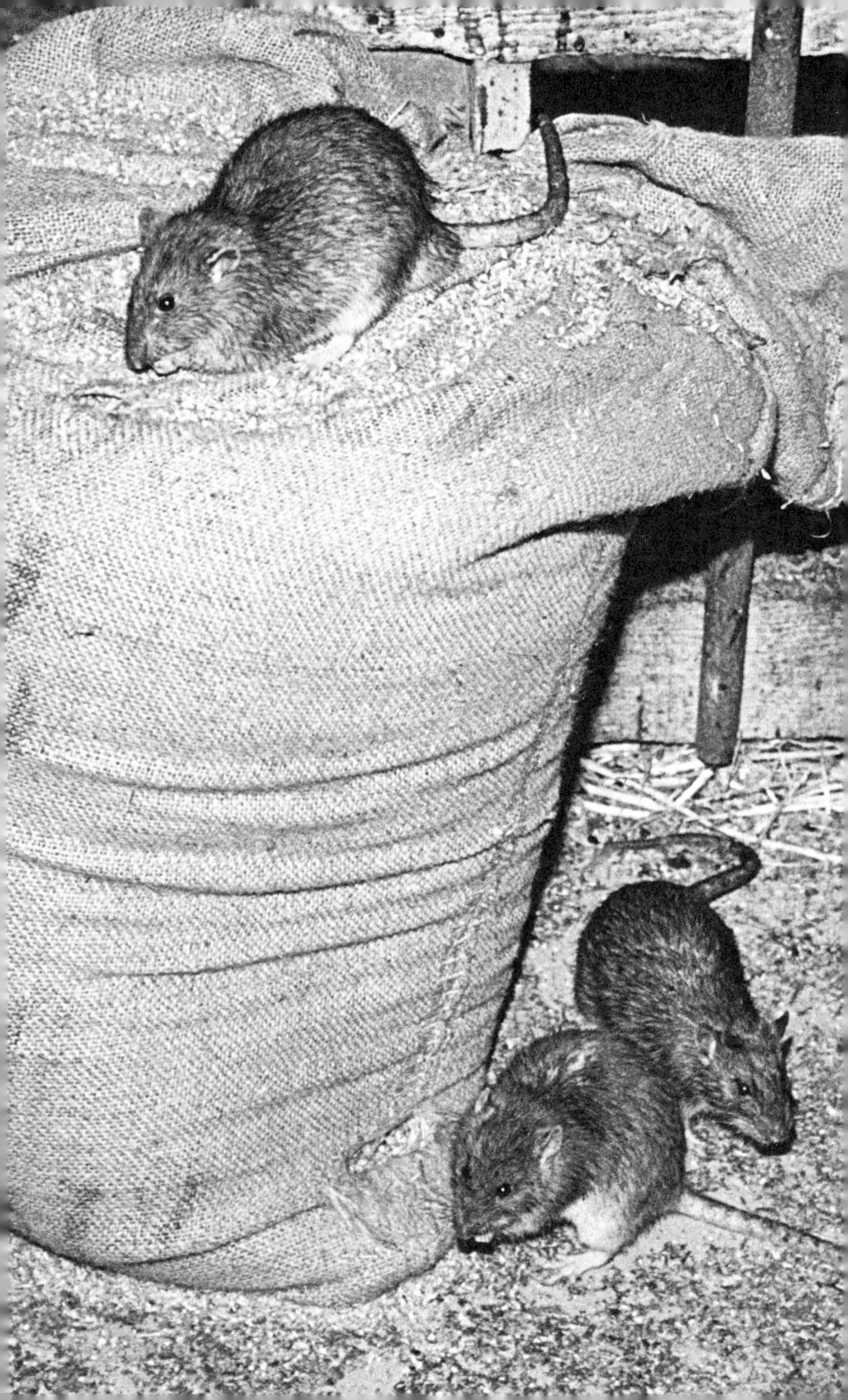

Flight from the plague. Woodcut, 1630.

In most parts of Europe black rats have been completely eliminated, but they continue to arrive in ships from overseas and are therefore still present in certain large ports. They are associated with man to an even greater extent than the brown rat, but being more warmth-loving they do not occur out in the open in central and northern Europe.

When black and brown rats are living in the same building, the former keep to the upper storeys, while the brown rats live on the ground floor and in the cellars. The black rat can live in much drier places than the brown rat, and it jumps and climbs better. It can, for example, walk along a telephone line between one house and another.

Like the brown rat the black is essentially a social animal which lives in groups. It is not so prolific as its relative and it produces fewer and smaller litters.

Black rats are omnivorous, but they prefer a vegetarian diet, particularly cereals and seeds.

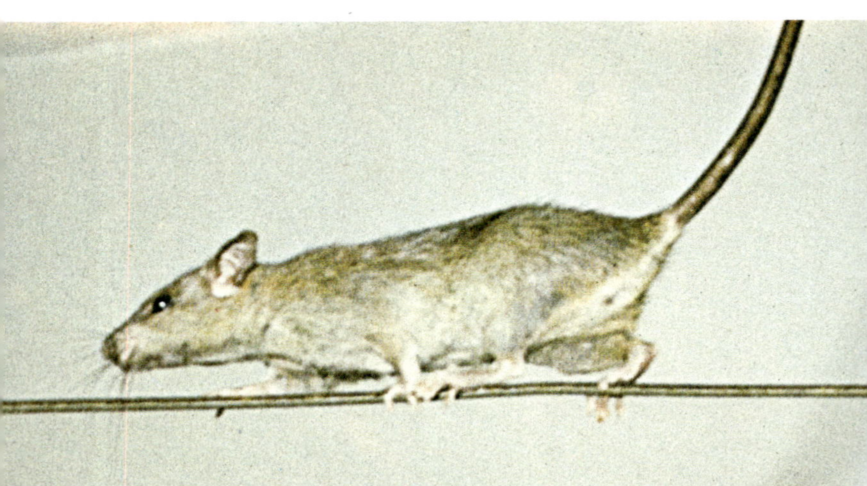

Rat proofing and eradication

In most civilized countries serious attempts are made to control and eradicate rats, and in some places regular inspection of properties is required by law.

All means of access should be made secure against rats. Windows should either be completely glazed or fitted with galvanized wire netting with a mesh of 1–2 cm, the wire itself having a diameter of at least 0.7 mm. Ventilation ducts opening to the outside should also be fitted with netting. Doors should close tightly and any holes or cracks in the floor and walls should be filled with cement. Holes made in walls for pipes and ducts must be covered with a close-fitting plate or secured with netting and cement.

Man-holes should be fitted with rat-proof covers, and drainpipes from the roof and outlets from the kitchen sink should also be inspected to ensure that they are not providing access routes for rats.

Rats which manage to get into houses very often enter via the drainage system, either because the drains are old and crumbling, or because the new drains have been badly installed.

Rat catcher, 17th century

Naturally rats cannot enter if the drains are below a well-cemented cellar floor, but if there is a badly finished join between the floor of a room and the earth they will often manage to dig their way up.

When the presence of rats has been confirmed the normal practice is to put down poison, but if they are under the floors it would be better to catch them in traps, as dead rats produce a dreadful smell.

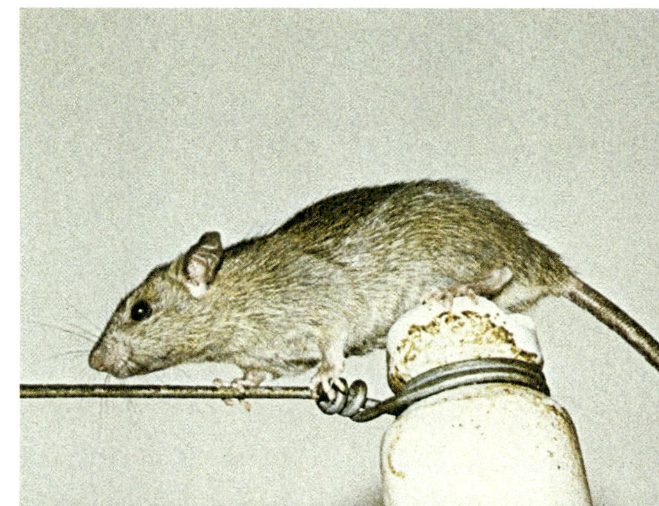

Black rats are brilliant tightrope artistes. Using the tail for balance they can easily walk along a taut wire.

PREVENTION OF DAMAGE BY PESTS IN KITCHENS AND FOOD FACTORIES

As in so many other situations prevention is better than cure, and a kitchen or store should be built so that conditions are as unfavourable as possible for animal pests.

During the actual construction of a building care should be taken to avoid leaving any cavities or cracks in which dust and scraps of food can accumulate and which are too inaccessible for proper cleaning. Such places may be ideal for certain pests. Book-cases and cupboards should either fit tightly to the floor or they should be free-standing with a clear space below them. Cupboards and drawers should close properly and it is better to avoid panelling on walls and ceilings with cavities behind. In food factories the covers to machinery should be easily removable, so that frequent and thorough cleaning presents no problem.

Foodstuffs must be kept as cool and dry as possible. In a store the goods should not be stacked right up against an external wall, but placed on low racks so that there is ventilation from all sides, and it is possible to sweep underneath them.

Cleanliness and tidiness are all important and it just does not pay to leave dust and waste in cracks and crevices to provide favourable breeding grounds for all sorts of pests.

In a kitchen or dining room it is best to store foodstuffs in tight-fitting containers, but there is no guarantee that they have not been infected beforehand. Many animal pests have an incredible ability to find their way into containers that are apparently sealed. Foodstuffs should not be kept longer than is absolutely necessary, especially if there has been a previous history of pest infestation in the kitchen. It may be better, at first, to buy food in smaller amounts and to keep those items most liable to attack in the refrigerator until one is quite sure that the pests have been eradicated.

As already mentioned (p. 10) pest animals must come from somewhere and one way of preventing their spread is to go out and look for the source of infection. In a factory such animals often arrive with raw materials. Suspicious looking parcels should therefore be examined and possibly treated before they come into the work area or at any rate kept separate from the finished goods for as long as possible. Returned goods and packing, empty sacks and containers with production waste are also a common source of infection. Here again the same principle applies, and they should be kept well apart from raw materials, finished goods and packing material.

Sometimes pests are found in groceries in the house. If such animals are observed in newly purchased items it is in the interests of the grocer to tell him about this so that he can examine his store and isolate any infected goods. In a block of flats the animals may also come from other flats via ducts and piping.

Netting over windows and doors can be very effective in keeping occasional flying insects out of food factories or houses. In cases where the doors have to remain open owing to the volume of traffic it is possible to install a kind of air curtain, the opening having a continuous stream of air through which the insects cannot fly.

It will always be easier to keep insects and mites out of food factories if a belt (about 2 metres broad) around the building is kept free of vegetation. If it should be necessary to spray or powder with poison in order to keep away undesirable intruders this can be done in such a belt, without adversely affecting the surrounding fauna.

Signs of gnawing by:

Warehouse moth larva in almond

mealworm beetle larva in corn

flat grain beetle larva in wheat

lesser grain borer in wheat

grain weevil in wheat

rice weevil in rice

coffee weevil in coffee beans

common bean weevil in brown beans

white-marked spider beetle larvae in peas

house mouse in oats

brown rat in oats

rat in maize

CONTROLLING PESTS IN KITCHENS AND FOOD FACTORIES

When one has identified a pest species, possibly with the help of the keys, tables and descriptions, the next step is to find out the goods it is likely to attack.

In a factory the control of pests will usually require expert assistance. In a house, on the other hand, one can sometimes do it oneself and the following lines of action are suggested.

a) empty the cupboards and perhaps throw away any lining paper.

b) thoroughly clean all cupboards and shelves, preferably with a vacuum-cleaner which can remove insects and dirt from cracks and crevices. Laundry should be properly dried, as damp encourages most pests.

c) examine the goods before putting them back in place. It is usually best to throw away any that are infested.

d) if the goods are only slightly infested or if one has any doubts, it is often possible to save them by warming them in an oven; a temperature of 80° C will kill all stages in the life cycle within a few minutes. The same result can be achieved by putting the goods in a deep-freeze for a week.

e) in spite of thorough cleaning it will sometimes be necessary to treat inaccessible cracks and crevices with an insecticide. It is obvious that the strictest precautions must be taken if such substances are to be used in a kitchen or food store. In most cases insecticides based on pyrethrum (p. 219) will be the most suitable for use in the kitchen.

Animals that attack Textiles

Wool, fur and feathers consist primarily of keratin which is one of the most indigestible proteins. There are, however, some insects which are adapted for feeding on this diet. Special conditions in their gut enable them to break down the sulphur linkages in the keratin and thus render it digestible.

In the wild insects that can digest keratin probably feed mainly on the remains of animals left by carrion-eaters, but they are also found in nests and lairs containing down or hair. However, keratin alone does not provide a sufficient diet for the normal development of an insect. It lacks, for instance, certain vitamins. In the wild the insect will have plenty of opportunities for supplementing its diet, but this is not possible if it is feeding on a completely clean textile. If it is to thrive it must be able to eat small amounts of food remains or traces of sweat and urine.

In addition to the true specialists there are many animals occurring indoors which occasionally gnaw textiles. This may be because there are stains on the material to which they are attracted, but they may also do so in order to pupate. Mice and rats often cause serious damage by gnawing textiles, particularly in stores and warehouses, when they are gathering nest material.

Small moths

Many of the smaller moths are superficially very similar in appearance. Some attack textiles, some are pests of agricultural crops, while others infest foodstuffs (p. 63 *et seq*). In everyday life, however, the moths most commonly encountered are those that attack clothing, and these must have been a nuisance to man for a very long time. As soon as our ancestors started to store skins the moths must have arrived immediately and exploited this new and rich source of food. Evidence that moths have been one of man's pests over a long period can be found in several places in the Bible. Thus, in Job XIII. 28: 'And he, as a rotten thing, consumeth, as a garment that is moth eaten.' Also in the Sermon on the Mount, Jesus says 'Lay not up for yourselves treasures upon earth, where moth and rust doth corrupt' (Matthew VI, 19).

Common clothes moth,
Tineola bisselliella
(Pages 23 and 105)

This small moth, now common in human habitations in temperate countries, came originally from warmer parts of the world. It was probably not very abundant until houses started to be warmed more or less efficiently. It does not, therefore, live outside in temperate regions, and it is not one of the insects that fly in through an open window.

A female clothes moth lays about 100 eggs, which are difficult to see as they are very small and whitish, and they are usually deposited in the folds of clothing or in among the hairs of carpets and furs. After a few days the eggs hatch and each larva immediately starts to spin a fine

tube around itself as a protection against desiccation. The tube becomes covered with gnawed scraps of the material that the larva is living in, together with faeces. It is worth noting that the faeces which are the same colour as the food and more or less spherical are often mistaken for the moth's eggs.

The development from the egg to the adult moth may take anything from one month to over a year, depending upon the temperature, the humidity and the quality of the food. The optimum temperature is around 25° C. In a centrally heated house one can therefore reckon on 4 generations in the year. The larvae require a supplement of food other than keratin so they search for spots and stains on the material and will also feed on flour, meat and dead insects.

Clothes moths have been decreasing in number since the 1950's. This is due to several factors, including the use of effective impregnating materials, an increase in the use of synthetic materials which are not eaten by the moths, vacuum cleaners and the drier climate in our houses also help to keep the moths down.

[top] *Clothes moth larvae usually gnaw irregular holes and produce much silk and faeces. The round balls of faeces are up to ½ mm in diameter.*
[bottom] *Pests of textiles cannot live on the pure wool alone. Here a clothes moth larva has obtained the necessary dietary supplement by eating its way through a dead housefly.*

A case-bearing clothes moth larva has crawled part of the way out of its case and is 'browsing' on a fur

Case-bearing clothes moth,
Tinea pellionella
(Pages 23 and 105)

Unlike the common clothes moth this is an insect which does live outside in temperate regions. For instance, it is not uncommonly found in birds' nests.

The adult case-bearing clothes moth is very similar in appearance to the common clothes moth. The larvae of the case-bearing moth are, however, easy to recognize, for they spin a small tubular case, which becomes covered with fragments of wool or feather. They creep around in this case and withdraw into it when threatened. Clothes moth larvae, on the other hand, attach their tube firmly to the substrate.

The case-bearing clothes moth larva pupates inside its case. In other respects its habits and life history are similar to those of the common clothes moth, but it requires a higher humidity, and it has become less common as a pest in recent years.

Case-bearing clothes moth larvae crawl around protected by a small case. The presence of these characteristic cases will always show when these insects have been at work. Their faeces resemble those of the common clothes moth.

Brown house moth,
Hofmannophila pseudospretella
(Pages 23 and 105)

This is another moth that is very similar to the clothes moth, but it is larger (up to 1.5 cm long).

Under favourable conditions the female can lay 500–600 eggs and the larvae feed on many different types of material. They are found in stores of cereals and seeds and may attack practically any kind of vegetable matter. They also gnaw

This is actually an old tennis ball, which has been gnawed by the larvae of the brown house moth

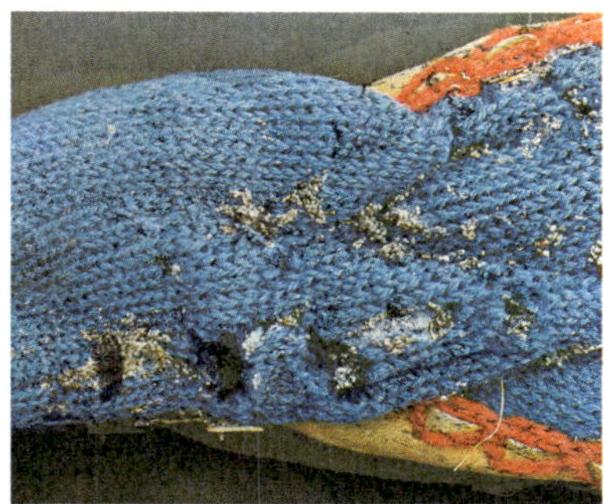

The brown house moth is more destructive than the clothes moth. Its faeces are oblong and larger than those of the common clothes moth.

woollen goods, often causing severe damage.

The larvae are sometimes found in birds' nests where they feed on food remains and on the nest material. The adult moths may fly indoors from birds' nests built under the eaves. The larvae, however, are very sensitive to desiccation, so if the humidity is constantly below 80%, they cannot complete their development. They will, therefore, only cause damage in damp rooms or cellars. When conditions become unfavourable the development of the larvae may come to a standstill for a period of time. They then go into a resting phase, which may be the result of low temperature or low humidity, and activity is only resumed when the conditions again become favourable. The pupal stage is spent in a torpedo-shaped, brownish cocoon.

Tapestry moth,
Trichophaga tapetzella
(Page 23)

This is the largest of the moths that attack textiles, and it has a tendency to feed more on coarser materials than the other textile moths, including such things as horse hair, coarse furs and skins.

Like the preceding species it thrives in humid conditions, and nowadays it is found especially in outhouses and stables. It does not attack wallpaper, but is a serious pest of tapestries hung on damp external walls.

When the tapestry moths emerge the larval cases and the remains of the empty pupae protrude from the material

Dermestids (hide and bacon beetles)

This is a family of beetles, the members of which live mainly on the dried remains of animals and plants (p. 73). The more specialized of them can also, like clothes moth larvae, digest hair and feathers.

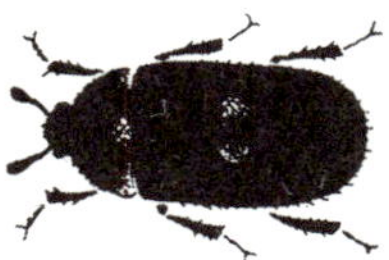

Carpet beetle, *Attagenus pellio*
(Pages 25 and 105)

This beetle is easy to recognize for it has a white spot on each of the otherwise black elytra. The adults fly around outside during the summer and land on flowers where they feed on nectar and pollen. They often find their way indoors.

The eggs are normally laid in the nests of mice and birds, and the larvae, which have a characteristic tuft of hairs at the rear end, feed on hair, feathers and offal. In the house this beetle may lay eggs in woollen textiles or in other places where there may be food for the larvae, as for example in cracks in flooring or panelling where scraps of wool may accumulate. They may also gnaw skins, furs and stuffed animals.

Museum beetle larvae can live on dead insects, and cause serious damage in entomological collections

A collection of stuffed mice destroyed by museum beetle larvae

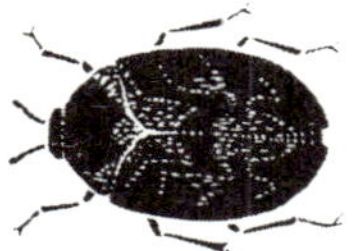

Museum beetles, genus *Anthrenus*
(Pages 25 and 105)

The museum beetles are somewhat like small ladybirds. However, they are not glossy, but have an attractive matt pattern formed by numerous small, black and reddish-yellow scales.

The larvae, which are yellow-brown and hairy, are known as 'woolly bears'. At the rear end they have a tuft of long hairs, which can be erected when the larva is threatened. The adult beetles are seen especially in the spring. Like the preceding species they often sit on flowers where they feed on the pollen and nectar.

The eggs are laid in birds' nests and in other animal homes or in dry carrion, where the larva can feed on feathers, hair and fragments of meat. They will also eat dead insects and are much feared by insect collectors. These are common insects and

as the adults fly well they can be found almost everywhere.

The larvae sometimes wander about quite a bit and when they appear in large numbers in a house the source of infection may, for example, be a bird's nest under the eaves, a felt carpet underlay, forgotten woollen cloths in a box of cleaning materials, or perhaps merely a collection of dead insects in a spider's web.

In spite of their varied diet, when they attack textiles museum beetles are usually very fastidious, for they prefer clean new materials such as fine woollen curtains or bunting or soft, expensive knitted goods such as cashmere sweaters. In many places these insects are regarded as new pests of textiles, but this is probably because in former times they were grouped together with the numerous moth pests. It is, in fact, quite likely that our ancestors knew them. For example, it has been suggested that Odysseus had museum beetle larvae in mind when on his return home he took up his old bow which was made of horn and turned it around to see whether the horn had not been eaten by worms (Homer's Odyssey, song 21, verse 395).

A couple of museum beetle larvae on a woollen curtain. These larvae usually gnaw regular small holes and do not leave visible signs in the form of silken threads or faeces.

Spider beetles, Family Ptinidae (Page 26)

As mentioned on p. 75 these beetles attack a little of everything and they do not go out of their way to gnaw textiles. Their gnawing activities can normally be recognized by the small, regular, round holes and the absence of silk.

Signs of gnawing by spider beetle larvae, with pupal cocoons

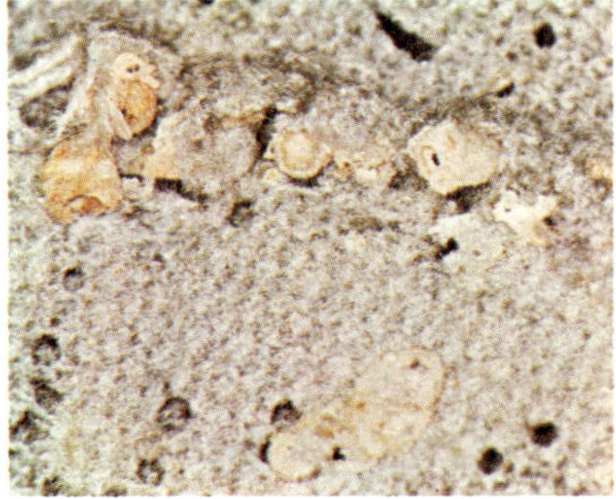

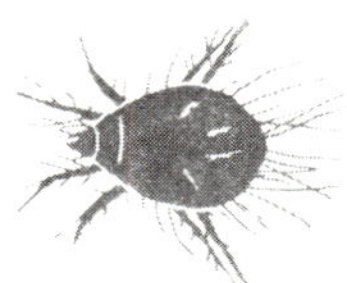

Common house mite,
Glycyphagus domesticus
(Page 20)

These small mites are very similar to those that occur in foodstuffs (p. 56), but under a lens they can be recognised by the long hairs at the rear end. They may occasionally occur in foodstuffs, but they are primarily found in upholstered furniture, which has been kept damp for some time so that the stuffing has rotted. House mites then feed on the fungus, and multiply in large numbers. They occur particularly in upholstery stuffed with fibre derived from palm leaves. Nowadays these mites do not present any serious problem, but they may be a nuisance in very new houses which are still damp and in holiday houses which remain unheated for most of the year. Like all the other mites they quickly die if they become desiccated.

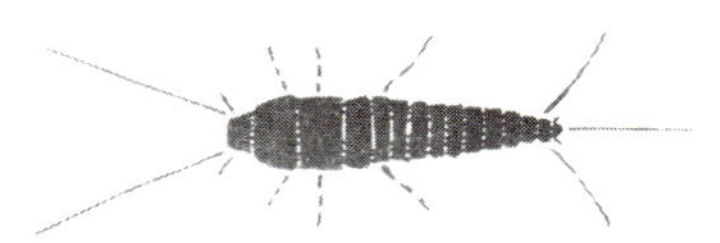

Silverfish, Order Thysanura
(Page 20)

These are omnivorous insects which occasionally gnaw textiles. They will, for example, attack artificial, cellulose-based silk, such as the red ribbon used in Christmas decorations and in gift wrappings.

Other insects which occasionally attack textiles include cockroaches and mealworms, which sometimes feed on soiled linen.

On account of their size, mice and rats often cause serious damage to textiles when they are collecting nest material. In empty holiday houses which mice may enter during the winter it is a good idea to move mattresses and bedding to a place where the mice cannot get at them. For precautions against mice, see also p. 87.

Red artificial silk ribbon damaged by silverfish

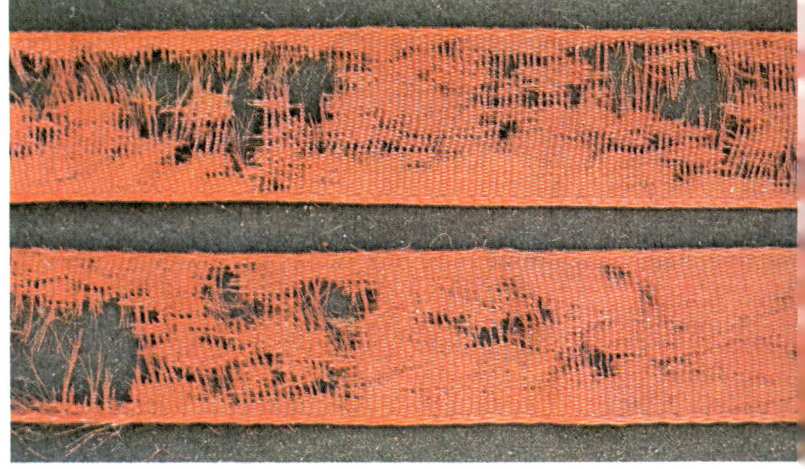

A woollen winter coat badly damaged by mice, which use the fragments as nest material

PRECAUTIONS AGAINST ATTACKS BY PESTS OF TEXTILES

Clothes moths and other insects which attack textiles are, in general, shy of the light, so woollen goods that are stored away in cupboards and chests are especially at risk. However, carpet beetle larvae form an exception, for they do not go out of their way to shun the light, and they may, for example, feed on woollen curtains.

The eggs of insect pests are easily destroyed by brushing, beating or vacuum-cleaning, so textiles which have lain undisturbed for a long time are the most likely to be attacked.

As mentioned on p. 94 insects that feed on wool are dependent upon a dietary supplement in the form of 'dirt' on the material. It is, therefore, important that clothes should be clean before they are stored away for any length of time. Materials that are newly washed, chemically cleaned or pressed with a warm iron will be free of pests and will need no further protection apart from being packed carefully in plastic or paper bags which are properly sealed. Under such conditions it should not be necessary to take any further precautions, but in the case of clothes kept in cupboards or chests, which are not hermetically sealed, it is advisable to protect them by spraying with a suitable insecticide. The insides of wardrobes, including all cracks and crevices, should also be sprayed. Such treatment should protect clothes for 1–2 years, depending upon the extent to which the insecticide layer is subjected to sunlight, heat, polishing and cleaning. Mothballs, which consist of naphthalene or paradichlorbenzene, are useful, but only if the packaging is well sealed to prevent the fumes escaping. The fumes are relatively heavy so the mothballs should be placed at or near the top of the clothing. It is advisable to use plenty of mothballs, perhaps about 1 kg per cubic metre, which would be roughly the volume of a large wardrobe. Nowadays, many materials and carpets are impregnated against moths during manufacture. This is done with toxic substances which are introduced during the dyeing process or in a special bath. The poison becomes incorporated in the wool fibres and it kills the insect larvae when they start to feed. If the treatment has been effective there should be little damage before the insects have acquired a lethal dose.

CONTROL OF TEXTILE PESTS

In many cases it will be sufficient to wash or clean the infested materials or to spray them with one of the many good insecticides available on the market. These substances contain a contact poison dissolved in petroleum or mineral turpentine. They can be sprayed by the appropriate vacuum-cleaner attachment or by an aerosol where the insecticide is packed under pressure and released by pressing on a knob. Aerosols are, of course, more expensive to use and are not really suitable for the treatment of furniture.

Upholstered furniture should be sprayed until the covers are quite damp, and this may require, for example, at least half a litre for a sofa.

Large objects which are difficult to treat at home can be sent for gas treatment, but this may be expensive, depending upon the distance to be travelled. Such treatment should involve the use of cyanide gas or methyl bromide.

Treatment by gas will kill eggs, larvae and adult insects, but it will not protect against a fresh infestation.

A severe period of frost can also be used, the furniture being placed outside when the temperature is likely to fall to at least —10° C, at least during the night. The furniture should be brought into the warmth again during the day. This process should be repeated for a couple of days, for although moths can tolerate low temperatures for quite a long time they are quickly killed by alternating heat and cold.

An example of accidental damage. A mealworm beetle larva has found its way into a chest and has bitten holes in the clothing.

Animals in Paper, Leather and Plastics

Many animals gnaw paper or cardboard, some, for example, doing this in order to get in or out of paper bags or packaging.

There are, however, only a few species, such as boring beetles and silverfish, which actually feed on a diet of paper, which consists almost entirely of cellulose (see p. 107). Glazed paper also contains glues which may, for example, attract cockroaches, and finally damp paper will provide a substrate for the growth of various kinds of fungus, and this makes it a good food source for animals such as wood-lice, earwigs and certain moth larvae.

Various dermestid beetle larvae feed on raw hides, but freshly tanned leather is a very poor source of nutriment. Here, as with paper, damp leather which goes mouldy becomes more attractive as a food.

To an increasing extent artificial materials such as nylon and other plastics are replacing natural products in everyday life. Many of these plastics can be broken down by bacteria and fungi, and thus re-enter the natural chain of events, and this is to be welcomed, but there are still no animal species which have become adapted to feeding on such materials. This is not to say that animals cannot gnaw them, for several mammals and some insects with biting mouthparts can damage the softer plastics, sometimes because they want to get through them, or to nest in them.

Slugs, genus *Limax*
(Page 18)

Slugs are peaceful and in general completely harmless animals. In very damp places they may, however, damage paper when feeding on the moulds growing on it. In wine cellars slugs often cause havoc by eating the labels off the bottles.

A piece of damp textile damaged by slugs which have left their slime trails

Wood-lice,
Order Isopoda
(Page 18)

Like slugs, these familiar crustaceans prefer damp conditions. They do not normally feed on paper but if, for example, a pile of damp, mouldy newspapers is left lying on a cellar floor, wood-lice will more or less destroy them.

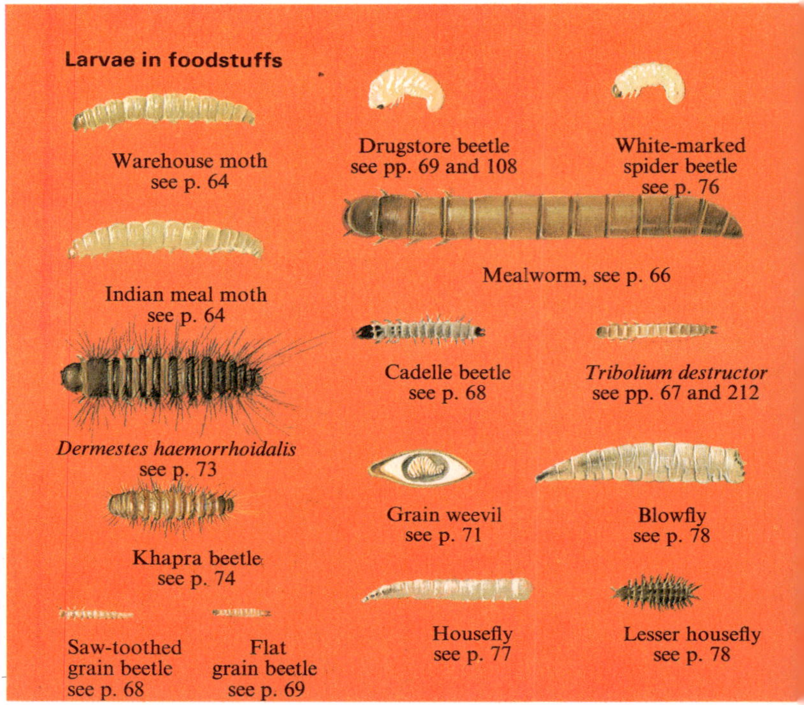

Larvae in foodstuffs

Warehouse moth
see p. 64

Drugstore beetle
see pp. 69 and 108

White-marked
spider beetle
see p. 76

Mealworm, see p. 66

Indian meal moth
see p. 64

Cadelle beetle
see p. 68

Tribolium destructor
see pp. 67 and 212

Dermestes haemorrhoidalis
see p. 73

Grain weevil
see p. 71

Blowfly
see p. 78

Khapra beetle
see p. 74

Housefly
see p. 77

Lesser housefly
see p. 78

Saw-toothed
grain beetle
see p. 68

Flat
grain beetle
see p. 69

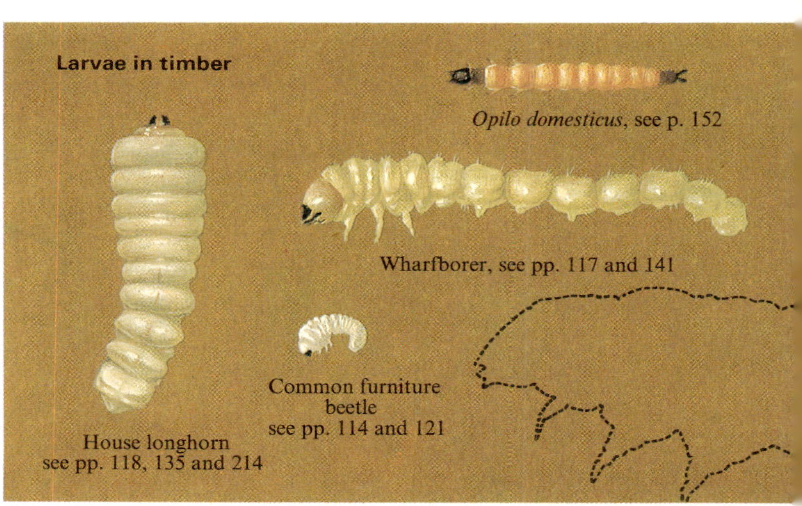

Larvae in timber

Opilo domesticus, see p. 152

Wharfborer, see pp. 117 and 141

Common furniture
beetle
see pp. 114 and 121

House longhorn
see pp. 118, 135 and 214

PLATE 16

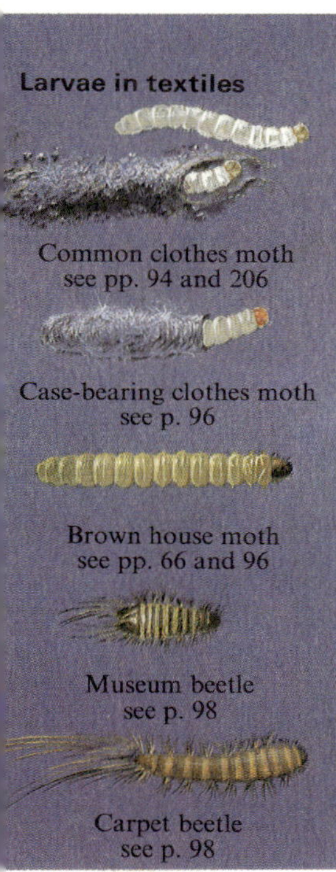

Larvae in textiles
Common clothes moth
see pp. 94 and 206
Case-bearing clothes moth
see p. 96
Brown house moth
see pp. 66 and 96
Museum beetle
see p. 98
Carpet beetle
see p. 98

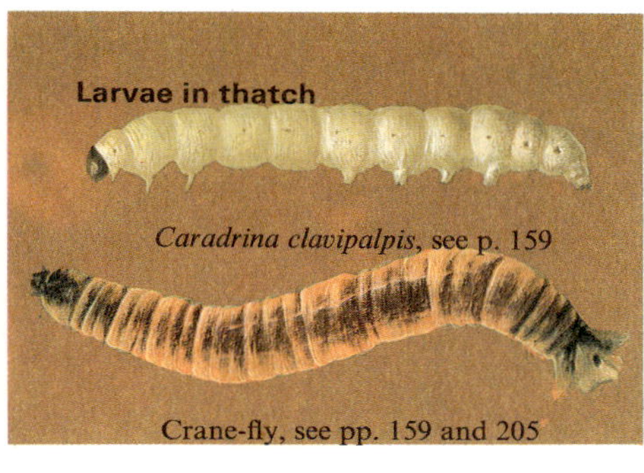

Larvae in thatch
Caradrina clavipalpis, see p. 159
Crane-fly, see pp. 159 and 205

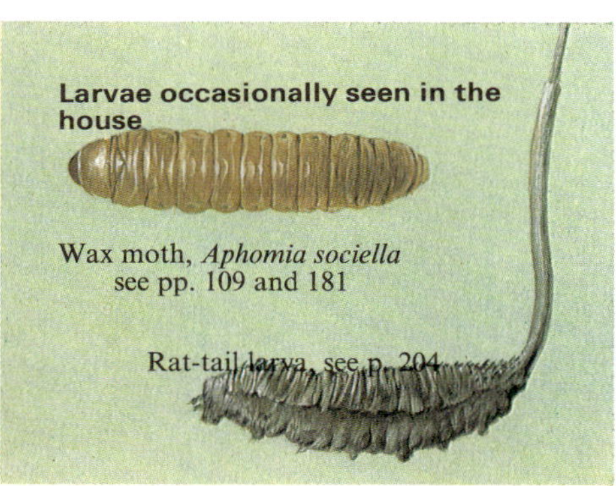

Larvae occasionally seen in the house
Wax moth, Aphomia sociella
see pp. 109 and 181
Rat-tail larva, see p. 204

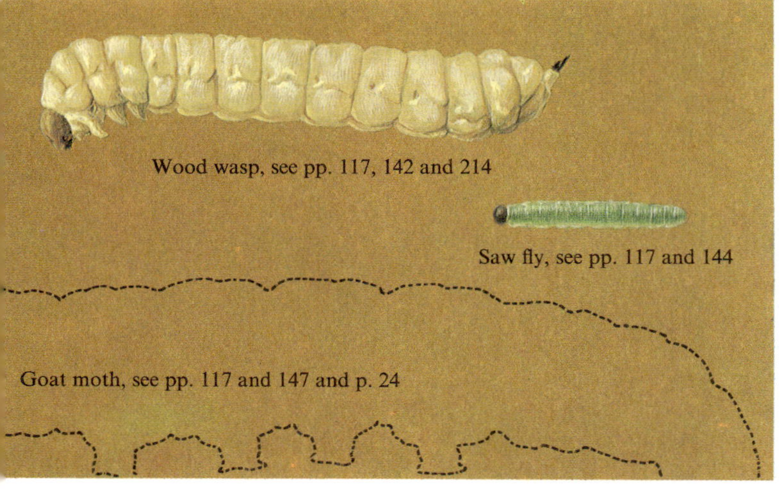

Wood wasp, see pp. 117, 142 and 214
Saw fly, see pp. 117 and 144
Goat moth, see pp. 117 and 147 and p. 24

All larvae shown twice natural size

Silverfish are normally harmless, but they sometimes cause damage, as here in a stamp collection

Copper engraving from Robert Hooke: Micrographia, *1665*

Silverfish, *Lepisma saccharina*
(Page 20)

It is probably about 300 million years ago that the first animal looking somewhat like a silverfish saw the light of day. It was doubtless very widely distributed and occurred in enormous numbers, and it has been suggested that primitive animals of this type may well have been the ancestors of all the different insect types alive today.

Some insects, including silverfish, have remained more or less unchanged over long periods. Indeed, it is likely that there were primitive insects of this type when the first fish went up on to land, that they crawled around the feet of the dinosaurs, and they are still with us. Silverfish can, in fact, be regarded as living fossils, comparable with the coelacanth.

In spite of their antiquity, silverfish have succeeded in exploiting the new opportunities created by man. In southern Europe and in parts of Asia they live out in the open, under stones and in crevices, but elsewhere they are almost exclusively associated with human habitations – houses, stables, outhouses and so on. Most people must have seen these small silvery insects run to shelter in the evening when the light is turned on in the kitchen, or may have found them in a bath or wash basin. They do not, as many believe, come up the drainpipe, but they become trapped after sliding down the smooth walls of the bath while searching for food during the night. They are particularly prevalent in kitchens and bathrooms for they require a high humidity or access to water.

Silverfish are pleasant animals which are easy to keep in captivity and they live for quite a long time, sometimes over 5 years. On the other hand, they are not very prolific, for a female will only lay about twenty eggs during the course of her life. The eggs are deposited in cracks and crevices and the young resemble the adults, except in size. Under favourable conditions they become sexually mature at an age of about six months.

Silverfish will thrive on the tiniest scraps of food, preferring starchy foods such as flour and bread (p. 59), but they also gnaw meat and are not above eating dead members of their own species. They are capable of digesting cellulose and may therefore attack books and documents. In such cases damage is not usually very serious unless the goods have been kept in a damp condition.

Tunnels in an old book of Danish ballads gnawed by furniture beetle larvae

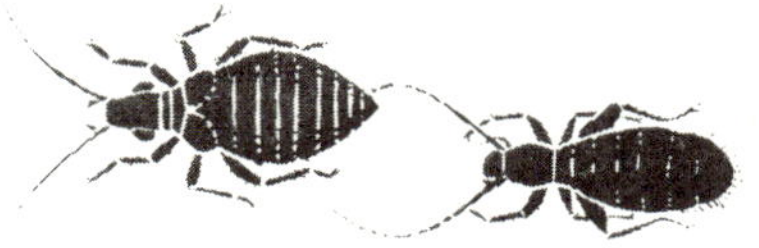

Booklice, Order Psocoptera
(Page 21)

The names booklice and dustlice are used somewhat indiscriminately. Booklice are light-shy insects that thrive best when the humidity is over 75%. There are several species. Some, such as *Liposcelis divinatorius*, have no wings and cannot fly, while others, the so-called winged booklice, e.g. *Atropus pulsatorius*, have small but non-functional wings.

Booklice run about actively when disturbed, with characteristic jerky movements, and they can also make small, rather clumsy, jumps.

As the name implies, booklice are found between sheets of paper in libraries and archives, and also behind loose wallpaper and in herbaria. They do not eat the paper itself, although they may feed on the glue in glazed paper, but they subsist primarily on the moulds growing on the paper. Indeed, the presence of numerous booklice is a sign that the paper is being kept too damp.

Some booklice can produce a ticking sound by striking the abdomen against the substrate (p. 214).

In the present context, the term bookworm refers to the larvae of certain wood-

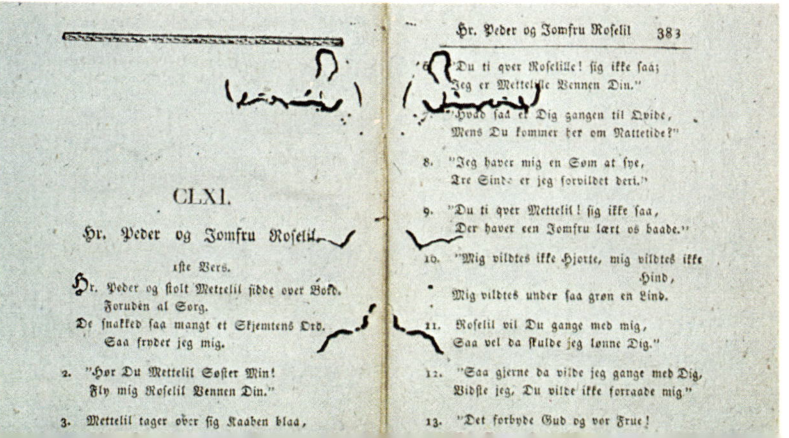

CLXI.

Hr. Peder og Jomfru Roselil.

1ste Vers.

Hr. Peder og stolt Mettelil sidde over Bord.
Foruden al Sorg.
De snakked saa mangt et Skjemtens Ord.
Saa fryder jeg mig.

2. "Hør Du Mettelil Søster Min!
Fly mig Roselil Vennen Din."

3. Mettelil tager over sig Kaaben blaa,

Hr. Peder og Jomfru Roselil 383

6. "Du ti qver Roselille! sig ikke saa;
Jeg er Mettelille Vennen Din."

7. "Hvad saa er Dig gangen til Qvide,
Mens Du kommer her om Nattetide?"

8. "Jeg haver mig en Søm at sye,
Tre Sinde er jeg forvildet deri."

9. "Du ti qver Mettelil! sig ikke saa,
Der haver een Jomfru lært os baade."

10. "Mig vildtes ikke Hjorte, mig vildtes ikke Hind,
Mig vildtes under saa grøn en Lind.

11. Roselil vil Du gange med mig,
Saa vel da skulde jeg lønne Dig."

12. "Saa gjerne da vilde jeg gange med Dig,
Vidste jeg, Du vilde ikke forraade mig."

13. "Det forbyde Gud og vor Frue!

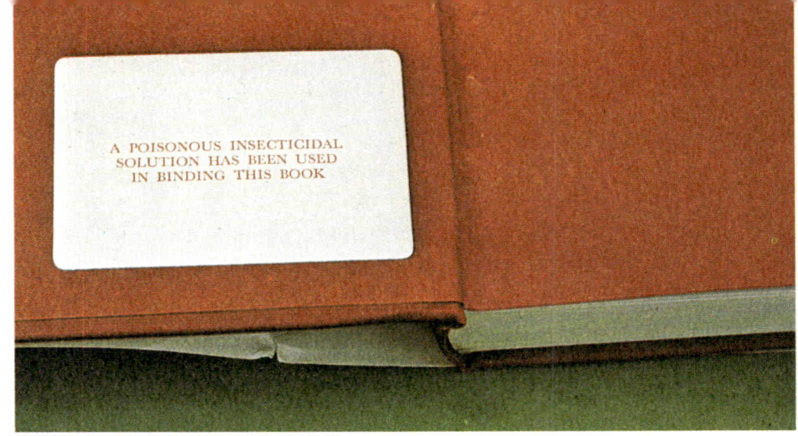

A label inside a binding saying that it has been treated with insecticide, a precaution that is particularly necessary against termites in the tropics

boring beetles which feed on paper (p. 122). These larvae require a high humidity and nowadays they rarely attack books. They only occur in books which stand undisturbed for years in cellars or lofts.

Beetles and other insects with wood-boring larvae may, when they make their way out of timber, gnaw holes in paper that is nearby, as for example wallpaper.

Drugstore beetles, tobacco beetles, spider beetles, dermestid beetles and moth larvae, to name only a few, will gnaw

A pattern of tunnels and holes in the bottom of a plastic bucket, made by drugstore beetle larvae. The bucket had been filled with powdered soup, in which the beetles had developed.

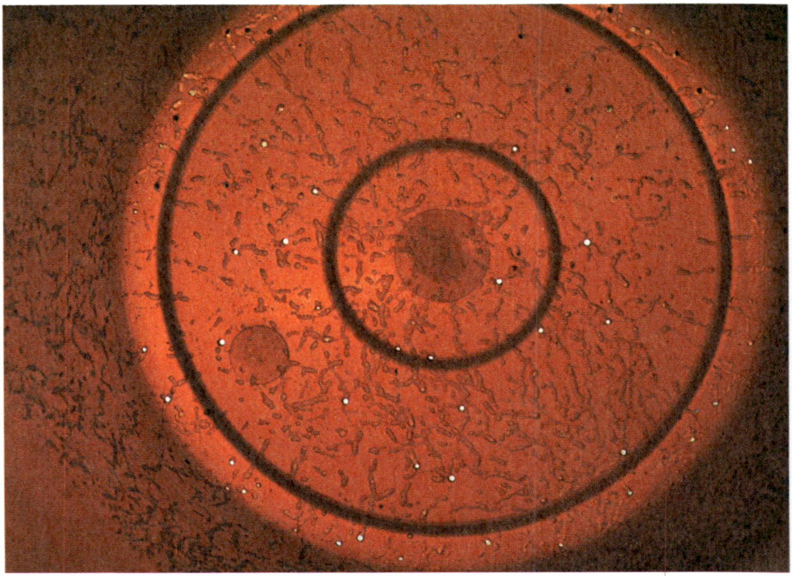

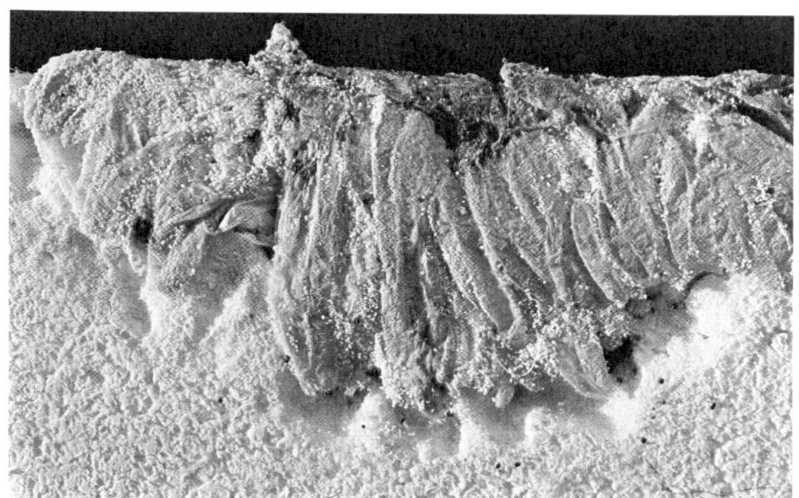

Foam plastic is easy to gnaw. Here waxmoth larvae have made their pupal chambers in a sheet of insulation material.

Jet black ants normally build their nest in timber (p. 145). Here they have used a sheet of foam plastic under a floor. The ants have gnawed tunnels in the insulation and have reinforced these with their usual nest material, wooden chips and soil particles mixed with saliva.

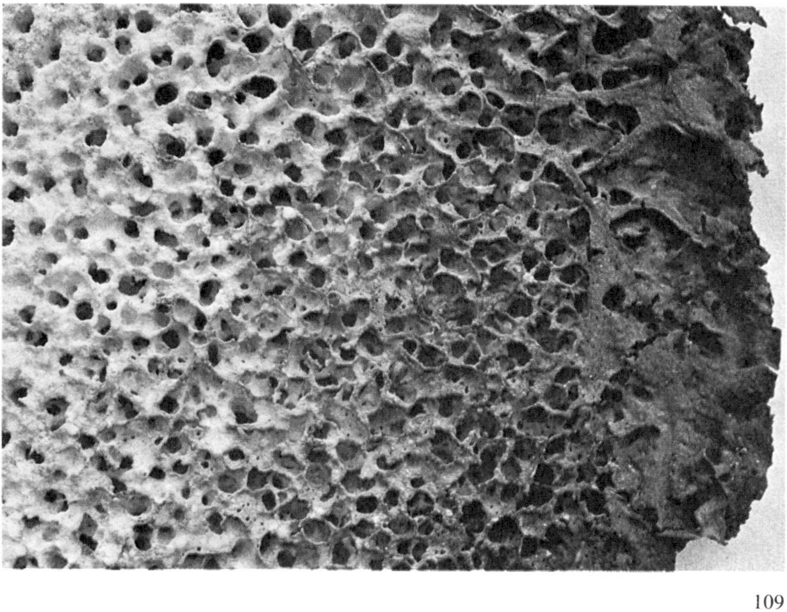

through paper, cardboard and plastic packing, and holes in the packaging will often be the first sign that the goods contain live animals.

Mice and rats sometimes cause a great deal of damage to paper and plastic. They can easily gnaw through packaging made of these materials and often use the fragments as nest material.

The activities of these rodents can be recognized by the tooth marks (p. 84), which can always be identified, even in the thinnest sheet of newspaper. They might be confused with holes torn by a cat or a marten, but here one would normally see distinct claw marks.

[*top*] *A bank note gnawed by a house mouse which found its way into a cash register. The toothmarks can be clearly seen.*
[*bottom*] *Just before a short circuit. A rat has gnawed through the plastic insulation of an electric cable. The broad toothmarks show it was a rat and not a mouse.*

Animals in Timber

Timber is in many ways a remarkable material, and an understanding of its nature is essential for those who wish to use it correctly. Under certain conditions timber is one of the most durable materials known to man. In Norway, for example, they are still using timber churches built about 1000 years ago. On the other hand, when conditions are different timber may disappear without trace in a few years, destroyed by a variety of animals or by fungus.

It is a perfectly natural process that dead trees not only accumulate, but are broken down by other organisms, and it is only when we want to preserve the timber that we regard the process as injurious.

Timber is, in fact, very poor in nutrient, and there are only a few organisms which have become adapted to digesting its principal constituents, which are lignin and cellulose. The bacteria and fungi which live on wood produce digestive enzymes which are able to break down the lignin

The wooden church at Borgund in Norway, dating from the 12th century

and cellulose to substances, such as various sugars, which can be absorbed as food.

A few insects which feed on timber secrete the same kinds of digestive enzymes in their gut (this applies, for example, to the larvae of the house longhorn beetle), but the majority have a different method, for they have established an association with micro-organisms which help to break down the wood. Finally, there are some species, such as the powder post beetles, which are dependent upon the presence in the wood of starch or sugar.

The structure of timber

When a tree trunk is sawn through one can see first the outer layer or bark and then a thin growth layer. It is this layer that is responsible for the growth in thickness of the trunk or branch of a tree, for it forms bark outside and wood inside. A new growth ring is added every year. During the spring, large thin-walled cells are formed which are adapted for the transport of water, while later in the summer the cells formed have walls that are thicker, and often darker. While the tree is growing the cells in the outermost annual rings are living and it is here that the transport of liquids from roots to leaves takes place. This part of the wood is called the sapwood, while the inner part, the heartwood, consists of dead cells. Right in the centre is the pith.

There are certain structural differences between coniferous trees, e.g. pine or spruce, and deciduous trees, such as oak or beech, and it is often difficult to distinguish these two types on external features. The surest method of distinguishing them is on the presence or absence of true vessels. These are present in deciduous trees, but absent in conifers. These vessels are specially adapted for the transport of

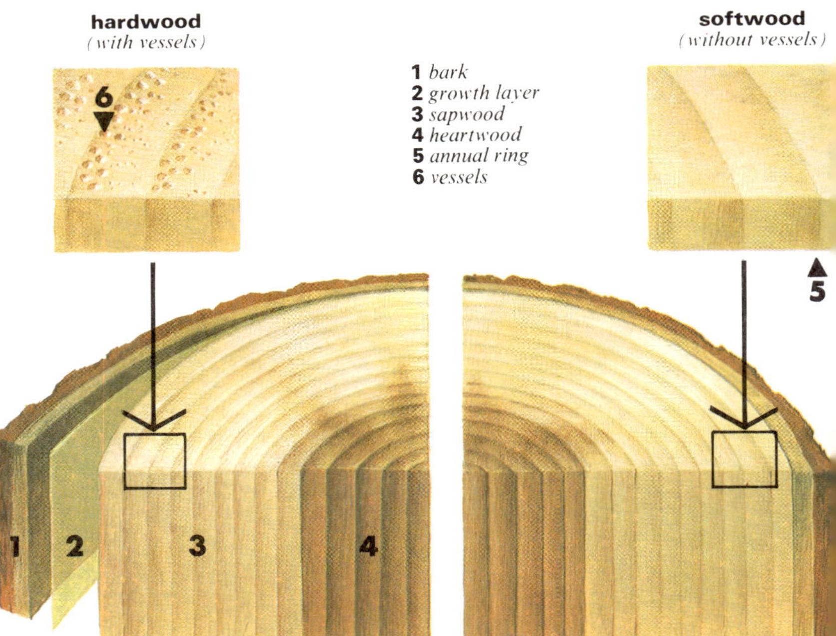

water. In some species these are visible to the naked eye in a cross section. Oak and ash, for example, have large vessels.

In some deciduous trees, such as birch and beech, the vessels are more uniform in size throughout the season, and are generally quite small. Normally the darker colour of the heartwood is due to waste products, such as tannins, and to some extent these serve as a protection against fungal infections and the attacks of various animals. On the other hand, the heartwood is not receptive to impregnation with timber preservatives.

ANIMALS THAT GNAW TIMBER IN BUILDINGS

In the forest, trees are attacked by many different kinds of animal. There are some which eat the leaves, but in the context of the present book we are more interested in those insects which attack the timber itself. Some of these attack only healthy, living trees, whereas others specialize exclusively in weakened or dead trees. Certain species live only in the growth layer immediately beneath the bark, whereas others penetrate right into the sapwood and the heartwood. Among those which attack dead trees, some species live in dry timber, and in the wild these will be found in dry branches or dead trunks which remain standing, whereas others will only thrive in damp, rotting timber.

When man began to use timber from the forest for equipment and houses certain of these insects must have entered his home. Some of them are merely transferred from the forest as eggs or larvae, and cannot live in timber that has been worked.

The species which had the most chance of survival, and which have become serious pests of timber, were those which could thrive in dry wood, for this is what is used in houses. In addition, there are several species which occur in places where timber structures have been damaged by damp and by fungus.

Identification of pests in timber

With a few exceptions it is the larvae which attack timber, but normally these are difficult to find, and even if one does manage to extract one, it is difficult to identify with any degree of certainty.

The adult insects only appear for a short period, usually in summer, and so in most cases the culprit has to be identified from the tracks and signs it leaves in the timber. The type of tree, whether deciduous or coniferous, and its age and condition, may also provide clues.

EXIT-HOLES IN TIMBER

All the exit-holes on this and the following pages are shown natural size.

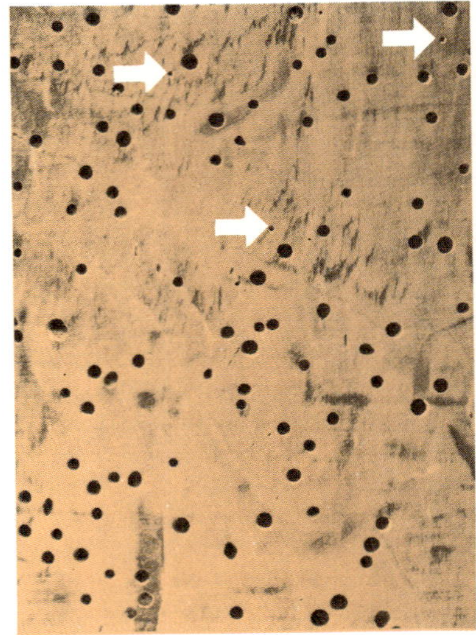

Chalcids

The exit-holes have a diameter of less than 1 mm (see arrow). They are always found close to the holes made by furniture beetles, on which the chalcids live (see p. 152).

Common furniture beetle

The exit-holes have a diameter of 1.5–2 mm. This beetle occurs in many kinds of deciduous and coniferous trees. The tunnels are most often in the sapwood, but they may enter the heartwood. The wood dust is a uniform colour and feels gritty. The faeces are almost cigar-shaped. This is the species commonly found as woodworm in furniture and structural timber (see pp. 121 and 163).

Ernobius mollis

The exit-holes have a diameter of c. *2 mm. This species occurs only in softwood (conifer) timber, but only in the bark and the outermost sapwood, and the exit-holes always penetrate the bark. The faeces are spherical, and they contain pale and dark particles, depending upon whether the larva has been feeding on bark or sapwood. Very common in houses where bark-covered timber is used (see p. 122).*

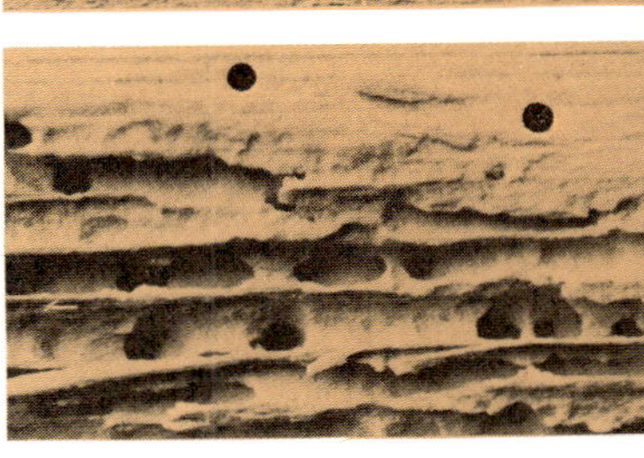

Dendrobium pertinax

The exit-holes have a diameter of 2–3 mm. This species is found almost exclusively in softwood that has been damaged by damp. It works mainly in the spring wood, while the summer wood remains behind in the form of lamellae. The wood dust is similar to that left by the common furniture beetle, but usually darker. The faeces are cylindrical (see p. 123).

Death-watch beetle

The exit-holes have a diameter of 3–5 mm. The larvae occur almost exclusively in oak damaged by damp, both in the sapwood and the heartwood. The faeces are large and lens-shaped (see p. 125).

Fan-bearing wood-borer

The exit-holes have a diameter of 1.0–1.5 mm. The larvae are found in the sapwood of deciduous trees. The wood dust is very fine and rather like talc (see p. 125).

Powder post beetles

The exit-holes have a diameter of 1.0–1.5 mm. The larvae most frequently occur in the sapwood of oak, but may also be found in various exotic deciduous timber, and in bamboo. The wood dust is extremely fine and feels like talc (see p. 125).

Lymexylon navale

Very small exit-holes, less than 1–2 mm across, usually in oak. Some of the tunnels are completely empty, others have very tightly packed wood dust. The tunnels frequently enter the heartwood and unlike those made by ambrosia beetles they do not have a dark lining (see p. 128).

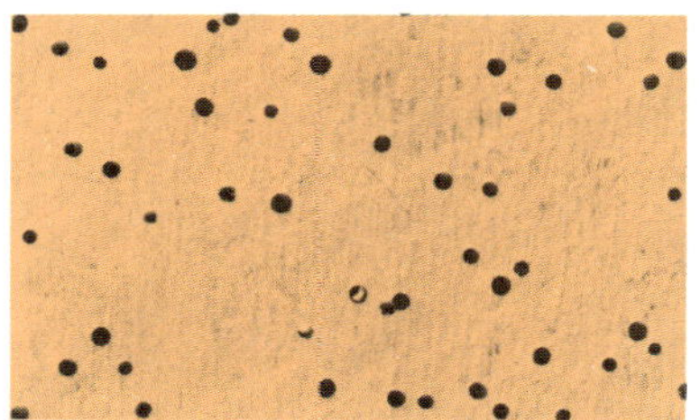

Wood-boring weevils

The exit-holes have a diameter of 1–2 mm. The larvae of these beetles only attack timber damaged by damp. It is typical that many of the tunnels break through the surface of the timber. The wood dust is finer than that produced by the common furniture beetle (see p. 128).

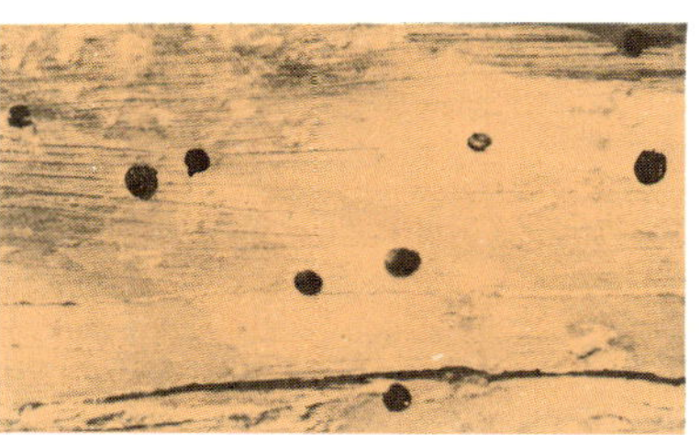

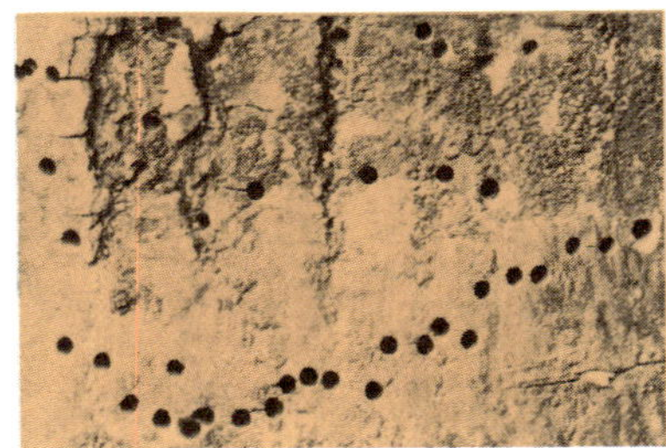

Ash bark beetle

The exit-holes have a diameter of c. *1.5 mm, and they always emerge through bark. This species only occurs in ash and the characteristic tunnels, which are full of dark wood dust, can be seen when the bark is removed (see p. 130).*

Ambrosia beetles

Tunnels of this beetle that reach the surface may be confused with the exit-holes of the common furniture beetle. However, they contain no wood dust and usually have a distinct darkish lining due to the ambrosia fungus. The colour of the lining varies from pale brown to almost black, and it may be restricted to a narrow zone or extend out into the timber. Several species of ambrosia beetle occur in imported hardwood used for furniture, panelling, etc. The diameter of the tunnels depends upon the species concerned (see p. 131).

Trypodendron lineatus

Common in softwoods used as structural timber. The tunnels, with a diameter of 1–2 mm, run in a very characteristic way (see p. 132), and not at random as in the common furniture beetle.

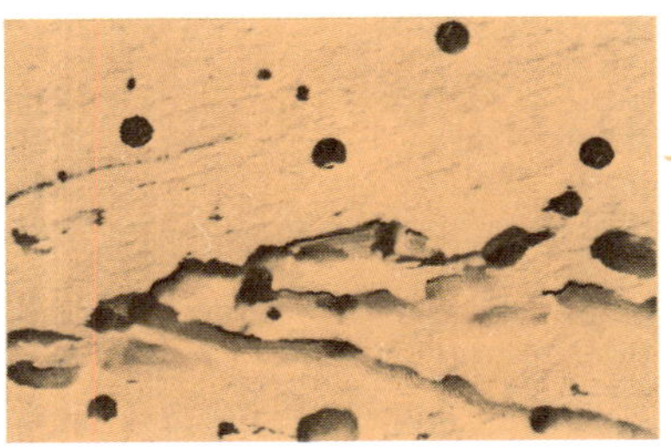

Bostrychid beetles

Many species of tropical boring beetles of the family Bostrychidae occur in imported timber: in boxes, carved figures, baskets, etc. The exit-holes have a diameter of 1–5 mm, depending upon the species. Unlike the work of the powder post beetles they make distinct larval tunnels, circular in cross section. The wood dust is powdery, but coarser than that made by powder post beetle larvae and more tightly packed (see p. 128).

Wood wasps

The exit holes have a diameter of up to 1 cm. They are circular, with completely smooth edges, and look as though they had been bored with a 10 mm drill. Wood wasps occur only in conifers, the larval tunnels being made in both sapwood and heartwood. The coarse wood dust is so tightly packed that it may be difficult to scrape out of the tunnels (see p. 142).

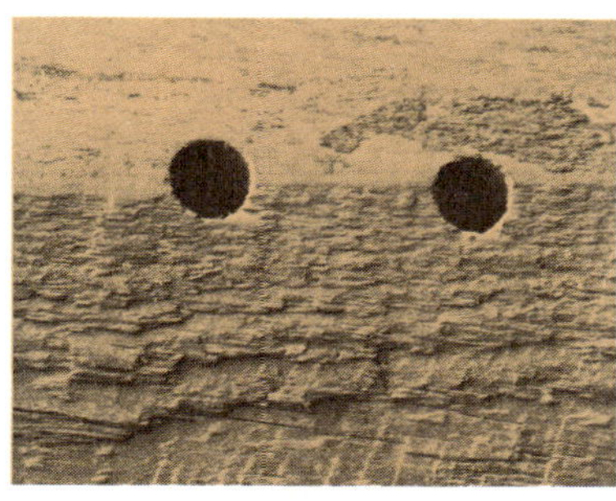

Sawflies

The larvae may gnaw into timber when they are about to pupate. The tunnels are c. *2 mm in diameter. It is obvious that they have been gnawed from the outside, and there are often several attempts, each a few mm deep. The attack always takes place on external timber work, and normally on new houses which are near to uncultivated areas with weeds (see p. 144).*

Goat moth larvae

Larvae of the goat moth may gnaw their way into timber when ready to pupate. The holes are circular with a diameter of up to 2 cm. Unlike those made by wood wasps these holes are somewhat frayed at the edge, and they are usually found in mouldering timber (see p. 147).

Wharfborer

The exit-holes are irregular, oval or circular, up to 6 mm in diameter, and they occur mainly in softwood. They may be confused with those made by the house longhorn beetle but the present species only attacks damp timber, and it is typical that the larval tunnels contain numerous pieces of wood fibre (see p. 141).

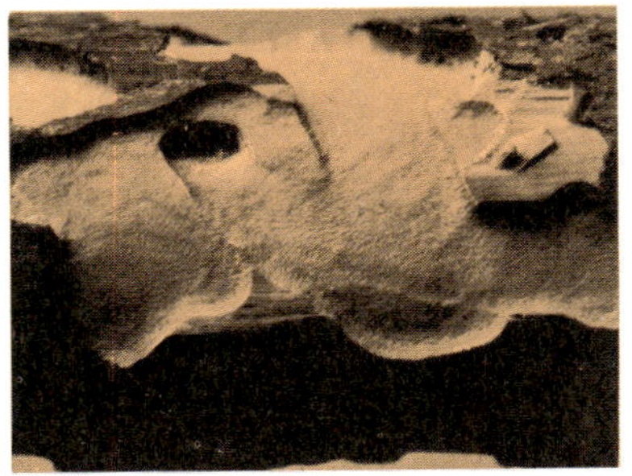

Callidium violaceum

The oval exit-holes measure c. *6 × 3 mm. The species is found only in softwood. The larval tunnels, which lie just under the bark, are full of wood dust, with a mixture of dark and pale particles. The exit-holes are always in the bark, the oval holes in the sapwood being the openings of the pupal chambers. Very common in timber which still has the bark on (see pp. 132 and 163).*

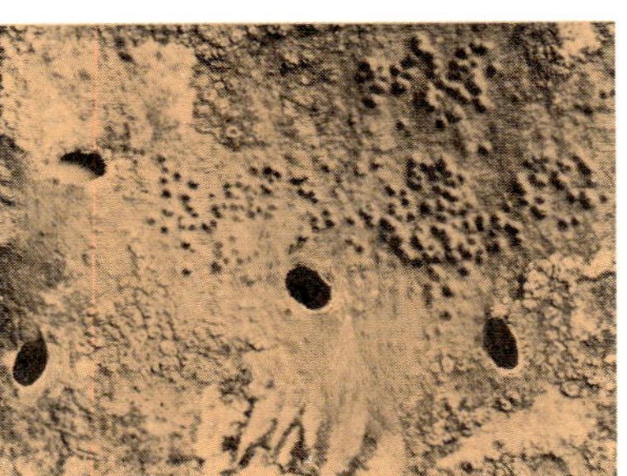

Phymatodes testaceus

The oval exit-holes measure c. *6 × 3 mm. This species only attacks timber from deciduous trees. The larval tunnels lie just below the bark and are full of wood dust, with a mixture of dark and pale particles. The exit-holes are always in the bark, the oval holes in the timber itself being the openings of the pupa chambers. Common in wood logs (see p. 134).*

House longhorn

The exit-holes are mostly oval, but usually irregular with frayed edges. Their size is variable, but is normally c. *6 × 3 mm. The larval tunnels often extend right out to the surface, but a thin outer layer of wood is always left. The tunnels are full of uniformly coloured, yellowish wood dust. The faeces are cylindrical (see p. 135).*

Tetropium luridum

This species attacks softwoods almost exclusively. In timber that has been planed the pupal chambers will often be seen. They are oval, measuring 6 × 4 mm, without wood dust but often containing a few coarse wood fibres. The larval tunnels, which are full of uniformly coloured, dark wood dust, run in the bark, with only a slight trace in the wood. The exit-holes are oval with smooth edges, 6 mm long and 4 mm across. They also open out through the bark and so are not found in worked timber (see p. 138).

Criocephalus rusticus

The exit-holes are oval, with smooth edges, and with a maximum diameter of 0.5–1.3 cm. This beetle only attacks conifers, especially pine, damaged by damp. The larval tunnels which occur in both sapwood and heartwood are oval and strikingly broad. The wood dust is extremely firmly packed in the tunnel and difficult to scrape out *(see p. 139).*

Pine sawyer

The round circular exit-holes have a diameter of 5–8 mm, and normally open out through the bark. Worked timber often shows larval tunnels that the plane has cut through.

In cross section, the tunnels are oval, measuring c. *8 × 3 mm. They are therefore similar to those of* Criocephalus *but contain no wood dust* *(see p. 139).*

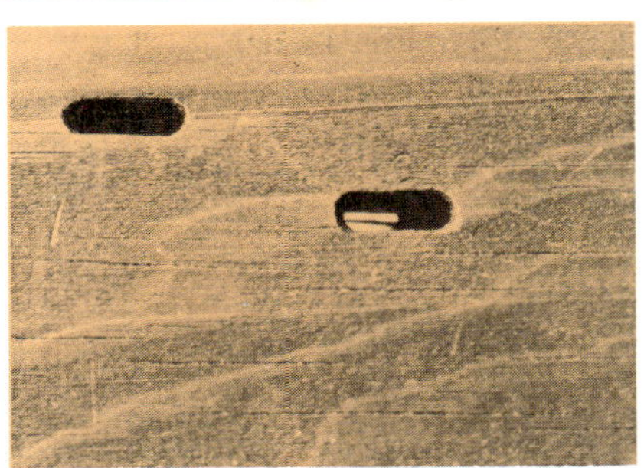

Leptura rubra

The circular exit-holes have a diameter of 5–8 mm, and may therefore be confused with those made by wood wasps. This beetle only attacks conifers damaged by damp and the larval tunnels are almost oval in cross section and full of firm wood dust which is not, however, so firm as that left by wood wasps. The faeces are cylindrical with rounded ends *(see p. 139).*

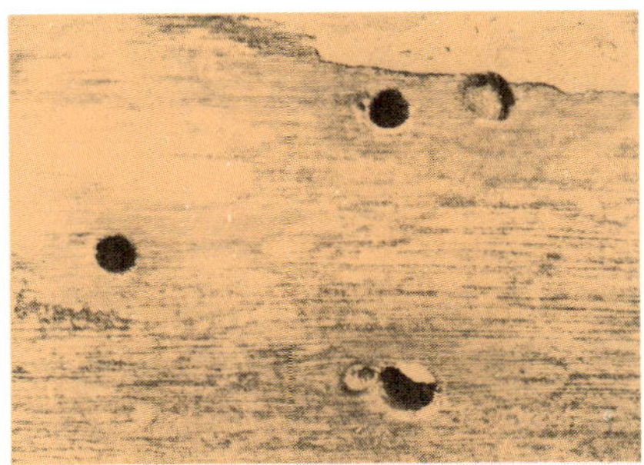

Gracilia minuta

Small oval exit-holes in the bark, almost always in willow. The larval tunnels lie between the bark and the wood *(see p. 139).*

Small black ant

These ants form labyrinthine tunnel systems in soft, crumbling timber which has been attacked by fungus or possibly by wood-boring beetles.

The surface of the timber takes on a typical rounded and polished appearance. When the colony is deserted the tunnels are completely empty (see p. 145). There are other ants which also attack timber (see pp. 120 and 145).

Termites

Termites excavate trees, leaving behind the hard summer wood in the form of lamellae. There is no wood dust in the tunnels, but one finds the nest chambers, which are built of earth particles cemented together (see p. 149).

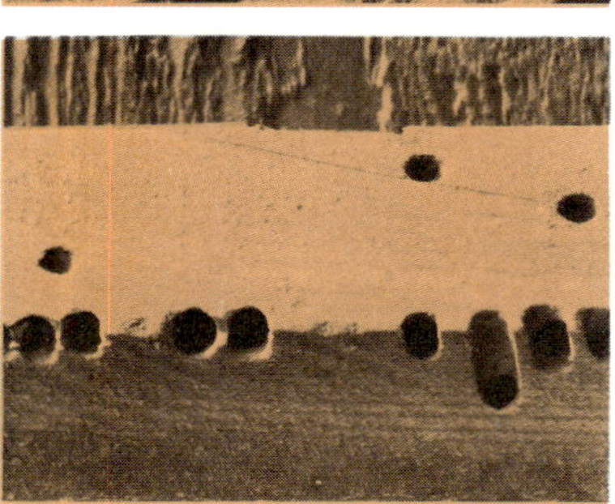

Larder beetles

The larvae of many beetles and moths sometimes gnaw their way into timber when they are about to pupate. The pupal tunnels are gnawed from the outside and usually end blind, but if there are many of them the timber may be riddled with a labyrinth of tunnels. There is no wood dust in these tunnels, but empty larval casts are nearly always found.

The pupal tunnels of larder beetles are circular in cross section, with a diameter of c. *4 mm (see p. 120).*

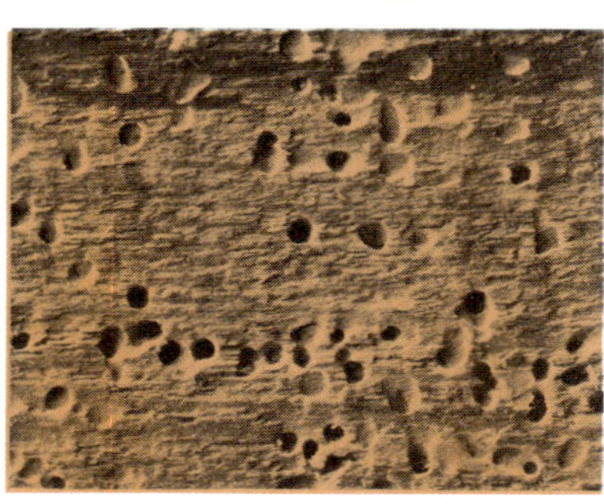

Australian spider beetle

The pupal tunnels are circular in cross section, c. *2 mm in diameter. They are normally not very deep and are often only pits in the surface of the timber (see p. 120).*

Death watch beetle

Furniture beetles, Family Anobiidae
(Page 26)

The larvae of these beetles live mainly in timber. The adults are very small and brownish with an almost cylindrical body. It is typical that the thorax is arched to form a hood which almost conceals the head.

The larvae of the different species of furniture beetle are soft, curved, with very small legs, and they are difficult to distinguish from one another. They are known colloquially as woodworms. During the mating season the adults communicate with each other by banging the thorax against timber (p. 214).

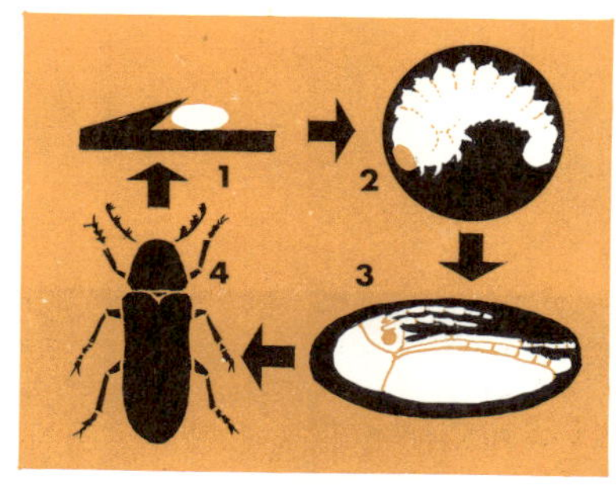

Life cycle of the common furniture beetle. 1. the eggs are laid in crevices in timber; 2. the larvae that hatch from the eggs gnaw the wood and eat it; 3. after 2–3 years each larva pupates in a pupal chamber just below the surface; 4. a couple of weeks later the pupa metamorphoses into the adult beetle which gnaws a circular exit-hole in the thin surface layer and emerges. After mating the females start to lay their eggs. Other wood-boring beetles have a similar life cycle.

Common furniture beetle,
Anobium punctatum
(Pages 26 and 104)

This is a very common pest of timber and furniture and is or has been present in most old houses. The adult beetles emerge during the summer months by gnawing their way out from the infected timber through circular exit-holes. It is at this time that wood dust falls out of the timber. The beetles, which only live a couple of weeks, can fly and are often confused with small flies. Shortly after emergence they mate and the female starts to lay. The eggs are never deposited on smooth surfaces but in crevices, on the end grain, or on unplaned timber, and very often in old exit-holes. The eggs hatch after 3–4 weeks, and the tiny larvae start immediately to gnaw into the timber. They leave the undigested parts of the timber in the tunnels in the form of small, oblong balls of faeces. As the larvae grow the diameter of the tunnel gradually increases. The larvae do not leave the timber and cannot therefore wander from one piece of furniture to another. Their development takes 2, 3 or more years, depending upon the temperature, the humidity and the type of timber.

The most favourable temperature for the development of the larvae is 22–23° C, but they can live at lower temperatures, and even outdoors in Europe. The water content of the timber is important for the well-being of the larvae. The damper it is

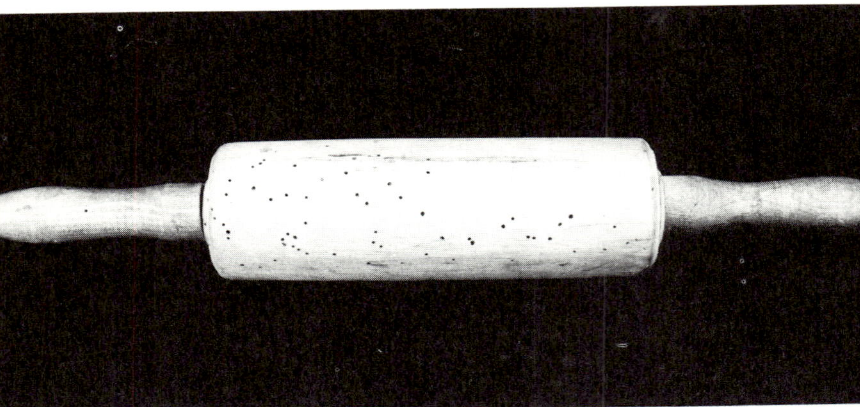

Worm holes, the exit-holes of the common furniture beetle, are often regarded as proof that an article is antique

the better, provided the timber is not soaking wet over a long period. Serious attacks by this beetle often occur, therefore, in kitchens, cellars, outhouses and stables which are sometimes rather damp. This species does not thrive if the air humidity is constantly under 50%, so it will not survive in the dry climate of a modern centrally heated building. It prefers softwoods but can live in practically all types of timber. It does not, however, attack sound heartwood.

Bookworms are beetle larvae that live in paper (p. 107). The fact that these larvae can develop in all these materials, and even in pure cellulose, is due to the presence in the gut wall of special yeast cells which break down the cellulose to digestible sugars and provide the larvae with the necessary supplement of vitamins and nitrogen.

Ernobius mollis

Ernobius mollis

(Page 26)

In this species the outer skeleton is softer than in the other furniture beetles. A clothing of short, fine hairs gives the beetles a pale, golden-brown colour. The life cycle is very similar to that of the common furniture beetle but the female only lays eggs in the bark of fallen or dead conifers. The newly hatched larvae gnaw their way into the growth layer and feed partly on the innermost layer of bark, partly on the outermost zone of sapwood.

If the bark is removed the larval tunnels can be seen as furrows (*c.* 1 mm deep) in the wood. Just before pupating the larvae gnaw a little deeper and at right angles to the ordinary larval tunnels (p. 114).

This beetle is very common and can be found practically everywhere that timber with the bark still on is used in house construction. The damage done is purely superficial and will not affect the mechanical strength. On the other hand, if such timber is covered with sheets of any kind the emerging beetles will gnaw their way out and leave unsightly holes. The position is more serious when the timber is covered directly with roofing felt or lead sheets. The beetles will then gnaw through the roof covering and their exit-holes will allow the entry of rain, thus supplying a substrate for the growth of moulds.

Dendrobium pertinax
(Page 26)

This species is a little larger and darker than the common furniture beetle. The females lay only a few eggs (*c*. 10), usually in spring, in cracks and crevices in the timber. Development normally takes 2–3 years. When fully grown the larvae pupate and a couple of weeks later they metamorphose into adult beetles. This usually takes place during the autumn, but the beetles do not then emerge, but overwinter in the pupal chambers and gnaw their way out in the following spring.

This species attacks rotting branches or

In this case a veneer with an edging of bark has been used, with the result that a number of beetle larvae (Ernobius mollis) *have gnawed their way out through the veneer*

When timber is kept continually damp and becomes infected with fungus the beetle Dendrobium pertinax *often completes the destruction*

trunks of conifers, and when found in houses it is always in timber which has been softened by fungi. In some cases the infected timber is almost completely reduced to powder, with only the hard summer wood remaining in the form of thin lamellae.

An attack by this beetle will only be successful if the timber is damp, so the first step in controlling it is to find the source of the damp. Even when this problem has been solved the larvae may still go on developing in timber that has been damaged by damp, so any infected timber should be treated or even replaced. The beetles cannot live in healthy dry timber.

A specimen of Dendrobium pertinax *on a wooden plank showing exit-holes*

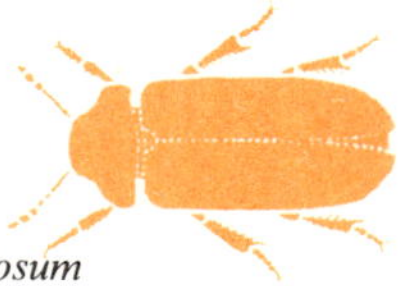

Death-watch beetle,
Xestobium rufovillosum
(Page 26)

This is one of the larger wood-boring beetles. The female lays up to 50 eggs in April-May. In structural timber the larvae may take 5–10 years to complete their development. They pupate in the autumn and metamorphosis to the adult takes place a few weeks later. As in the preceding species the beetles remain in the timber until the following spring, when they gnaw their way out through characteristic exit-holes. In nature, the eggs are usually laid on dead branches of various deciduous trees. In buildings, they are almost always laid on oak. The larvae can only survive in timber that is damp enough for fungi to flourish on it, so preventive measures should be the same as those recommended for the preceding species.

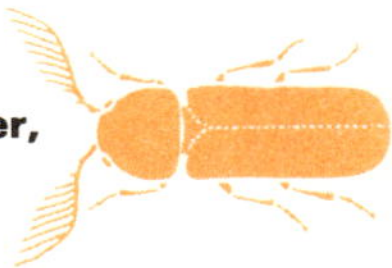

Fan-bearing wood-borer,
Ptilinus pectinicornis
(Page 26)

This species, which is not so common as the other wood-boring beetles, mainly attacks deciduous trees, e.g. beech, birch, oak. It is easily recognizable by the large, comb-like antennae. Unlike the other wood-borers here the adult beetle also gnaws timber. The wood dust is very fine and similar to that produced by the powder post beetles.

Powder post beetles, Family Lyctidae
(Page 25)

These beetles are very slender, brown and 2–5 mm long. They are particularly as-

An oak beam in a 700-year-old church in Jutland damaged by death-watch beetles

[*top*] *Souvenirs from tropical countries are frequently attacked by timber pests. This wooden beaker from Tanzania has been attacked by one of the powder post beetles,* Minthea ruficollis. *Bostrychid beetles also attack this kind of object.*
[*opposite*] *Powder post beetles may also attack bamboo. Here the species* Lyctus brunneus *has attacked a table mat made of split bamboo.*

sociated with deciduous trees that have large vessels, e.g. oak, ash, walnut, and with many tropical species, as well as bamboo. The female usually lays her eggs in the sapwood in the vessels themselves. The larvae feed on the starchy contents of the sapwood cells and gradually reduce the timber to a powdery mass surrounded by a thin shell. When fully grown the larvae gnaw their way towards the surface and pupate in an oval chamber. The adult beetles emerge through small circular exit-holes. Development normally takes one year.

In recent years powder post beetles have assumed some considerable importance. This is due in large measure to the way the timber is treated nowadays. In former times it was left to cure for years, and so the cells still living in it had a chance to use up their content of starch. In recent years there has been an increase in the practice of drying the timber by heat soon after the tree has been felled. This method kills the

cells but preserves the starch in them. Timber treated in this way will therefore continue to be very attractive to many insect pests.

The species *Lyctus linearis* is fairly common in Britain and Europe, but it is the related *Lyctus brunneus*, rare as a native species, which is most often seen in houses. This beetle attacks parquet floors and oak panelling, which it may completely destroy. It frequently arrives in imported hardwoods from the tropics.

Lymexylon navale
(Page 25)

This beetle attacks old oaks in the forest and oak beams in timber yards. It has, on occasion, done considerable damage in shipyards, and is especially famous from Linnaeus' account of its depredations in the naval dockyard at Gothenburg in 1747.

Bostrychid beetles,
Family Bostrychidae
(Page 25)

The members of this family are predominantly tropical. They are somewhat similar to the Anobiidae, for their downturned head is almost completely covered by the arched thorax, but in contrast to the Anobiidae this 'helmet' is beset with tiny spines or knobs.

In their habits they are more like the powder post beetles for they also attack deciduous trees rich in starch, and exclusively the sapwood. The females lay their eggs on newly felled trees, but many of the species only do so when the bark is still on. They never attack dry, seasoned timber, though some of the species are able to continue their development in the timber even though it starts to dry out, and they may even emerge from furniture.

In Europe bostrychid beetles occur mainly in imported goods. Wooden chests from the east are often almost reduced to powder by the time they arrive.

Exotic wooden sculpture, as well as baskets and other woven objects, may also be infected, and in many cases the species concerned is *Bostrychoplites cornutus* (Plate 8, p. 25).

Some species, such as the small *Dinoderus minutus* (Plate 8, p. 25), are common in bamboo.

There is, of course, no risk that the beetles might move from one object to another, but they may completely destroy the timber they are in. An attack can be stopped by heat or by freezing.

Weevils, Family Curculionidae (Page 28)

The weevils form the largest family in the animal kingdom, with more than 40,000 known species. A few of them can be regarded as minor pests of worked timber. One of the species concerned, *Codiosoma spadix*, is 3–4 mm long and brownish-black with a very short, powerful snout. It only attacks timber which has previously been infected with fungus, and may thus be regarded as a secondary pest.

Pine weevil, *Hylobius abietis*
(Page 28)

This beetle may occasionally be found indoors, sometimes in large numbers, although it really has no reason to be there. The larvae live in tree stumps and in the roots of diseased or dead conifers. The adult beetles may cause some damage outdoors because they gnaw shoots and twigs, but indoors they are quite harmless.

The beetles occur particularly in new timber houses, and they are possibly attracted by the scents given off during the first few years.

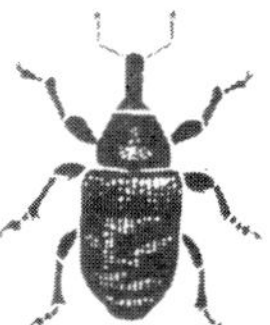

Pine weevil

Black vine-weevil

This species may easily be confused with the black vine-weevil (p. 203). Both are about the same size and have patches of yellow hairs on the elytra, but the snout is considerably larger in *H. abietis*.

Bark beetles, Family Scolytidae (Page 28)

These are small, cylindrical beetles with a large thorax. They can be distinguished from the furniture beetles by their angled antennae. The adults emerge in the spring and search for diseased or newly felled trees, where they gnaw their way into the bark. After mating the female makes a tunnel in the bark and forms an egg-gallery with small niches, in each of which she lays an egg. When the larvae hatch each one gnaws its own tunnel at right angles to the maternal egg-gallery.

These tunnel systems are often seen when the bark is removed from dead branches or trunks. Some bark beetles keep exclusively to the bark, others work in the layer between the bark and the wood, and each species produces its special pattern. True bark beetles are only seen indoors when brought in with timber that still has the bark on, e.g. firewood, and they cannot attack worked timber.

Tunnels made by bark beetle larvae

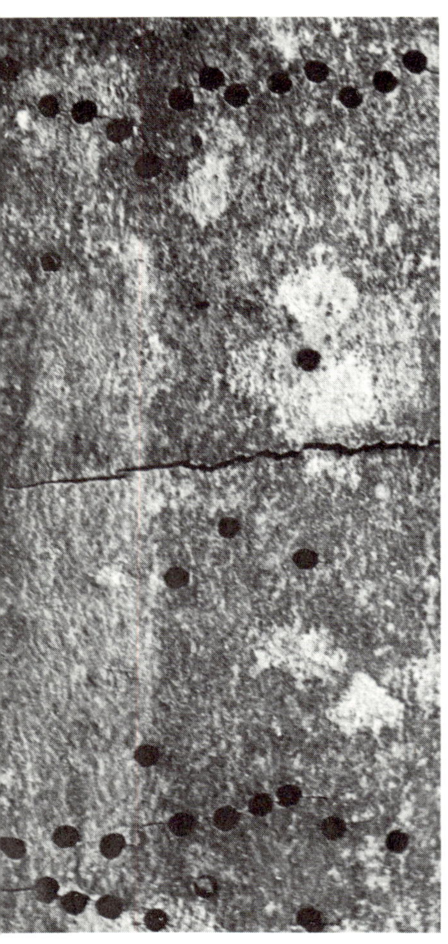

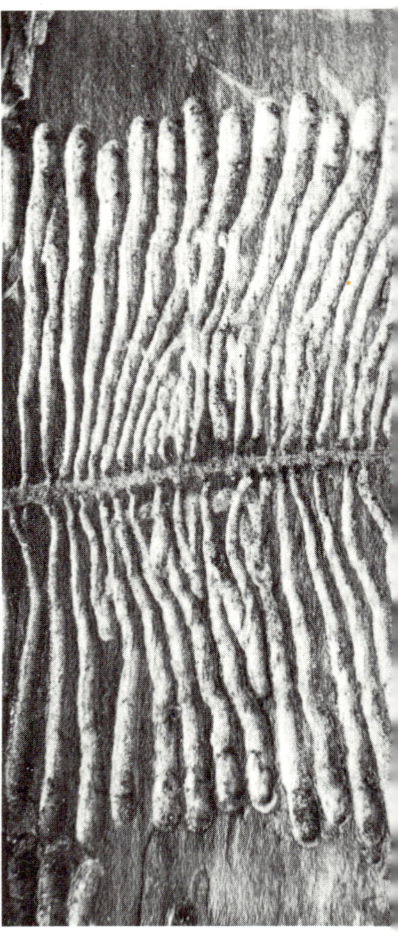

Ash bark beetle,
Hylesinus fraxini
(Page 28)

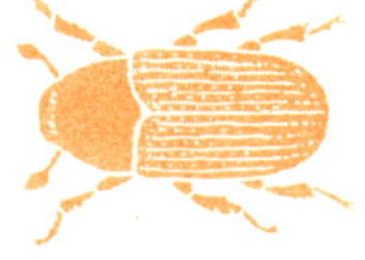

This is the scolytid most commonly seen in houses, where it may suddenly appear as a swarm of small, yellow-brown, spotted beetles. These will always have come from ash logs, and the round exit-holes quickly show where they have come from.

[*left*] *A piece of ash log with exit-holes of the ash bark beetle.* [*right*] *The same piece with the bark removed showing the decorative system of galleries*
[*opposite*] *Timber attacked by* Trypodendron lineatus. *The holes are the female tunnels cut through by the plane. The dark staining round the holes indicates the work of ambrosia beetles.*

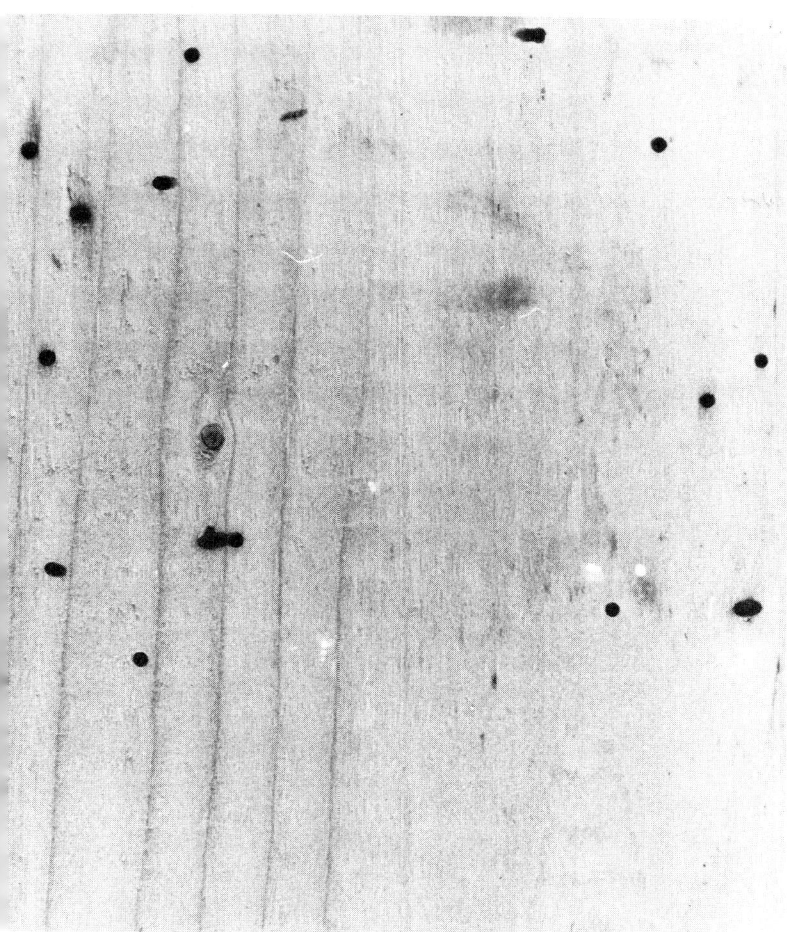

Ambrosia beetles

These are scolytid beetles that are not completely typical for they make tunnel systems in the wood itself. The adults gnaw their way into the wood, bringing with them the spores of special fungi which germinate and grow on the insides of the tunnels. The fungi are able to digest the cellulose in the wood and they produce nutritious spores on which the beetles and their larvae feed. This food is known as ambrosia.

In Greek mythology ambrosia was the food of the gods, and their drink was nectar.

When the tree dries out the fungi can no longer thrive and the attack dies out, so in normal circumstances this is not an economically important pest of building timber. If timber is directly exposed to wind and rain the holes made by the beetles will provide an entry for various moulds. When timber is valued for its aesthetic appeal, as when used for making furniture, the holes and discoloration produced by an attack by ambrosia beetles will considerably reduce its commercial value. On the other hand in some cases the workings of the beetles may be utilized as part of a decorative pattern, for they can be quite attractive.

Traces of the workings of ambrosia beetles can often be seen in imported hardwoods from the tropics.

Trypodendron (= Xyloterus) lineatum
(Page 28)

Timber showing the activities of this ambrosia beetle is quite commonly seen in Europe. It lives in conifers; others are associated with deciduous trees.

After mating the female drives a short tunnel into the trunk of the tree, and from this she makes two or three horizontal egg-galleries, which usually follow the annual rings. She then gnaws small niches in the roof and floor of the galleries and lays an egg in each one. When they hatch the larvae somewhat enlarge the niches but they do not gnaw true tunnels in the wood, for they feed on the fungal growths already mentioned. Each larva pupates in its own chamber and the adult beetles emerge from the tunnel system by the same route as their parents entered.

Galleries of Trypodendron lineatus *in a piece of split wood. The horizontal gallery is made by the female, and the short larval tunnels branch off from it.*

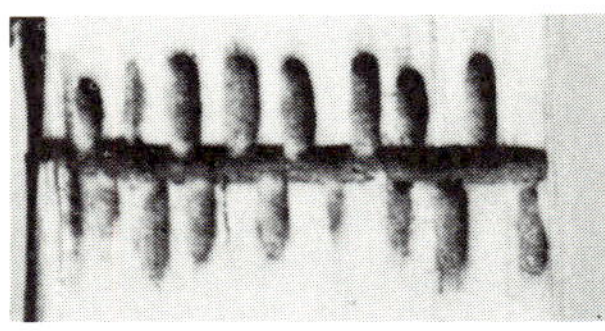

Longhorn beetles,
Family Cerambycidae
(Page 27)

These are mostly quite large beetles, often with very long antennae.

The larvae of the different species, which are difficult to distinguish from one another, are pale, plump, rather flat, and broadest towards the head which has powerful, dark jaws.

The females lay their eggs in bark crevices or splits in the timber, and the larvae feed on the wood. Their development may take several years. When fully grown each larva prepares an enlarged pupal chamber, often lined with coarse wood fibres, in which it pupates and later metamorphoses to the adult beetle.

The different species vary widely in their choice of timber. Some can thrive only in hardwood, others exclusively in softwood, some attack fresh, newly felled timber, while there are certain species which require timber that has been damaged by damp.

Callidium violaceum (Page 27)

This is probably the species that is most commonly seen in the house, though not as serious a pest as the house longhorn (p 135). It lays eggs exclusively in softwood and only in dead or felled timber that still has its bark on. The larvae live in the growth layer and if the bark is removed their tunnels can be seen as broad furrows on the surface of the timber, with the marks made by their jaws showing as fine stripes.

Larval development takes one to two years and when they are fully grown the larvae bore obliquely into the timber for a distance of 3–5 cm. At the bottom of this tunnel they make a chamber in which they

[opposite] The larval tunnels of Callidium violaceum *showing the fine markings left by the gnawing larvae*

pupate having sealed it with wood fibres.

These pupal tunnels might suggest that the attack has also gone deep, but it is not difficult to test with a screwdriver that these end blindly, and as each larva only makes one such tunnel during its life this does not seriously affect the mechanical strength of the timber.

When the beetles emerge – normally in the spring – they wander back through the pupal tunnel and gnaw their way out through the bark, making an oval, smooth-edged hole (p. 118).

The larvae are often brought into the house with bark-covered timber, and are common in firewood (only softwoods), and in planks of pine or spruce that still have the bark on.

The larvae can thrive in timber until the whole of the layer between bark and wood has been used up, but the attack cannot spread to timber without bark. The best method of stamping out an attack is simply to remove the bark.

As in the case of *Ernobius mollis* (p. 122), this species may also cause damage when panels or roofing are placed up against bark-covered timber. When the beetles emerge they sometimes gnaw their way out through the covering panels.

Phymatodes testaceus
(Page 27)

There are different colour variants of this beetle, some having yellowish elytra, some blue. The life cycle is the same as that of the preceding species with the sole exception that the present species only attacks hardwoods, such as beech, birch and oak. In a house the first sign will normally be the adult beetles, seen crawling around the room, and as they must necessarily have come from bark-covered timber the first place to search is the log basket. The exit-holes are oval (p. 118).

This beetle is in no way a menace in the house, but if hardwood is being kept for carpentry work it is always advisable to remove the bark, as an attack by these beetles renders the outer layer of timber unusable.

Phymatodes testaceus *at its exit-hole on a piece of birch log*

House longhorn, *Hylotrupes bajulus*
(Pages 27 and 104)

From the economic standpoint this beetle is one of the most important pests of structural timber, but it is not widespread in Britain. In the wild the larvae live in old and completely dry coniferous trees. The adult beetle, which is only rarely seen, emerges in lofts in the warmest part of the summer, mates, and the female starts to lay. She may produce up to 400 eggs and with the help of the very long, flexible ovipositor these can be deposited deep down in cracks and crevices in the tree. The eggs hatch in about 14 days and the larvae bore straight into the wood where they continue to feed for the next couple of years. The actual period of development and the final size of the larva depends upon the temperature and the nutritional content of the timber. The average length of the larval life is probably about 3–4 years, but it can be much longer. The larva feeds mainly on the sapwood and often gnaws outwards towards the surface until only a thin papery layer separates it from the outside world. When fully grown it pupates in a special pupal chamber which is sealed with coarse chips, but just before doing this it gnaws an exit-hole through which it will later leave the tree as a beetle (p. 118). The exit-hole, the wood dust and the chips which the larva often push out are usually the first visible evidence of an attack by this beetle, although the actual infection may have taken place several years before. However it is possible to listen for evidence before the attack has got as far as this. By standing quietly in a loft on a warm summer day it is possible to hear quite distinctly the rasping sound

Larvae of the house longhorn have removed most of the sapwood from this rafter, leaving behind the knots and heartwood

made by the larger larvae as they gnaw (see also p. 214).

This beetle is now thought to be established in the southern parts of England, but it is not often seen in woodland, which is not surprising as it does not attack green timber.

The temperature must be at least 25° C before the adults become active, so in northern Europe it is only in some years that they actively disperse by flying from buildings already infected. There is little doubt that the dispersal of this beetle is mainly effected by man himself. Sometimes the timber may become infected in the merchant's yard before it reaches the builder, or infection may spread from boxes or furniture which have previously been stored in an infected loft.

This species occurs primarily in roof timber, because this is where it finds the high temperatures it requires, but it can easily spread to other timber in the house.

Larva (below) and pupa (bottom right) of the house longhorn in their tunnels
[*top*] *House longhorn larvae normally leave a thin outer layer of timber. Here some of this paper-thin layer has been removed to show the extent of the damage beneath.*

Tetropium luridum
(Pages 27 and 118)

The females of this species visit old or diseased woodland trees and lay their eggs in crevices in the bark. They also lay in fallen trees or stumps, almost always choosing conifers, particularly spruce. As in the case of *Callidium*, the larvae live in the layer between the bark and the wood, but gnaw more of the bark. The tunnels, which have a diameter of up to 1.5 cm, are full of wood dust. The larva first gnaws 2–4 cm directly into the tree and then turns and follows the grain of the wood, the tunnel having a total length of 4–6 cm. When fully grown the larva makes a slightly enlarged chamber, which it closes behind it with coarse wood fibres, and then pupates. When the adult beetle emerges it finds its way back along the tunnel, gnawing an exit-hole if there is still bark on the tree, and flies off. The total development normally takes a year.

The larva can complete its development even if the tree is felled and used as timber, but as the female beetle will only lay eggs in the bark and not in dry wood the infection cannot spread indoors, and will soon die out.

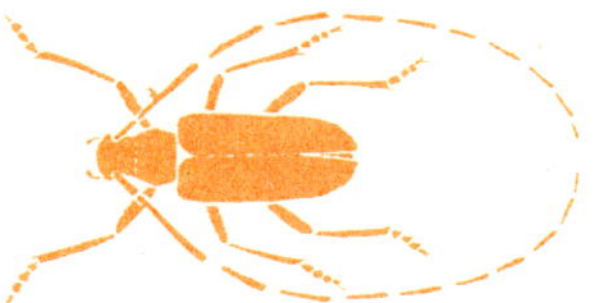

Pine sawyer, *Monochamus sutor*
(Pages 27 and 119)

This beetle is widely distributed in the conifer forests of northern Europe. The development normally takes one year. The eggs are laid in a depression which the female gnaws in the bark and the larva eats its way from there into the wood. Metamorphosis into the adult beetle takes place in the following spring in a special pupal chamber close to the surface of the tree, and the beetle gnaws its way out through an almost circular hole. This species is regarded as a very serious pest in Sweden where it causes damage to softwoods before they reach the sawmills.

The trees are always attacked while still growing and the larvae are unable to live for long in worked timber so there is no risk of the infection spreading indoors.

Leptura rubra
(Pages 27 and 119)

This beetle is easily distinguished by the attractive yellowish-red coloration. The females lay their eggs in damp softwood, often in diseased or dead branches. The larvae live exclusively in the sapwood and their development normally takes two years.

When seen indoors this beetle has usually flown in from adjacent woodlands, but it may also emerge from damp posts or planking. Softwood logs which have lain at the bottom of a stack may also be a source of infection. The female does not lay in dry timber, so there is no risk of this species becoming established indoors.

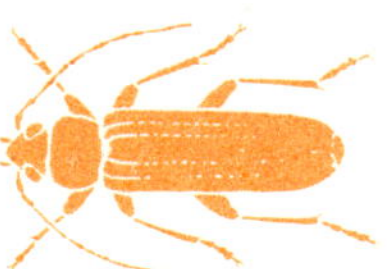

Criocephalus rusticus
(Pages 27 and 119)

This is another pest of conifers, particularly pine, and is commoner in the north of England and in Scotland than further south. It requires the timber to be damp if it is to thrive. The larvae normally live in pine stumps, but may also attack dead or felled trees, or damp planking at the base of a stack.

When the beetles are seen indoors they may have come from pine logs or from timber damaged by damp. In many cases worked timber may show signs of an old attack in the form of larval tunnels exposed by the plane. This would mean that the timber had been damp but had since dried out, and would be quite suitable for use provided it was kept dry with good ventilation.

If a building suffers a serious attack by this species the structural timber must be too damp and this should be rectified.

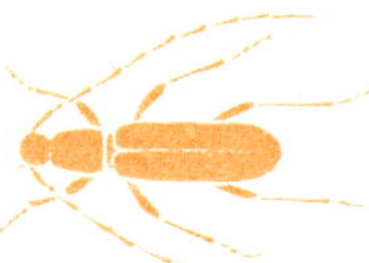

Gracilia minuta (Pages 27 and 119)

This beetle is specialized for living in the thin branches of various deciduous trees. It is a very small species occurring mainly in southern Europe, whence it may be introduced further north in basketwork made out of willow with the bark still on. Development normally takes a year. In northern Europe this species could certainly continue to breed in baskets kept indoors, but would not damage other objects.

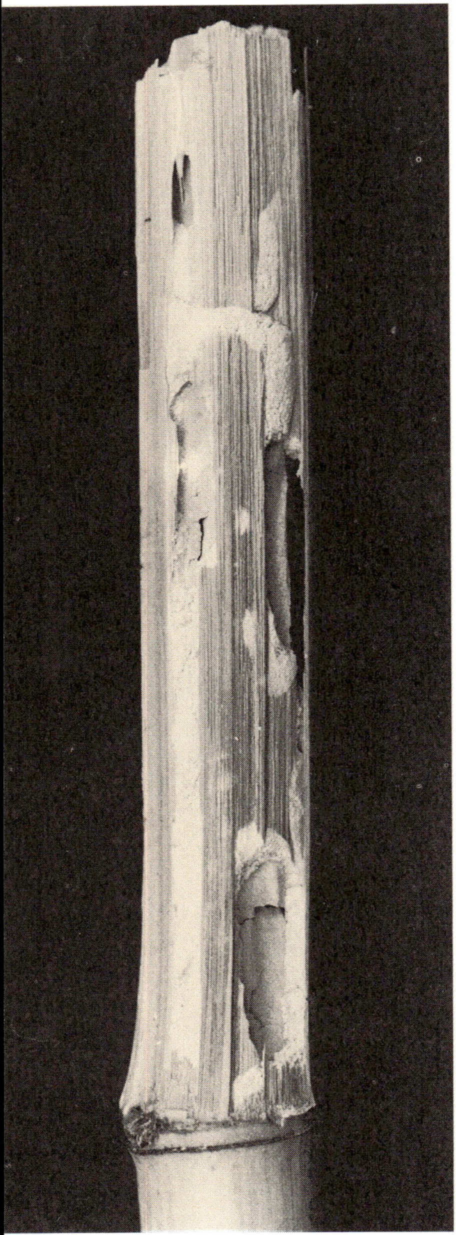

Chlorophorus annularis
(Page 27)

This is a beetle from south-east Asia, which feeds mainly on bamboo, and it may be a very serious pest where this is used for building houses. Occasionally bamboo imported into Europe may contain the larvae. In dry bamboo the larval development takes several years so it may be a long time after the purchase of bamboo furniture before the adult beetles gnaw their way out. The larvae will not, however, attack other timber in the house.

Clytus arietis
(Page 28)

The larvae of this beetle live in dead, dry deciduous wood. They do not attack timber indoors, but may be introduced with logs, and when the adult beetles are flying in mid-summer, they sometimes come in through doors and windows. They attract attention because of the striking colour pattern, which is somewhat reminiscent of a wasp.

Wharfborer, *Nacerda melanura*
(Pages 26 and 104)

This species is rather like a cerambycid, having long antennae, but it actually belongs to a completely different family. It is thought to have come originally from the Great Lakes area of the U.S.A., but has now been carried to all parts of the temperate zone by ships. The adult beetle is seen in summer, and it often occurs in large numbers during the middle of the day and sometimes enters houses. After mating the females lay eggs on damp timber.

The larvae prefer softwood provided it is not dry. Probably such timber will have been to some extent attacked by fungi, but it must not be so rotten as to be falling apart.

When seen in a house this beetle may have come in from outside, having emerged from ships' timber or wharves, and it also thrives in piling and in structural timber in damp cellars.

It is not uncommon for such timber to be so damaged as to require replacing. The new timber should be impregnated and efforts made to reduce the humidity, possibly by improving the ventilation.

[*opposite*] *Bamboo damaged by larvae of* Chlorophorus annularis
[*right*] *A freshly emerged wharfborer sitting on a badly damaged piece of oak. When the water table drops, as happens in many large cities, e.g. Copenhagen, air can reach the timber piling and this is followed by attacks by fungi and wharfborers.*

A split oak pile with a wharfborer larva. The tunnels are mainly in the soft spring wood. The fibrous fragments are characteristic.

[opposite] *Wood dust left by wood wasp larvae is very tightly packed, and it remains in position when the timber is split (see also p. 117)*

Wood wasps, Family Siricidae
(Pages 28 and 105)

Two of the commoner wood wasps in European forests are the horntail, *Urocerus gigas*, and the related *Sirex juvencus*. Adult wood wasps are active on warm, sunny days, when they search for freshly felled or diseased trees. The female has a large ovipositor at the rear end, with which she bores through the bark and lays eggs in the wood, one or two in each hole. The presence of fungi in the tree probably makes the wood more digestible for the larvae. At any rate, when the eggs hatch the larvae start to feed, gnawing their way through the wood. Under normal con-

ditions they are fully grown in 2–3 years, but if conditions are unsuitable, as when the wood is too dry, then the development may take much longer.

Wood wasps only lay in trees that still have their bark on, so they are unlikely to enter a house, except in timber already infected. It would, in fact, be possible to buy furniture containing these larvae. There is no risk of these insects spreading in the house, and it is very unlikely that they will be present in such numbers as to weaken the furniture. On the other hand, they may well cause damage when they emerge as adults. They can, for example, gnaw through floor boards and floor coverings or through roofing felt, or even lead sheeting (p. 163).

In some places wood wasps cause considerable damage in the forests. This is why timber exported to Australia has to be guaranteed free from wood wasps.

These insects have a rather frightening appearance but in fact they never attack man and do not sting.

Ametastegia glabrata
(Pages 28 and 105)

The green larvae of this sawfly live on various weeds, such as sorrel, dock and willow herb.

A sawfly larva has tried in vain to gnaw a pupal hole in a piece of timber, and is now on its way to try a new place

Normally, the fully grown larvae gnaw ıeir way into dry plant stems where ıey pupate, but occasionally they try sewhere. When they attack wooden rticles in the house they may become a uisance. Very often they give up gnawing nd try elsewhere, leaving a number of alf-finished holes in the timber (see p. 17). It is very often new houses that are ıbjected to the attacks of these otherwise ompletely harmless insects. This may be ue to the fact that the gardens have not et been cultivated so that the ground is overed with the various weeds on which ıe larvae feed.

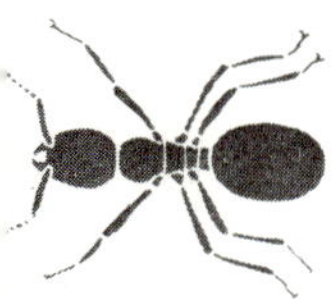

mall black or **garden ant,**
canthomyops niger
'age 30)

everal of the ants which otherwise live in e ground will occasionally build their ests in damp timber in the house, and ese include the garden ant.

They will only start to gnaw their way to timber which has already been subject damp and has been broken down by ngi and possibly by the attacks of beetle rvae. On this ant see also p. 81.

et black ant,
'anthomyops fuliginosus
age 30)

ıese shiny, black ants normally live in es, and they have a distinct smell of oranges. They can establish themselves in the dead parts of trees, in stumps and in wooden floor boards damaged by damp.

They gnaw extensive tunnels and holes in the timber and fill them with a dark papery material which they make by mixing gnawed wood fragments with saliva and particles of earth or other available material. The timber these ants live in need not necessarily be damaged by moisture, and sometimes they spare the harder parts so that the summer wood remains as lamellae. When present in a house, there will usually be ceaseless troops of these ants moving in line between their nest and food sources in the kitchen.

Hercules ant,
Camponotus herculeanus
(Page 30)

This very large ant occurs on the continent of Europe, but not in Britain. The nest is normally built in timber, sometimes in a living tree, occasionally in timber in the home. These ants prefer conifers, but they sometimes also live in various deciduous trees. In living trees the nests can be found up to a height of 10 m from the ground. The ants gnaw their tunnels in the soft spring wood, and leave the summer wood alone, so that in a transverse section of the tree trunk the tunnels appear as numerous regular rings. In a longitudinal section the summer wood remains as a series of lamellae, pierced here and there by openings which connect the different tunnels.

There have been cases where whole nests of Hercules ants have been built in with the timber of a new house, and in

forest areas they sometimes enter and become established in a house.

This is one of the ant species in which a single mated queen can found a completely new colony. The species is sometimes a serious pest in Central Europe and in parts of Scandinavia.

[left] Hercules ant nest exposed by the plane. The ants leave lamellae of hard summer wood and the knots.
[right] A piece of wooden partition wall in a tannery. In the course of time numerous larder beetle larvae have wandered out from hides and have gnawed into the timber. The holes lie in rows because the larvae have preferred the softer spring wood.

Goat moth, *Cossus cossus*
(Page 24)

From time to time one finds remarkably large circular holes in timber, particularly if there are willows or poplars in the vicinity. These holes are always in the surface timber of structures such as doors and window frames, and they are made by goat moth larvae. The female lays her eggs in crevices of the bark of various deciduous trees, particularly willow and poplar, but sometimes also in fruit trees. The larvae live and feed in the wood for 2–3 years and when fully grown they sometimes leave the tree they have been living in and seek a suitable place for pupation. This usually happens in the autumn when the larvae may be up to 10 cm long, and they may choose any soft timber to provide them with protection. They metamorphose into moths in the following summer.

DERMESTID LARVAE (p. 120) usually wander away from the material they have been living in when they are fully grown (p. 73) and then gnaw into some other material and pupate there. In buildings they often attack timber, and in stores of hides or dried fish which have been attacked by the larder beetle the woodwork may, in the course of time, become completely riddled with holes.

SPIDER BEETLE LARVAE (p. 104) behave in the same way as dermestid beetles, but their pupation tunnels are smaller.

WOODLICE (p. 18) are among the animals which often stray indoors. They occasionally try to gnaw timber, but are incapable of doing so with any degree of efficiency unless the wood is completely rotten, and are therefore not important, although unwelcome (see also p. 196).

A floor board in a loft damaged by Australian spider beetle larvae. In corn lofts various moth larvae gnaw similar holes in which to pupate.

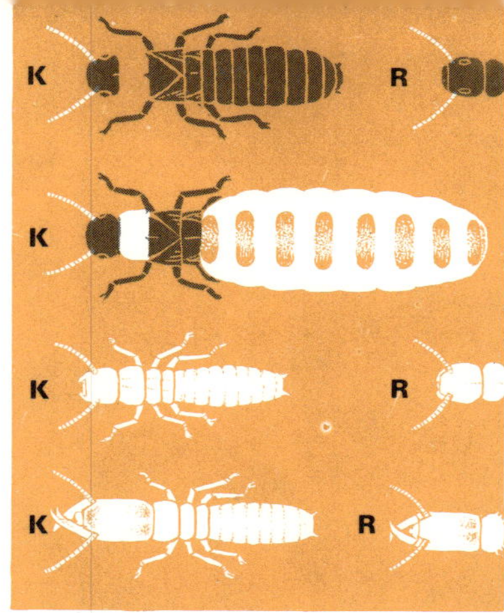

K = *Kalotermes*
R = *Reticulitermes*

Termites, Order Isoptera
(Page 20)

On a world scale the termites are by far the most serious pests of timber. There are about 2000 different species, but they require warmth and a high humidity and therefore only thrive under tropical conditions.

Like ants and bees, termites live in colonies which consists of so-called kings and queens, concerned with reproduction, workers which do the practical work and form the most numerous caste in the colony, and in some species there are soldier termites which defend the colony.

Two species, *Reticulotermes lucifugus* and *Kalotermes flavicollis*, occur in Europe, but do not extend north of Paris. For some years a few colonies of *Reticulotermes flavipes* have managed to survive in harbour warehouses in Hamburg, which they presumably reached in goods imported from America. Termites of various kinds probably arrive in other ports in northern Europe, but normally they would not become established.

Many of the wood-boring beetles seen indoors come from firewood

Woodpeckers

These birds are specialized for life in trees. They climb with the help of strong claws and use the powerful chisel-shaped bill for chopping a way through bark and soft wood in order to reach insect larvae, and also for making their nest holes.

They can seldom be regarded as pests but in certain cases they have been known to turn their attention to the external timber of a house. This is mainly done by the black woodpecker *(Dendrocopus martius)* and the great spotted woodpecker *(Dendrocopus major)*.

Normally woodpeckers hack timber in order to reach food, but sometimes they will attack fresh timber, and nearly always do this in order to make a chamber to spend the night in. In some cases they apparently run amok and hack one hole after another. The most likely explanation is that if the result is not satisfactory they will try again and again. Desperate house-owners have been known to shoot woodpeckers, even though they are now totally protected in most countries.

Normally woodpeckers can be deterred from these attacks by hanging up strips of aluminium foil or by stretching nylon threads back and forth across the parts of the house that are attacked.

Mammals

Among the mammals that occur indoors it is only the true rodents, mice and rats, which attack timber. They can, however, cause a lot of damage, but much of this can be avoided if metal plates are fixed at the base of each outside door. Rats and mice always start to gnaw timber at an edge or in a corner where their teeth can get a grip. The size of the hole and the toothmarks will sometimes serve as clues to identify which species has been at work (see p. 84).

[left] *Great spotted woodpecker (Elvig Hansen photo)*
[bottom] *Typical rat holes in a barn door. A metal plate nailed to the bottom of the door would have prevented this.*

Natural enemies of timber pests

It might be thought that animals living the greater part of their lives in timber would be well protected against enemies but this is not always the case. Wood-boring beetle larvae fall prey to many species of parasite and predator, and when an attack by such beetles is thought to have died out on its own, this is very often the work of these natural enemies.

The occurrence of such animals should, in fact, provide a warning that there are timber pests in the house.

Chalcids
(Page 29)

Several species of small chalcids lay their eggs in the larvae of wood-boring beetles. They may directly hunt the larvae in their tunnels and one can often see these nimble little insects flying in and out of the holes in the timber, but some can lay their eggs through the timber with the help of their ovipositor. The chalcid larva lives as a parasite on the beetle larva and eventually kills it. There are records of up to 95 per cent of the beetle larvae in roof timbers being attacked in this way. When the adult chalcids emerge they often find their way out through the old exit-holes of beetle larvae or they may make their own very small exit-holes. The adult chalcids are attracted by the light and can sometimes be found in large numbers on windows (see p. 114).

Opilo domesticus
(Pages 25 and 104)

This beetle can often be found in a loft where wood-boring beetles are attacking the timber. The adult beetle kills and eats many of the adult wood-boring beetles.

Larva (much enlarged) of Opilo domesticus, *a voracious predator and one of the worst enemies of furniture beetles (Steen Rasmussen photo)*

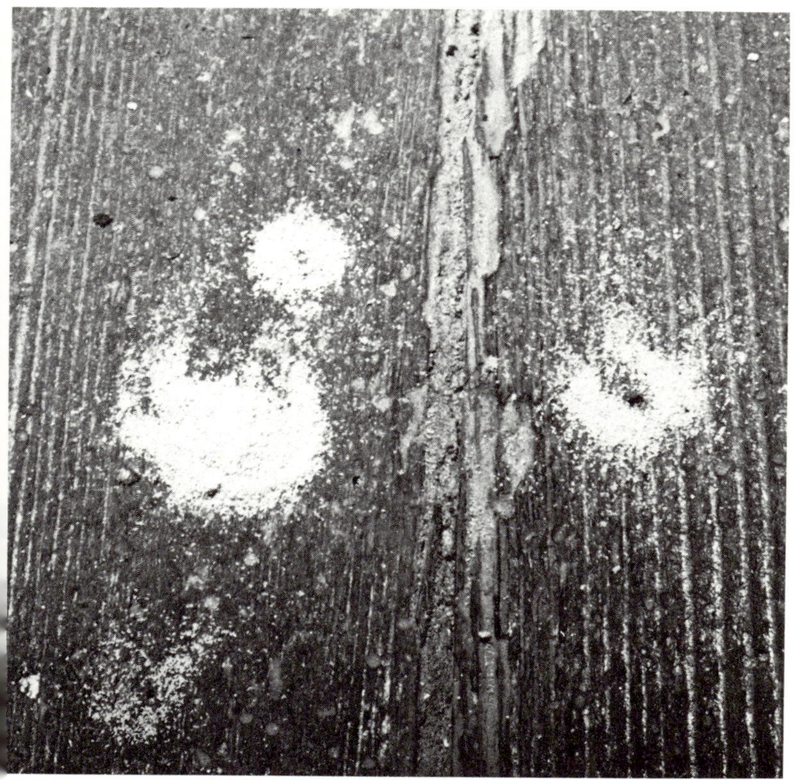

Small mounds of wood dust turned out by larvae of Opilo domesticus, *which hunt furniture beetle larvae, the so-called wood-worms, in their own burrows*

while its larvae hunt the larvae of wood-borers and house longhorns in their own tunnels. In doing so they have to dig their way through wood dust and in true mole fashion they eject this material through the exit-holes forming little 'mole-hills'.

Ant beetle, *Corynetes coeruleus*
(Page 25)

This beetle has very similar habits to the preceding species. Its larvae wander round in the tunnels and attack wood-boring larvae. They may also feed on the larvae of moths and larder beetles, for example in birds' nests, and like the copra beetles (p. 75) they are sometimes found on dry carrion.

Prevention of attacks by timber pests

The attacks of timber-eating insects can, to a large extent, be prevented by the same methods as are used in preventing fungal growths. For many timber pests only thrive in damp wood, which also provides the right habitat for fungi.

Normally it would not be an economic proposition to try to prevent all attacks by insects. In certain circumstances, of course, such as the replacement of timber in a building already infected, it would be worth impregnating the new timber under pressure or painting its surface with one of the many insecticidal preparations available on the market.

In the case of enclosed spaces, e.g. below some flat roofs, there should always be a means of access so that the structural timber can be inspected for possible traces of infection. It is usually advisable to avoid timber with bark edges, as in some forms of panelling. Several very common timber pests thrive in this type of habitat (p. 123 and p. 134). These would not normally cause damage in the sense of weakening the timber, but the adult beetles emerging from the timber often leave ugly holes in the panelling.

When repairing or modifying old property it is advisable to examine all the structural timber before it is enclosed behind ceilings or panelling, so that any necessary treatment can be carried out while it is still accessible. Sometimes money can be saved by using secondhand timber but if this is done it is quite essential to check that it contains no pests.

Control of timber pests

From the descriptions of the different timber pests it will be apparent that, in northern Europe, the only insects that warrant drastic measures are the house longhorn beetle *(Hylotrupes bajulus)*, which causes trouble in some countries, and in certain cases the common furniture beetle *(Anobium punctatum)* and the powder-post beetles (*Lyctus* spp.).

In attempting to control timber pests the difficulty is that the larvae, which account for by far the largest part of the population, are well protected inside the timber. They can be treated with gas or heat which penetrates the timber, or by spraying large enough quantities of insecticides.

Pests of timber can also be controlled by treating the surface of the wood with a contact insecticidal powder so that the beetles are killed when they emerge, and before they can mate and lay eggs. In many cases this would not be a very practical method because the timber would have to be treated over a period of several years owing to the long and varying duration of larval development.

For gas treatment the substances used are cyanide or methyl bromide. These gases have the ability to spread rapidly and to penetrate the timber. When the attack takes place in a house all openings (doors, windows, etc.) must be tightly closed before the treatment is started.

Smaller objects, such as furniture, can be taken away and treated in a gas chamber.

No insect can survive a temperature of 55° C for over half an hour, and this fact can be used in the treatment of timber pests. Provided they can withstand the heat small objects can be put in an oven at the appropriate temperature, in a steam bath (sauna) or in a carpenter's drying oven.

Roof timber can be treated with heat by piping warm air under pressure into the relevant space.

Treatment of infected timber with insecticidal liquids will normally provide the best answer to the problem. Numerous preparations of this kind are available on the market. It is essential that the timber should take up as much of the liquid as possible, and apart from spraying one can also inject the insecticide using a hypodermic syringe. It should, however, be noted that the wood worm holes show where adult furniture beetles have already emerged. Even so it may be worth injecting them as the liquid may then reach neighbouring holes containing live larvae.

Treatment of timber pests, particularly the house longhorn, is often such a serious matter that it is really advisable to seek professional advice, either from a government agency or from a commercial firm specializing in pest control.

In some parts of Europe, houses can be insured against the attacks of the house longhorn and if an insured house is attacked the insurance company has to undertake the necessary repairs and control measures without cost to the owner. Even though the responsibility lies with the insurance company it is nevertheless advisable to watch for the house longhorn because it invariably causes great inconvenience if the attack is widespread and a comprehensive programme of eradication has to be carried out.

FUNGUS IN TIMBER

Fungi are plants and therefore do not really belong in this book. Nevertheless they are often associated with animal pests and are therefore worth considering quite briefly.

There are several different species of fungus which attack timber in houses, but they only do so when the timber is damp. This may happen when timber is used before it has had time to dry out, but more often it is due to water coming in through the roof or from an overflowing drain, or through lack of ventilation.

Such fungi are most active when the timber has a water content of 30–50 per cent. Timber that has been attacked by a fungus is usually dark brown to black when wet. One of the common species is the yellow *Coniophora cerebella*.

DRY ROT is caused by the fungus *Merulius lacrymans* which can thrive in timber with a water content as low as 20 per cent, and once an attack has started the fungus can spread to dry timber, because it brings with it the water derived from the breakdown of the original damp timber.

Dry rot can spread several metres through cracks and over masonry and cement, which it cannot feed on, in order to reach timber. The fungus is also distributed by its spores, produced in millions, which cover the floor and furniture as a brown dust. The spores are also spread by the wind. Dry rot mainly attacks softwoods, but sometimes also beech and oak.

Many other fungi, known colloquially as moulds or mildew, attack timber through which they spread relatively slowly, without producing any fructification comparable to the familiar mushrooms and toadstools. It is interesting that quite a number of animal pests, mainly insects. will only attack timber that has already been attacked by fungus.

Certain dark mildew-like fungi produce a bluish discoloration of the timber. This occurs particularly in new timber with a water content of 50–80 per cent. The timber is not weakened mechanically.

Some moulds only grow as surface films, as for instance on wet timber and sometimes also on the inside of cold external walls where water condenses.

Prevention of fungal attacks

In order to prevent the attacks of fungi it is essential that all timber should be properly dried before it is used. Once it has been installed the next step is to ensure that there is adequate ventilation, particularly of roof spaces and of the space below the floor boards on the ground floor. Ventilation louvres should be installed and these should not be closed in winter.

Damp may also arise from leaking drains and gutters, and from condensation arising on the inside of external walls.

If such constructional measures are not sufficient to prevent fungal growth it may be necessary to resort to chemical treatment, using one of the numerous substances which render the timber unsuitable as a substrate for fungi.

Back of a door frame attacked by fungus. It is characteristic that the wood splits longitudinally and transversely.

The surface of the timber can be painted or sprayed with the chemical, or the wood can be immersed in it, if this is still possible. However, this will only protect the surface as the penetration of the chemical will be very limited, depending upon the type of timber, the nature of its surface and the degree to which it has been dried. The most efficient method of protecting timber is to impregnate it with the chemical, preferably under pressure, so that this reaches all parts. The heartwood of some trees cannot be impregnated but generally speaking this is protected naturally, e.g. in oak and pine.

Once the source of the damp has been traced and suitable countermeasures have been taken, it would be advisable to identify the fungus involved. This will usually involve consultation with an expert, although in some cases an experienced building craftsman may be able to help.

When dry rot has been identified it is essential that all the infected timber is removed and burnt in order to prevent the dispersal of the spores. In the case of panelling and floor boards it is advisable to remove about half a metre of timber beyond the infected area. Adjacent brickwork should be carefully cleaned and then scorched with a blow-lamp. Newly installed timber must, of course, be completely dry and it should have been impregnated under pressure.

The measures recommended above would apply in cases of serious attacks by other fungi, and here again the advice of professional experts can be sought.

Animals in Masonry and Insulation

There are no animals which actually feed on bricks, mortar or plaster, but there are many, such as woodlice, earwigs and spiders, which use the holes and cracks that appear in masonry as places to hide in or for laying their eggs. There are, however, some which actually dig their way into mortar.

Davies's Colletes, *Colletes daviesanus* (Page 29)

These are solitary bees (p. 180) which do not form true colonies although several may live close together. Like other bees they have a sting, but are not very aggressive. In the wild they live in chalk or clay, but they may also live in mortar if it is not too hard.

These bees dig cylindrical, horizontal tunnels in the mortar, but do not enter cavity walls. They nearly always choose a sunny aspect, and on the whole they are most active when the sun is shining. The diameter of the tunnels is about the same as a pencil and they are lined with a very fine, transparent material which is secreted by the bee's salivary glands. Each individual cell is *c.* 1 cm long and it is filled with a mixture of pollen and nectar. When it has been completed the bee lays an egg in it, seals it with a lid and starts on the next cell in the series. Normally there are 2–8 cells in each tunnel. The larvae which hatch from the eggs feed on the stored food, overwinter in the cell, pupate in the following spring and emerge as adult bees, usually in early July.

In normal circumstances the damage done by these bees is fairly restricted, but it can be annoying when plaster is being gnawed out the whole time, and in a serious attack when much mortar is being removed it may be necessary to take countermeasures.

Outside the period when the bees are flying (mid-June to mid-August) this can be done by simply scraping out the loose mortar together with the bee cells and larvae. If this is carefully replaced with a strong mortar containing cement it will not matter if some of the cells are still in place as any bees that emerge later will not be able to reach the surface.

On the other hand, if repair work has to be done during the period when the bees are on the wing they will need to be dealt with first otherwise they will be able to dig

A woodpecker hunting for Colletes *larvae has hacked away the mortar and exposed the bees' tunnels*

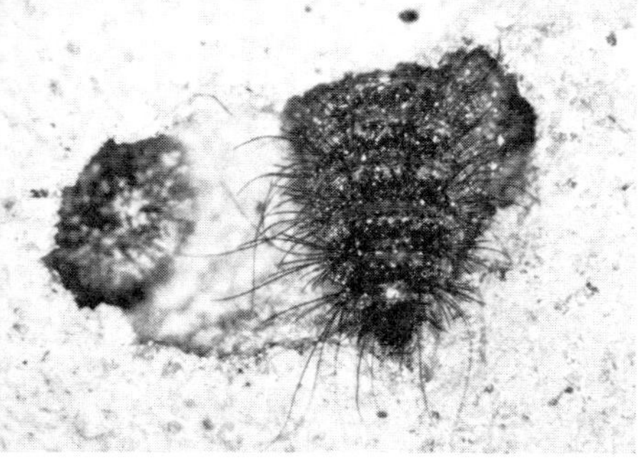

A larder beetle larva gnawing its way into the plaster on a wall, with only its rear end protruding

new holes before the mortar has hardened. Dusting the affected areas of wall with an insecticidal powder will usually solve the problem.

It should be remembered that even though the bees living in the mortar have been killed off there will always be a risk of a new attack so long as there are still areas of wall with loose mortar.

Now and again woodpeckers find out that there are fat, juicy bee larvae in the wall. Once they have learned the trick they will arrive and hack great craters in the mortar in order to get at the grubs. If one cannot tolerate this form of biological control it will be necessary to scrape out the larvae and make good the mortar.

Sparrows and tits often climb around walls searching for insects and spiders which they pull out of holes and crevices. Normally they do no damage to the wall, but sparrows and pigeons may peck lime out of the mortar and in some cases damage the bricks.

The larvae of dermestid beetles frequently gnaw their way into a variety of materials when they are about to pupate. It is rare for them to bore into plaster but they occasionally do so.

Glass wool used for insulation might not appear to be a very suitable material for building a nest in but in spite of this mice and rats will gnaw tunnels through it and construct their nests in it, thus reducing its effectiveness as an insulator.

Bumble bees may also establish themselves in insulating material, but the damage done will be local and not very serious.

When tufts of insulating material appear under the eaves it will normally be due to sparrows or starlings that have pulled it out to make a place for their nests.

Over the years house sparrows have damaged this masonry with their bills. The reasons for this type of behaviour are not known.

Animals in Thatch

Thatch is a very old roofing material that is still popular in some places. It not only blends well with the countryside but it also provides excellent insulation. As a result the house longhorn beetle *(Hylotrupes)* is unable to establish itself in the roof space below a thatched roof, which will not be warm enough for it during the summer.

However, one of the disadvantages of thatch is that it may be attacked by a variety of animals.

Caredrina clavipalpis
(Pages 24 and 105)

When a roof is newly thatched, whether with straw or reeds, thousands of grey-brown moth caterpillars may suddenly appear in the house.

In the wild these larvae live on grasses and reeds, and they reach the house in the thatching material. It is nearly always the fully grown larvae which appear in this way, as they wander out of the roof in the autumn to find a suitable place to spend the winter. Occasionally they gnaw their way into various materials where they retreat for the winter, and then pupate in the following spring and emerge as moths. The adult moths will not lay eggs again in the thatch, so the owner of the house experiences only a single generation and there is usually no need to take drastic action.

CRANEFLY LARVAE may also appear in thatch (p. 105). They normally live in damp earth, and so it is only in old, damp, mossy thatched roofs that they can thrive. They themselves do little damage in a roof that has already suffered, but it becomes more serious if rooks or other birds discover this source of food and start to pull at the thatch in order to reach the larvae.

House sparrows make nest holes in thatch and may badly weaken the roof

left] *The beech marten, which takes a toll of the birds and hedgehogs, may also seriously damage a thatched roof (Finn Kristoffersen photo)*
top] *Rat damage in a thatched roof, showing distinct runs between the holes (E. W. Kaiser photo)*

HOUSE SPARROWS (see also p. 84) often build in thatch. They pull out the straw and make tunnels in the roof, particularly in the eaves and along the ridge. The only effective, but not very attractive, method of preventing this is to cover these areas with galvanized chicken netting.

The BEECH MARTEN sometimes finds its way into lofts (see p. 188); it does not, however, occur in Britain. It is difficult enough to proof a house against martens and particularly so when it has a thatched roof. The marten tears holes in the thatch with its claws, and the edges of the holes are therefore frayed.

RATS (see also p. 88 *et seq.*) can also work their way through a thatched roof. In contrast to the beech marten they use their teeth and a hole made in thatch by a rat therefore has regular sharp edges.

Animals that Gnaw Metal

The outer casing or exoskeleton of an insect consists mainly of the tough, flexible material known as chitin, which is more or less strengthened with the horny material sclerotin. When completely hardened, as for example in the mandibles, this is the hardest material that the animal world has succeeded in producing. It is harder than lead, zinc, aluminium and copper, and this means that some insects are able to gnaw these materials.

The enamel on our teeth and on those of other mammals is almost as hard. It is scarcely so well adapted for gnawing hard materials, because it is relatively brittle. However, some rodents can gnaw the softer metals.

No animal will gnaw a metal for its own

[*top left*] *Exit-hole made in a lead sheet by the beetle* Criocephalus rusticus
[*top right*] *Lead roofing pierced by* Ernobius mollis, *because bark-covered timber has been used beneath it*
[*bottom*] *A lead cable damaged by house mice*

Metal plates fixed at the bottom of doors should be galvanized to prevent the entry of rats

sake, but they do so when for some reason it is in their way.

In some cases metal sheets are laid directly on timber and if the latter has been attacked by pests the metal may suffer damage when the adult insects emerge from the timber and gnaw their way out through the metal. The most serious damage occurs when a roof covering of copper, lead or zinc is laid on laths containing the larvae of wood wasps or of the beetle *Callidium*. The adult insects make large holes in the metal which allow damp to enter and the timber will then be attacked by fungus.

Wood-boring beetles may also work their way out through metal plates.

Insect pests of timber have been known to gnaw through electric cables and thus cause a short circuit.

Rats and mice also gnaw electric conduits, causing current failure, and they may do so even when the cables are protected by lead. They will sometimes gnaw food cans made of soft metals.

Sardine tin opened by rats, showing the marks left by the incisors

Animals that merely live in the house

Among the animals that live regularly indoors there are several which are interested neither in us personally nor in the stores of food and other commodities with which we surround ourselves. These include several animals that make use of the favourable conditions offered by houses. Some also use our houses as hunting grounds, feeding on the various invertebrate animals which they find there. As a rule these are animals which in the wild live in hollow trees, rock crevices or similar places.

Slugs

(Page 18)

These are molluscs which have lungs but no shell.

The yellow slug, *Limax flavus*, reaches a length of 7–10 cm, and is pale greyish with darker spots and a reticulate pattern.

Another species, the great slug, *L. maximus*, which sometimes enters houses, reaches a length of up to 15 cm. It is also greyish but often with a more reddish tinge, and the front part of the body is marbled, the rear part having dark stripes.

These slugs are found particularly in cellars and outhouses. During the day they normally remain hidden in damp places, but start to come out as the light fails. They are almost omnivorous, feeding both on plants and on dead animal remains. The eggs, which are very large, are laid during the summer in clumps under stones or logs where they are protected, and where it is damp.

Slugs themselves are quite harmless (but see p. 103), but they are annoying as they leave behind them a shiny trail of slime. This is normally a sign that it is rather damp, either in the room where the trail is seen, or in adjacent areas, such as the cellar or under the floor.

Slugs can also gain access to the house if the drains or outflows are faulty. Old lengths of piping which are no longer in use and which have not been removed or sealed off, will often provide good shelter for slugs.

Yellow slug, Limax flavus. *Opposite: Great slug,* Limax maximus, *with its slime tracks on a wall*

False scorpion, *Chelifer cancroides* (Page 19)

False scorpions have four pairs of legs and they move about very rapidly, both backwards and forwards. They can be found, for instance, in a pile of papers or books that has lain slightly damp for some time.

They somewhat resemble tiny scorpions because they have a pair of deadly pincers. When moving around false scorpions hold these up in front of them the whole time, and it is primarily the sensory hairs on the pincers which keep them informed about what is going on around them.

However, the pincers are not used solely as sense organs. In their lilliput world, false scorpions are voracious predators which hunt for any mites, springtails, booklice and other small invertebrates that come within their reach. Such prey is of course gripped by the pincers.

False scorpions also have venom glands which open at the tips of the pincers, and some species are evidently extremely venomous in relation to their size. They have been seen to bite prey considerably larger than themselves, and the prey has died immediately. However, they are never dangerous to man, for they are too small and cannot bite through the skin.

Several species are very common outdoors, where they live a sheltered existence under moss, among fallen leaves, and in similar places.

Some species are also common on dunghills where their prey includes the eggs and small larvae of flies. Sometimes they also attach themselves to the adult flies, not in an attempt to kill them or to suck their juices, but rather to use them as a convenient and rapid mode of transport to a new and tempting dunghill with fresh fly eggs and larvae.

False scorpions hunt mites and booklice

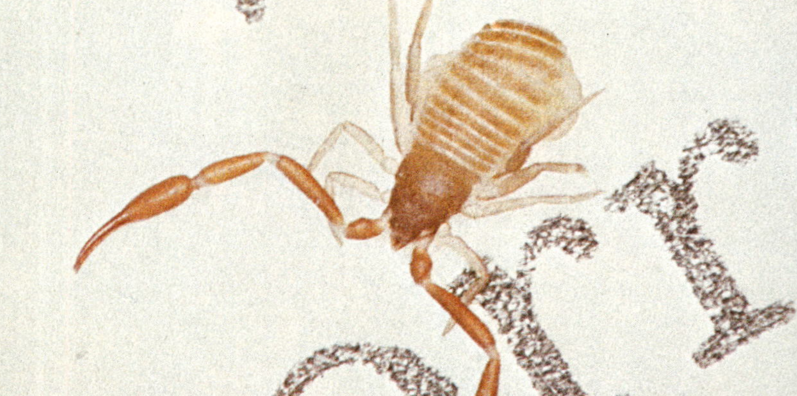

Harvestman on a cellar wall

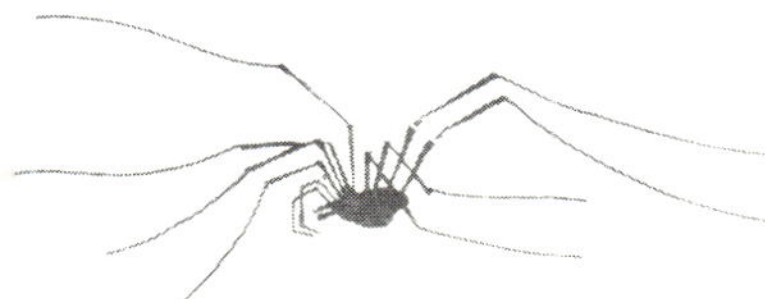

Harvestmen, Order Opiliones
(Page 19)

Harvestmen or phalangids are very easy to recognize by their small, circular body and enormously long legs. Two species, *Opilio parietinus* and *Phalangium opilio*, are very common in and around buildings, where they are active at night, searching for food.

Harvestmen live on many different kinds of food. They have been seen, for instance, to gnaw toadstools and pieces of cake, but they feed mainly on carrion and on any invertebrates they are able to overpower.

The method of hunting prey is rather like a game of blind man's buff. They move around their hunting area quite rapidly and find their prey by almost stumbling over it. The prey is seized with the tip of one of the supple, jointed legs and quickly transferred to the mouth where it is torn to pieces and thoroughly chewed.

Naturally, harvestmen themselves also run the risk of being hunted, and if they cannot hide or run away will sometimes cast off a leg which remains twitching on the ground long enough to distract the predator, while the harvestman runs off on its remaining legs. This is comparable with the tail-shedding of certain lizards, and it must happen quite frequently as many harvestmen are seen with fewer than eight legs.

Harvestmen have another method of defence, namely the production of an evil-smelling secretion from glands on the front legs. Even man, with his poor sense of smell, can detect this.

With its long legs the spider Pholcus phalangoides *resembles a harvestman. Its web is a tangle of very thin silk. (Steen Rasmussen photo).*

Spiders, Order Araneae
(Page 19)

Spiders are among the animals which some people find unplesant. Many untrue and misleading stories are told about them, but the truth is that spiders are venomous and that some species can be dangerous to man. This does not, however, apply to species living in the temperate parts of Europe.

Spiders play an extremely important part in keeping the populations of certain insects down to a reasonable level. An American spider expert has calculated that in many parts of the world man would have great difficulty in surviving, if there were no spiders to keep the insects in check.

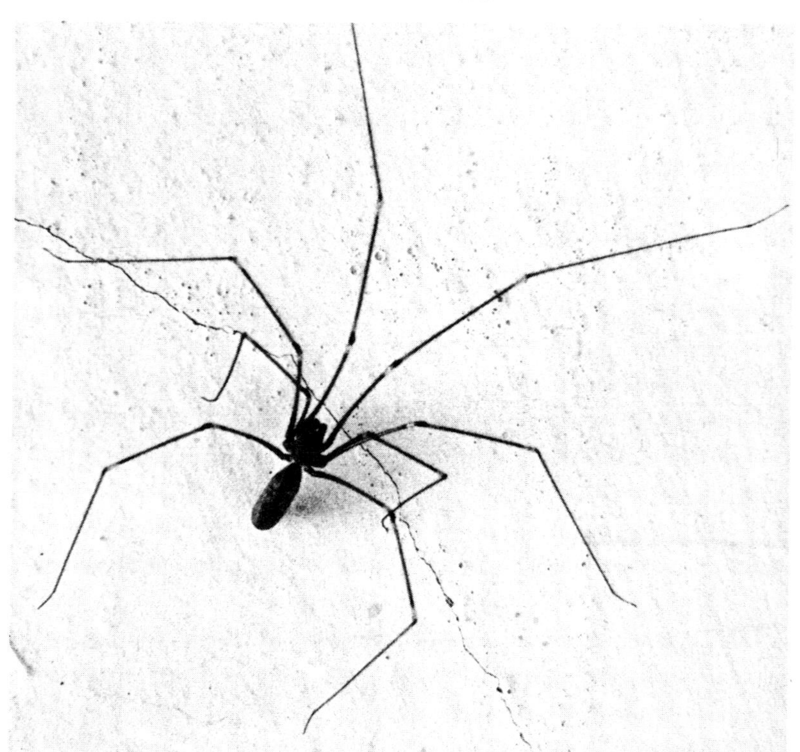

Common house spider,
Tegenaria domestica (Page 19)

This is one of the largest spiders found in Europe, and it also occurs in many other parts of the world. The body alone may be as much as 1 cm long and the long legs can give a span of 5–6 cm.

This spider can be found in all sorts of places where there is sufficient humidity, such as bathrooms and outhouses. It also occurs under the eaves of houses and in stone walls.

Unlike that of many other species, the web of this species is not a regular work of art, but consists of an apparently tangled mass of threads, often covered in dust. It is usually constructed in a corner and is then triangular, with the retreat hole where the spider lives right in the corner itself. The threads are not sticky, but when a fly or other insect lands on the web it tumbles around among the threads. This warns the spider which comes out and overcomes it.

Mating takes place in May-June and a little later the eggs are laid in a special cocoon, often covered with sand grains, which is suspended either in the web itself or in a suitable place nearby.

The common house spider, Tegenaria domestica, *an imposing animal which is sometimes taken to be a tropical bird spider*

Common house spider in its web

This very common spider can be found throughout the year. Specimens seen running across the floor are merely chance visitors, for they will scarcely be able to establish themselves in our living quarters, where the atmosphere is much too dry for them.

They have very poor vision and the best way to catch them is to hold an empty jam jar in front of them and give them a push from behind, and they will move straight into the trap.

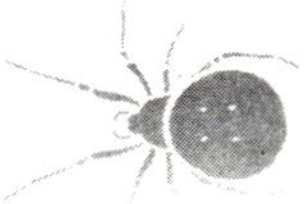

Steatoda bipunctata
(Page 19)

This spider is frequently seen in buildings, particularly outhouses, lofts and cellars. It is chocolate-brown, and the abdomen, which has a pale stripe across the front edge, shines as though oiled. The web consists of an open mesh with threads running either vertically or obliquely to the substrate. These threads are sticky at the ends which become attached to

Web of Steatoda bipunctata

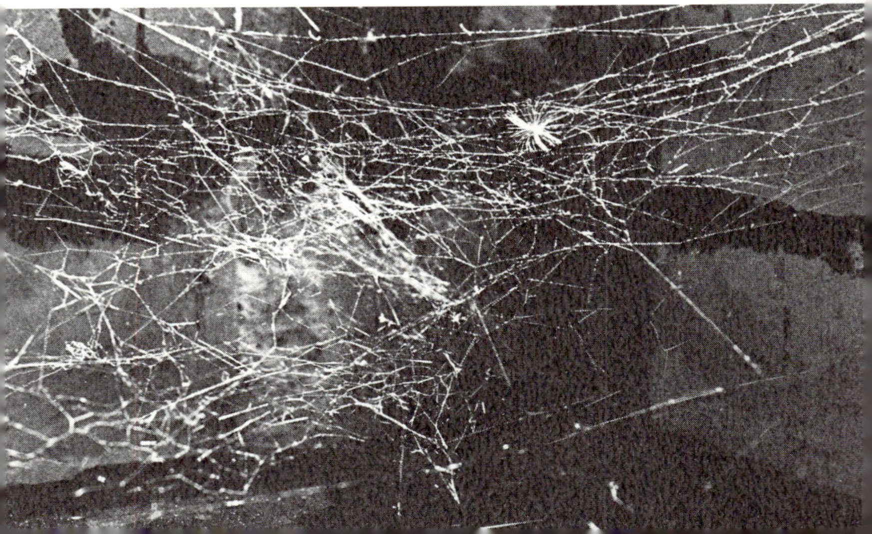

he substrate, and the web is thus adapted or catching the small invertebrates that un about there. The spider usually sits idden away in a crevice nearby. When small animal is caught in the threads he spider comes out, turns its abdomen owards the prey which it then envelops in a mass of sticky threads.

The eggs of this species are pink and they are laid in clumps of 100 to 150 which are attached by a fine thread of silk to a beam or similar object. They are protected by a sticky cocoon which envelops the egg clump without directly touching it.

teatoda bipunctata *with a fly which it has encased in a covering of sticky silk thread*

iniflo fenestralis
age 19)

common spider in cellars and outouses, on door-frames and walls; the eb is sometimes seen stretched across a indow pane. In addition to the normal three pairs of spinnerets, this spider (and many others) has an additional spinning organ, known as the cribellum, which has a large number of pores and has been likened to a sieve. The silk which emerges from the cribellum is combed out by the calamistrum, a row of small spines, on each of the front legs. This silk has a characteristic bluish appearance. The web is a tangle of threads firmly attached to the substrate.

The prey usually consists of crawling

Web of Ciniflo fenestralis *on a wooden garden wall. In the centre of the web is the hole in which the spider hides.*

invertebrates. When the net shakes the spider runs out, seizes the insect by a leg and drags it backwards into its retreat.

The eggs are normally laid in June. The female spins a spherical nest chamber in a sheltered place near the web and camouflages the nest with various foreign objects. In this completely enclosed chamber she lays her eggs and remains nearby, guarding them and taking no more food. In late summer old nests can be found from which the young have disappeared, leaving behind their egg cases and the empty casts from their first moult alongside the dead female.

Zygiella x-notata
(= Z. litterata)
(Page 19)

Spiders can build their webs in several different ways depending upon the species, but for most people a true spider's web will always be one of the elegant, circular, so-called orb webs, as spun by, for instance, the Common garden spider.

Zygiella x-notata is a smaller orb-web spider which is very common in the house, sometimes building its web in a window. The spider itself varies somewhat in pattern and coloration, but normally it is grey-brown with a greyish pattern on its abdomen.

In the circular web it is characteristic that a section is missing, and in this area the spider draws out a thread which leads to its hiding-place. This thread acts as a signal line.

The eggs are laid in a silk cocoon, sometimes in a corner. The cocoon, holding about fifty eggs, is flat on the side near the substrate, while the outer side is slightly arched. It is often covered with a dense tangle of white threads.

Web showing signal thread

'he stripes on a zebra spider serve as amouflage

:ebra spider, *Salticus scenicus*
Page 19)

ome spiders do not spin a web but hunt ieir prey actively. These include the hunt- ig spiders, and the zebra spider which is uite a small representative of this group an often be seen on the walls of a house, specially if the sun is shining. When a fly or other small insect lands nearby the spider's behaviour changes. It crouches down, turns the large, square front part of its body (the cephalothorax) with the four large and four small eyes towards the fly and starts to creep up like a cat. It does this so slowly that it may be difficult to detect that it is actually moving. When it is about a couple of centimetres away the spider makes a lightning jump and lands on the prey which it holds firmly with its powerful front legs and quickly kills with the poison-fangs or chelicerae. It is astonishingly skilful at outwitting the prey, but of course it sometimes misses its jump. Whatever happens it always lands again on the wall, which may seem strange, but there is quite a simple explanation. Like all spiders this species spins a safety line which it fastens to the substrate at regular intervals, and before it jumps it always takes care, like any other skilled mountaineer, that its line is properly attached.

zebra spider alongside its egg cocoon (Elvig Hansen photo)

House cricket, *Acheta domesticus*
(Page 20)

House crickets are closely related to the grasshoppers, and like them they have the hind legs modified for jumping. The adults are *c.* 2 cm long, and pale grey-brown with a black pattern on the head and thorax. They have two pairs of wings, of which the back pair is used for flying. At one time house crickets were associated with bakeries, but this is no longer so. Nowadays they are more likely to be found in warm ducts and in panelling behind heating installations, quite frequently in breweries.

House crickets often occur in new buildings and this is probably because such places provide good shelter and food, and half-finished houses are easy to enter. It is also possible that these insects may, in some cases, be brought in with building materials or packaging.

In northern Europe house crickets do not normally survive outside during the winter and most of them come indoors at this time. However, they can survive throughout the year, and will sometimes multiply in enormous numbers on refuse dumps where decomposing waste is producing heat.

They have a characteristic chirping which has been likened to the noise mad by very young chicks. In former time the cricket on the hearth was a familia 'domestic' animal, and a well-know character in many stories and fables.

It is only the male cricket that sings an he does so to attract the females. Eac male sits in its own little territory an sings, the actual sound being produced b rubbing part of one wing against the othe wing. The male also has a short, aggressiv piping note, which is heard when anothe male tries to enter its territory.

A love-sick cricket may sing for hours a time. One industrious zoologist foun that a single cricket chirped no less tha 42,000 times in a period of four hour Perhaps there are not many people Europe who now keep crickets, but ancient China the chirping was so high esteemed that the ladies of the Imperi Palace kept crickets in small golden cag on their pillows, so that they could fa asleep to the song.

Crickets feed on almost any kind organic matter. They prefer soft pla matter, but will also eat other insects ar carrion. On the whole it is true to say th crickets are quite harmless domes animals.

House cricket. The long ovipositor at the rear end shows that this is an adult female

The grasshopper Tachycines asynamorus *has an arched back, very long antennae and very powerful hind legs. It comes from the warmer regions of the world, but sometimes occurs in greenhouses in Europe (Elvig Hansen photo).*

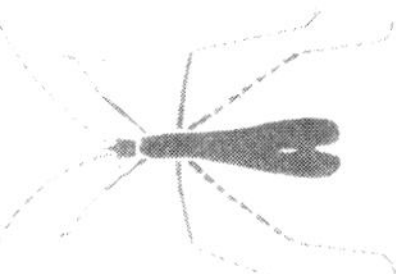

Empicoris culiciformis
(Page 22)

This is a reduviid bug (Order Hemiptera) which in spite of its very delicate appearance is an active predator. It frequents damp places, such as old walls, thatch and low herbage, where it catches small insects and feeds by sucking their body contents.

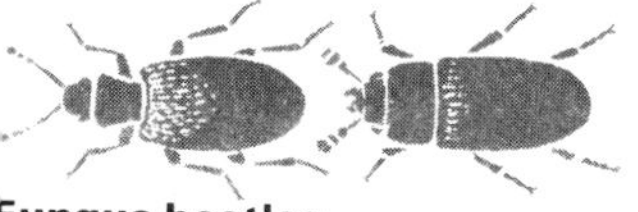

Fungus beetles
(Page 25)

This is a group of small beetles which have a somewhat unusual way of life. Both the adults and the larvae feed predominantly on moulds and they therefore live where these are to be found growing. They occur in cellars, outhouses and store-rooms where the humidity is high, and it is not uncommon for them to be seen in new houses, before the walls have dried out. They sometimes also live in damp parts of houses that are otherwise quite dry. For instance, if a cupboard is standing up against a cold external wall, mould may grow on the wall itself and on the back of the cupboard, and this will provide food for the beetles and their larvae.

Damp corn, hay or straw in a loft may encourage the multiplication of these beetles, and their larvae may then appear in their thousands in the rooms below, where they will be looking for a suitable place to pupate.

These beetles do not normally destroy anything, but now and again they may damage foodstuffs such as dried fruit.

The only rational method of control is to make the environment so dry that the moulds on which they feed disappear.

The first cell of a colony, built by the queen wasp

Queen wasp at the first cell of her colony

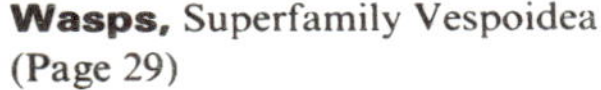

Wasps, Superfamily Vespoidea
(Page 29)

There are seven different species of social wasp in Britain and northern Europe, and they all have the same general appearance with the black-yellow barring, and the same habits. The wasps usually seen in or near houses are the common wasp *Vespula vulgaris*, the German wasp, *Vespula germanica*, and the hornet *Vespa crabro*.

In social wasps, as in many bees and ants, the characteristic feature is a division of labour within the colony. Among the wasps the queens and males are occupied with reproduction, while the workers build the nest, feed the larvae and defend the colony. Worker wasps are actually females with undeveloped reproductive organs.

Unlike the honey bee, wasps have not developed methods of storing food for the winter, and in temperate regions their colonies only last for one season. Each colony starts to break up in the autumn, and the workers die of cold.

However, before this has happened new queens and males have developed and these have swarmed out of the colony to mate. The males die soon after mating, but the young fertilized females search for a sheltered spot where they can spend the winter. Such dormant queens can often be found during the winter in lofts or outhouses.

The queens normally emerge from their winter quarters in mid-April and each one starts to search for a suitable site for its future colony. This may be a cavity in a wall, in a loft or under the eaves of a house. The queen starts the colony by building a spherical cell about the size of a walnut. Inside this she constructs 10–20 hexagonal cells and lays an egg in each. The eggs have to be attached firmly because each cell has its opening facing downwards. As soon as the eggs have hatched the queen is kept busy fetching food for the larvae, and after about a month (end of May) the first adult workers emerge from their pupae. The queen can now concentrate on egg-laying, while the workers take over the care of the larvae and the enlargement of the nest. Later in summer a successful wasp colony may hold 5,000–6,000 individuals.

Wasps can often be seen sitting on fences or telephone poles gnawing the timber. They chew the fine wood splinters with their own saliva to form a superior paper with which they construct the nest, both the outer protective casing, which comes to resemble an oval football, and also the hexagonal cells in which the larvae develop.

Each stripe represents material brought back to the nest by a single individual wasp

The larvae have an exclusively animal diet, consisting mainly of flies and moths which the workers can catch in the air. The wings of the prey are cut off by the workers' powerful mouthparts and the remains are divided up and chewed into round food balls, which are carried home to the larvae.

The workers themselves feed on liquid food. They can be seen drinking nectar from flowers and the juices of ripe fruit, and curiously enough they are also fed by the larvae. In exchange for fly flesh the larvae regurgitate a sugary liquid which the workers eagerly lick up. In addition to providing the workers with a form of energy this mutual feeding also has a social function, for it serves to bind the colony together.

During most of the summer, therefore, the worker wasps are kept busy maintaining the colony, and one sees surprisingly little of them, even when they have a colony in the house. By late summer, however, they stop rearing larvae and start to move around in search of sweet substances, and this is when they are noticed. They are usually just an annoyance but they can be a serious problem in bakeries, fruiterers and other food establishments.

In private houses wasps are noticed particularly when jam is being made, and during picnics. As they also visit carrion, dustbins and similar places they, like houseflies, may possibly spread disease.

They can also, of course, sting (p. 50) and in certain cases it may be advisable to exterminate a wasp colony when it has been built actually in part of the house. There are several ways of doing this, and two will be mentioned here. It is always best to undertake this task in the evening when all the members of the colony have returned home; also wasps are not so aggressive in the dark and when the temperature falls in the evening. If the nest happens to be in a place where it would be

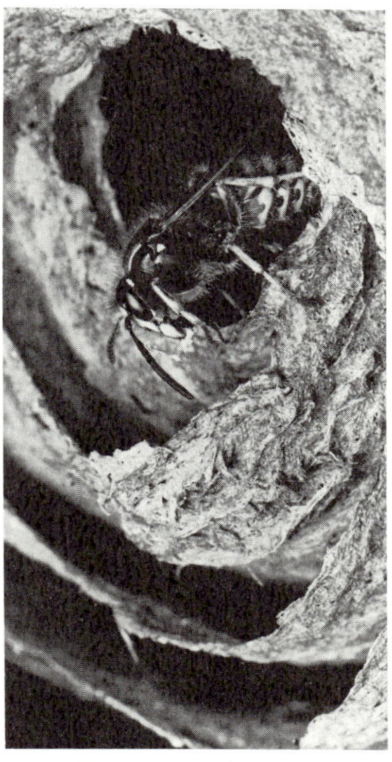

As the wasp net is enlarged it becomes enclosed in more outer layers of 'wasp paper', which provide good insulation (Elvig Hansen photo)

safe to set it on fire, then this would naturally be the quickest and most effective method of destruction. Alternatively, the nest can be carefully treated with an insecticidal powder, which should be blown into the entrance hole from below. In cases where the nest itself is inaccessible the powder should be blown into the cracks and crevices used by the wasps when flying in and out of the nest. It is not a good idea to stop up these holes, as the wasps are then quite likely to find their way into the house. In cases where a house proves to be a favourite nesting site for wasps it is always advisable to inspect it early in the summer and to destroy any nests before they become too large.

Light traps (p. 217) can be effective in catching wasps, e.g. in bakeries and food factories.

A wasp nest does not always hang free. Here a colony has been built in a lumber room between the wall and a mattress. The latter has been badly stained by the larval faeces.

Bees, Superfamily Apoidea (Page 29)

Honey bee, *Apis mellifera* (Page 29)

This is one of the few, if not the only insec species to have become a true domestic animal. The ancient Egyptians had beehives some 5,000 years ago. The importance of honey bees as pollinators canno be over-estimated, and their honey has always been much sought after.

Honey bees live in colonies with a highly developed social organization, which gc on from one year to the next. Each colony consists of a queen, a small number of males or drones, and a large number of workers, perhaps 10,000 to 20,000. As the central figure in the colony the queen is continuously fed and tended by the workers, as she concentrates on the production of up to 2,000 eggs per day. The work carried out by the individual worker bees depends largely upon their age. The first couple of days after emergence from the pupal state are spent in cleaning the colony. This is followed by a period in which the workers tend and feed the larvae. After this they turn to a period of constructional work, producing wax from special glands on the underside of the abdomen which is used for building new cells, and they also look after the pollen and nectar brought into the colony. The latter part of their lives is occupied in foraging for food to support the colony.

From time to time the workers build a few special large cells in which they rear new queens. As honey bees have evolved the habit of having only one queen in each colony the old queen usually leaves the colony when a new one emerges. A number of the colony's workers accompany her, forming what is known as a swarm which founds a new colony.

A swarm is usually taken by a beekeeper who provides it with a hive, but i is does not happen the swarm will re-ain wild. Originally honey bees probably uilt their colonies in hollow trees, but owadays a wild swarm may well establish self in a cavity wall, provided there is itable access.

The presence of a bee colony in such a tuation is not necessarily a disadvantage. n bright sunny days there will be a fan-stic amount of activity in and around the ole in the wall. Bees fly out and others turn home, heavily laden with nectar id with big masses of pollen on their nd-legs. A small number of bees are ationed at the entrance hole, keeping a ontinuous check on the traffic, and in-ecting those that are returning to the olony. These are guard bees who ensure at only the true inmates of the colony e allowed to pass, and if necessary they n call up reinforcements.

The bees fly off in all directions, ap-rently at random, but this is not actually . They can in fact tell one another where ere is a rich source of nectar. When a raging bee has found a good source, it turns to the hive and performs a special ance on one of the vertical frames that old the wax cells. According to its form is dance can communicate to the other orkers not only the direction in which ey should fly but also the distance of the ctar source. The type of flower con-rned is communicated by the scent hich still clings to the finder.

A bee has to visit up to 1000 flowers in der to fill its crop with nectar, and on a nny day it may make up to 10 foraging

trips. The production of a pound of honey would require 20,000–30,000 trips.

When observing bees it is best to keep a few metres away and naturally not to stand in their line of flight. Even though modern bees by selection over many generations have become remarkably peaceful, they may occasionally become aggressive (p. 51) and attack humans.

Bumble bees
(Page 29)

Unlike the honey bees, in which the whole colony survives the winter, a bumble bee colony only lasts for a single season. This means that all the workers die in the autumn, so that only a few young mated queens survive and spend the winter in hibernation.

The bumble bees seen in March flying low over the ground are usually these young queens, just emerged from their winter quarters, and now searching for suitable places in which to establish new colonies.

In northern Europe there are about 10 different species of bumble bee. The majority of these build their nests in the ground, in a deserted mouse hole or in between stones in a farm wall, but an empty nest box or a sparrow's nest under the eaves may also be used. The species which nest most frequently in houses are *Bombus lapidarius* and *B. hypnorum*.

Once the queen has selected the site she starts to build her nest. If the space is too small she extends it – up to about the size of a clenched fist – and lines it with dry plants, moss or mouse hair. She builds a couple of small, neat cells out of wax, each about the size of a thimble, one for stores and one to lay eggs in. The larvae which hatch from the latter are fed by the queen, who also has to fetch pollen and nectar.

When fully grown the larvae pupate and

Bumble-bee nest showing individual cells

a few days later they emerge as the first worker bumble bees of the year. They are sometimes very small, simply because their mother, the queen, has not been able to fetch sufficient food for them, but they now start to help with the building work and with collecting food, while the queen occupies herself more and more with egg-laying.

Later on in the summer a bumble bee nest is well established with larval cells and stores alongside each other. It does not have the regular cells and the neat arrangement characteristic of a honey bee colony, nor is it so large, having at the most 400–500 occupants.

Besides being rather attractive bumble bees are beneficial to man, as they act as pollinators of many fruit trees and other plants in which man requires the seed to set.

There is therefore every reason to conserve bumble bees and they would not normally be troublesome in a house. They can, of course, sting (see p. 51), but only do so when seriously provoked.

Solitary bees

There are about 200 different species of solitary bees in northern Europe. Although they may live gregariously, e. *Colletes daviesanus* (see p. 157), they a known as solitary bees because each i dividual female makes her own nest, la and tends her eggs and collects her ov food.

According to the species, solitary be may construct their nests in the ground, plant stems, in timber, or in buildin where crevices in masonry and woodwo offer good shelter. The nests may be bu of various types of material, such as mu plant material, or of substances produc by the bees themselves. The females fill t larval cells with pollen and nectar.

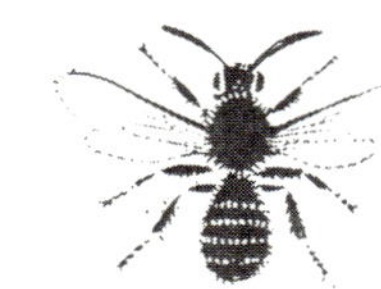

Patchwork leafcutter,
Megachile centuncularis
(Page 29)

This bee sometimes builds in the woo work of houses. It lines the cells wi regular oval pieces of leaf which it cu from plants with smooth leaves, som times roses.

The cells of the leafcutter bee are built fro pieces of leaf, and are often placed in o tunnels left by wood-boring beetles

mason bee using an old hole in masonry as
nest chamber

lason bee,
smia bicornis
'age 29)

nis is one of the solitary bees in which the st is built of mud, in a wide variety of es. On occasions the nest may be con-ructed indoors, possibly behind panel-g, in furniture or even in a key-hole, ovided there is constant access to the tside world.

Apart from the fact that it may some-nes block a lock with mud this is a mpletely harmless species.

e mason bee (above) has laid an egg and s closed the hole in the masonry with mud

A wax moth larva (Aphomia) *crawling on the brood's communal pupal cocoon*

Aphomia sociella
(Pages 24 and 105)

This is a moth which lays its eggs in a bumble bee nest, or more rarely in a wasp nest. There the larvae feed on any organic material, e.g. the wax cells and their content of nectar and pollen in a bumble bee colony, but they may also attack the bee larvae. When fully grown the moth larvae leave the nest in a body and in a sheltered spot nearby they then spin a communal cocoon, which may contain hundreds of pupae. These are commonly found, sometimes so firmly attached to the substrate that it is difficult to break them loose. The larvae may cause damage by gnawing the substrate to provide a suitable site for the communal cocoon, but otherwise they are completely harmless. The adult moths do not attack textiles or anything else in the house.

Each individual wax moth larva has gnawed its way into the underlay, in this case a plank

Bathroom fly,
Psychoda alternata
(Page 30)

These are small, dark flies which can sometimes be seen on the walls and in the basins in bathrooms and lavatories. They belong to a group known generally as owl midges.

Their wings are hairy and relatively large, but they do not fly particularly well. They move by a kind of hopping flight, or simply walk around.

The eggs are laid in the slime that accumulates in water-traps and outlets of basins. The larvae live in this coating of slime, which is continually damp but not covered with water the whole time, and they feed on any organic matter present and on bacteria, algae and fungi.

These little flies are naturally rather annoying to have around but they do not sting nor do they cause any damage. In the filters of purification plants they can be regarded as beneficial, because there the larvae help to break down organic waste.

In the house they are best controlled by removing the slimy deposit that the larvae live in. This can be done by pouring boiling water into the outlets and water-traps. A watch should also be kept on the overflows of basins as these provide excellent living conditions for the larvae.

Birds

Several birds have come to depend upon buildings when looking for a suitable nesting site. These are birds which have originally built on cliffs or in hollow trees, and each species chooses a position on the building which corresponds with its original nesting habits.

In most cases birds are regarded as welcome guests, and many give great pleasure. It should, however, be remembered that birds' nests may be the source of certain parasites and of some pests of textiles (see pp. 36, 41, 43, 45, 49 and 94 *et seq.*).

Swallow, *Hirundo rustica*

This familiar bird is very dependent upo buildings. It may nest inside a building, fc instance, under the roof of a stable wher there is continuous access to the outsid or it may build under the eaves.

The nest is in the form of a hemispher cal saucer of mud mixed with earth and little straw. Swallows are territorial, s there is usually a fair distance between th individual nests. They often return to th same nest year after year, and in Britai they usually start to lay in the middle c May.

They feed on insects, mainly flies, gnat midges, which are caught in the air.

Swallow's nest in a stable. Unlike the ne of a house martin this is a completely ope structure.

House martin, *Delichon urbica*

In the wild house martins build on cliffs but many make use of buildings. They always nest on the outside of buildings, often in small colonies, but occasionally there may be hundreds together. They build high up, rarely less than 3 m from the ground, and the nest which is constructed of mud is completely enclosed with a small entrance hole at the top.

The house martin normally builds outdoors, but may use a covered balcony

Swift, *Apus apus*

Swifts originally nested in hilly country, but they are now much associated with buildings, such as churches, silos and factories, where they build high up in sheltered, inaccessible places.

They arrive in Britain in late April and May and start to collect nest material. This takes place in the air, where they snap up scraps of dry grass, paper, feathers and anything else that is blowing around.

A pair remains together year after year, often using the same nest, which gradually accumulates a mass of material. Perhaps no other European bird spends quite so much time in the air, where it feeds exclusively, of course, on insects taken on the wing.

House sparrow, *Passer domesticus*

These familiar little birds are probably more dependent upon man than any other. They live in small colonies, and build their nests close together.

House sparrows are stationary birds, and after they have started to breed in a place they will remain there for the remainder of their life which may be 3–4 years. They use the nests to sleep in during the winter.

In March and April the breeding birds collect nest material, mainly dry grass, hair, feathers and scraps of paper, which they use to build their untidy, more or less spherical nests. A pair may rear two or three broods in the course of the summer.

House sparrows forage on the ground, often in flocks. The young are fed on insects, but the adults live mainly on seeds and in towns on household waste. In the country they frequently invade stores of grain and fodder. They cause serious damage to stored foodstuffs (see p. 84).

There are mixed feelings about having pigeons around. It may be attractive to have a pair walking up and down a cornice, but on the other hand they make an awful mess.

Rock dove, *Columba livia*

Wild rock doves build mainly on cliffs, often at a considerable height. The ordinary urban pigeons which nest on buildings in towns and cities belong to this species. They require very little nest material, and sometimes a nest consists only of a cake of droppings with a few straws or twigs. They start egg-laying quite early in the spring and may produce 2–3 broods during the season.

Domestic pigeons may cause considerable damage by fouling the buildings they nest on, and their nests provide shelter for irritating invertebrates which may then invade flats and annoy the occupants. They are also thought to be involved in the spread of certain diseases.

Various methods of controlling these ubiquitous birds have been devised, but most only work for a short time. The only efficient measure is to deny them nest sites by barring access to cornices, closing rooflights and so on.

Pigeon's nest on a balcony. These are very persistent birds, and if their nest is removed they will often start to build a new one.

In spite of the netting this pair of jackdaws has found a way down into the chimney. Below: Looking down into the same chimney a little later in the year (Elvig Hansen photo)

Jackdaw, *Corvus monedula*

In places without human habitation, jackdaws will build in hollow trees, but in towns and villages they find good nest sites on houses, and particularly in chimneys.

Kestrel, *Falco tinnunculus*

This bird of prey often builds on church towers in the country, and is by no means uncommon as a breeding bird in towns and cities, particularly in southern Europe. On occasion they also use the deserted nests of crows or magpies. They feed mainly on mice, but also take quite a few large insects, such as beetles.

Tawny owls often roost on buildings during the day (Elvig Hansen photo)

Owls, Family Strigidae

Among the owls that breed from time to time in buildings perhaps the best known is the barn owl *(Tyto alba)* which frequently nests in farm buildings or on church towers. In some areas the little owl *(Athene noctua)* will also nest in buildings, mainly in farming country.

Bats, Order Chiroptera

Bats, which are the only true flying mammals, are active by night, spending the day, and the winter, in sheltered places. Most of them probably live in hollow trees and caves, but some make use of buildings, where they are found mainly in lofts.

There are about a dozen different bat species in northern Europe, and of these the serotine *(Eptesicus serotinus)* and the pipistrelle *(Pipistrellus pipistrellus)* are perhaps the species most commonly found in buildings. Despite a certain amount of human distrust and aversion, bats are completely harmless lodgers, which neither gnaw nor in any other way damage the building.

In northern Europe bats feed on insects, which they catch in the air. When in flight they emit continual ultra-sonic sounds, which are reflected back to their ears by insects and other objects in the vicinity. Bats will bite if one tries to catch them.

They normally live in colonies, and if there are fifty or so in a loft they naturally produce rustling and piping sounds. It has been noticed that there is always a certain amount of unrest in a colony in the early evening, just before the bats fly out to hunt. Their droppings, which accumulate below their resting places, are somewhat similar to those of mice, but can easily be distinguished on closer examination (p. 209).

Bats can be driven away from a building if they are subjected to constant disturbance, or to strong-smelling substances such as naphthalene. However, they will often return and the only effective way of keeping them out of a building is to block all means of access.

Pipistrelle bat

Beech martens find easy access to lofts beneath an asbestos cement roof (Finn Kristoffersen photo)

Beech marten, *Martes foina*

In many parts of Europe (but not Britain) beech martens occur quite commonly on farms and in holiday houses in the country. They sometimes live in the lofts where they make their lairs in hay or straw, or even in the roof insulation. The 2–5 young are born in late April. The adults catch rats and mice, and also take quite a number of birds and their eggs.

Normally martens are not much seen, for they start to hunt about an hour or two after midnight, having first moved around the loft for an hour or so. They return home at 5–6 o'clock in the morning and go to sleep again, after another stroll. Apart from this habit of wandering around at night martens normally cause no great trouble. Sometimes, however, their droppings and the remains of their prey are a nuisance, and they also damage insulating materials when making their lair (see also under 'thatch', p. 161).

If martens do become a nuisance they can be driven away by laying down strong-smelling substances in the loft, such as naphthalene or ammonia. They are also sensitive to noise and will usually move off if continually disturbed over a period. Once they have been driven away their means of access must be blocked, otherwise new ones will quickly move in.

Beech martens are very skilful climbers, and they can get through gaps with a diameter of only 6 cm. They often find their way up to the roof by using espalier fruit trees, drainpipes or even large trees growing close to the house. Their route can sometimes be traced by the tracks or footprints they leave (p. 210).

Animals that come in for the winter

In temperate regions there is very little evidence of insect life outdoors during the winter. This is simply because the low temperatures render insects incapable of activity, and even if they could move around there would be nothing for them to feed on.

When autumn comes insects have to find sheltered places where they can spend the winter and for this outhouses and lofts are very suitable. They must also have reached a stage in their life history in which they can go without food and can withstand the unfavourable climatic conditions. The stage concerned will vary from species to species. Some overwinter as eggs, some as larvae and quite a few as pupae, e.g. cabbage white butterflies. There are others which spend the winter as adult insects, as for example lacewings, cluster flies and small tortoiseshell butterflies.

Lacewing, *Chrysopa carnea*
(Page 22)

With its large, translucent greenish wings, this is one of the most elegant insects. Seen in the right light the eyes shine like gold. During the summer lacewings live out in the open, flying silently around at night, and they are sometimes attracted into houses by the light. In autumn they start to look for a place to spend the winter, and some will then find their way into houses, and particularly lofts and outhouses. In the wild they spend the winter under bark or in similar sheltered spots. If their hiding-place becomes warm during the winter they will wake up, and this means that they will die quite quickly of hunger. If, on the other hand, the temperature remains low the lacewings will remain motionless throughout the winter, and will only wake up when it becomes warmer

Lacewing

in spring. In a house they will then try to move outdoors and they can then often be seen on window-panes, where they may die of hunger and thirst. If they do manage to get out they search for plants infested with greenfly and lay their eggs in clumps on the leaves. The larvae prey on other small insects, particularly greenfly. Lacewing populations fluctuate with the numbers of greenfly, and if the latter have been particularly abundant during the summer, large numbers of lacewings will be seen during the following winter.

Besides being attractive, lacewings are therefore beneficial insects, and they should not be destroyed. If they do happen to wake during the winter they should be moved to a cool place so that their activity stops, and in spring they should be helped to reach the garden.

Cluster fly, *Pollenia rudis*
(Page 31)

In many houses large, greyish flies may appear during the winter. In some places they may occur in their thousands, and constitute an absolute plague as they buzz around lamps and fall into the tea cups, and so on. These are the so-called cluster flies, which are actually related to the blowflies. They are not iridescent like the ordinary blowflies, but are more like large houseflies, and can be recognized by the numerous small, golden hairs on the thorax. Their life history is quite different from that of the ordinary blowflies, and they do not visit foodstuffs in the house.

They lay their eggs in the soil, and the newly hatched larvae bore their way into earthworms, where they live as parasites. During the summer the adult flies remain outside, often visiting flowers where they suck nectar. In the late autumn they look for a place to spend the winter and this is when they sometimes gather in large numbers on walls warmed by the sun before

A pair of cluster flies

they come indoors. They often gather in clusters in cool, unheated areas, including lofts. They have a tendency to return to the same house year after year, and they evidently prefer high-lying buildings. If the place they have chosen remains cool throughout the winter the flies will stay motionless until the spring, when they are woken by the warmth and move out into the light. On the other hand, if there is a warm spell during the winter these flies may become active and start to crawl around. This often happens when a holiday house is warmed for a spell during the winter.

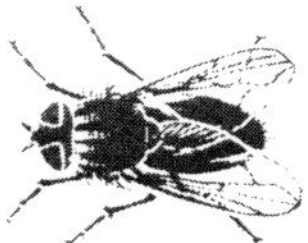

Musca autumnalis
(Page 31)

This is a relative of the common housefly, which it closely resembles, and indeed the two are difficult to distinguish. The eggs are laid in fresh cow pats in the fields and the larvae feed on the dung. The adult flies live around the cattle and are not seen indoors during the summer. In the autumn they sometimes enter outhouses and cool lofts where, like cluster flies, they hide away in cracks and crevices and remain inactive throughout the winter. In spring they become active again and move out into the open, but they may wake up in winter if there is a warm spell.

Indeed, it is not uncommon to see flies indoors during the winter. Sometimes these may belong to the two species just described, but in many cases they will just be common houseflies (p. 77). In northern Europe these do not overwinter in any particular stage. Many spend the winter in warm farm buildings, where they may breed throughout the year, and may therefore appear in the house even in the middle of winter.

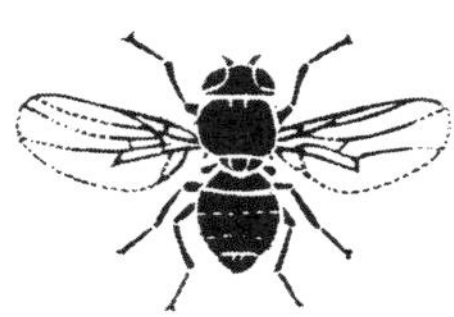

Thaumatomyia notata
(Page 30)

These are small, yellowish flies with black markings which enter houses in the autumn, sometimes in enormous numbers. They can easily be confused with vinegar flies (p. 80), but they are a paler yellow; they do not visit foodstuffs and, in fact, are quite harmless indoors.

These small flies will nearly always be attracted to the upper storeys of a house and very often to houses covered with ivy or Virginia creeper, for this type of dense vegetation is their natural habitat.

The larvae feed on various grasses.

Gnats and mosquitoes

These are normally summer insects (see p. 47 *et seq.*), but there are two species which are seen in winter, as they sometimes enter houses to spend the cold part of the year.

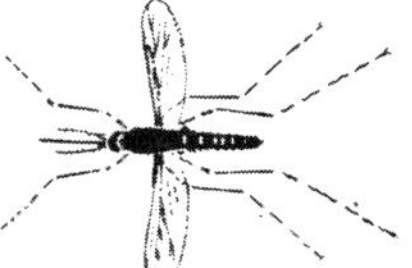

Theobaldia annulata
(Page 30)

This is a large grey mosquito with white rings on the legs. The fertilized females spend the winter in suitable cool places, but if disturbed they may wake up and even start to suck blood. In fact this is the species that is nearly always responsible for mosquito bites in the middle of winter.

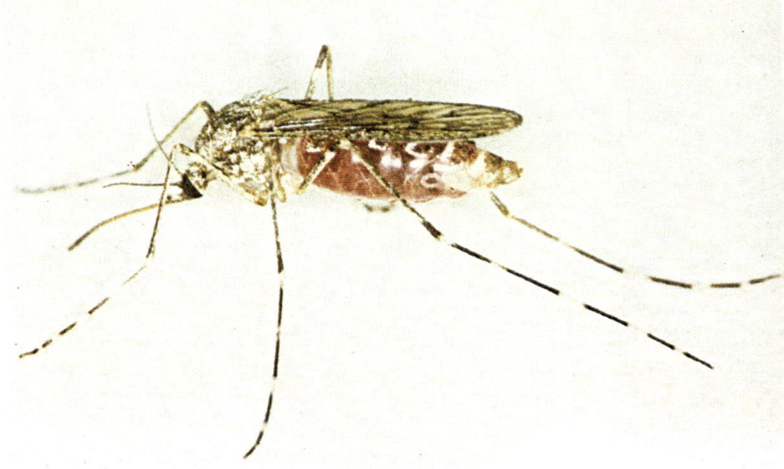

The large mosquito, Theobaldia annulata, *filled with blood*

Common gnat, *Culex pipiens*
(Page 30)

This is a small, brownish mosquito or gnat, often found spending the winter in large numbers in, for instance, damp cellars. Sometimes it will take to the wing during the winter if disturbed, but fortunately it seldom bites humans, evidently preferring the blood of birds.

Butterflies, Order Lepidoptera
(Page 24)

Butterflies sometimes spend the winter in houses, usually in lofts. The species that commonly do this are the small tortoise-shell *(Aglais urticae)* and the peacock *(Inachis io)*, which are seen in the typical resting position with the wings folded together over the back. They should not

Common gnat

Small tortoiseshell butterfly in its typical resting position with the wings folded on the back

be disturbed, for if they come into the warmth they will soon die. In spring many of the butterflies that have overwintered in the house will die because, being attracted by the light, they fly against the windows until they have used up their last reserves, so it is a good idea to open the windows and let them fly out.

Cabbage white butterflies, such as the large white *(Pieris brassicae)*, may overwinter, but in the pupal stage. These butterflies have more than one brood during the summer. The larvae of the last brood leave the plants they have been feeding on when they are ready to pupate. Sometimes roads and paths in the vicinity of a field of cabbages or swedes are alive with cabbage white caterpillars, searching for a sheltered place in which to pupate. They can be seen in their hundreds crawl-

Large white pupae together with the small yellow pupal cocoons of the parasitic braconid

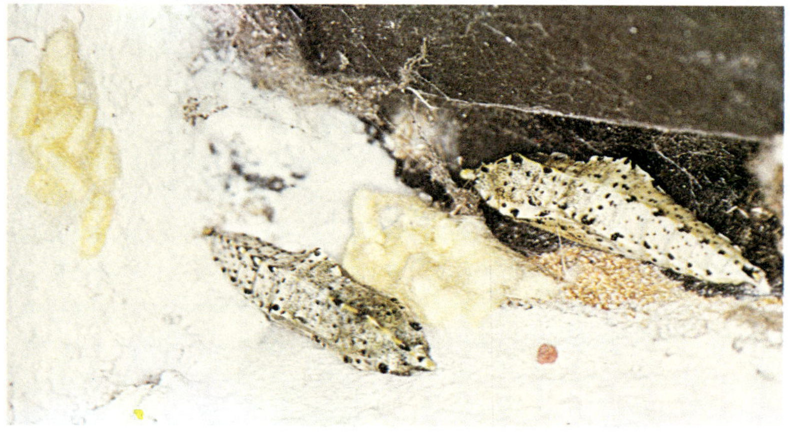

ing up tree trunks, wooden fences or the walls of houses. When a suitable place has been found each caterpillar makes a base of fine silken threads, and attaches itself firmly to the substrate with a loop around its body. The larvae then moults again to produce a hard, angular, immobile pupa (Page 24). These pupae can be found in houses and other sheltered places throughout the winter. The adult butterflies emerge from them in the spring and fly out into the open.

Sometimes, instead of pupating in the normal way, a cabbage white caterpillar will stop feeding and a mass of tiny larvae will crawl out of it; sometimes they come out of the butterfly pupa. These larvae will then pupate immediately, each in a tiny yellow cocoon (see photograph p. 193), alongside the now empty caterpillar skin or pupal case. They are parasitic hymenopterans known as braconids and they have developed from eggs laid in the living caterpillar by a female braconid. The larval braconids have simply eaten the whole contents of the caterpillar.

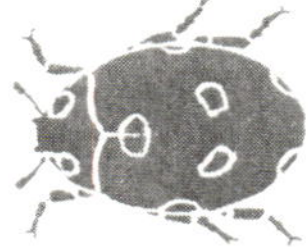

Seven-spotted ladybird, *Coccinella septempunctata* (Page 25)

In late summer ladybirds are often seen flying around in large numbers. They have come from the fields where the larvae have been feeding on aphids, and they gather in hedges and along the edges of woodland where they will spend the winter under bark or stones. They may also enter houses, where they are very commonly seen even in the middle of winter.

Wasps

Often when the loft is being cleared in

*A queen wasp just emerged from hiber nation. She has not yet cleaned the dust o*f *her body.*

winter one comes across a very drows*y* wasp hidden away in a well-sheltered spot This will be a hibernating young quee*n* (see p. 176).

Mice

When mice start to come into a house i*n* autumn they will usually be house mice wood mice or yellow-necked mice. Othe*r* species sometimes come indoors but the*y* usually do not survive very long.

For precautions to be taken to preven*t* such invasions see p. 87.

House mouse, *Mus musculus*

Many house mice spend the summer out i*n* the fields, but usually not far from houses Then from the middle of August onward they start to move indoors again, and th*e* peak of such an invasion will usually be i*n* the middle of September. See also p. 84 fo*r* more details on house mice.

Yellow-necked mouse, *Apodemus flavicollis*

Most yellow-necked mice spend the whole of the year out in the open, but some enter houses, usually later on than the house mice, about the end of October. They will eat stores of fruit in cellars or other places.

In the wild, yellow-necked mice feed on all kinds of seeds and they are very fond of hazelnuts and almonds. They are primarily woodland animals, which have spread to gardens and parks with scattered trees and bushes. They are common in many parts of Europe and also occur in southern England. The closely related wood mouse, *Apodemus sylvaticus*, is found throughout the British Isles and it also enters buildings in autumn.

A wood mouse, Apodemus sylvaticus, *on a kitchen shelf. Like its close relative the yellow-necked mouse, this species sometimes enters houses in the autumn (Elvig Hansen photo).*

Occasional Visitors

Many different animals may be brought into the house more or less accidentally, e.g. with fruit or flowers. It would be impossible to catalogue them all, but a few examples may suffice.

Grey worm, *Allolobophora caliginosa* (Page 18)

The principal external characteristic of an earthworm is the division of the elongate body into a series of distinct rings or segments.

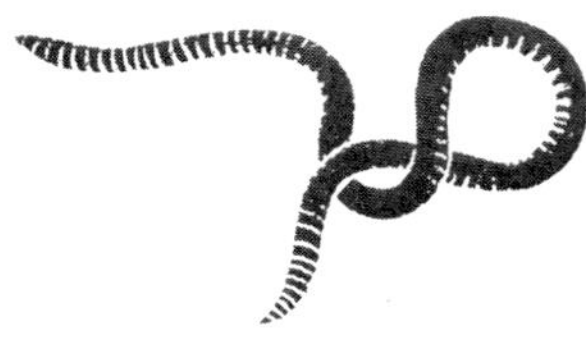

The skin of an earthworm is kept smooth and damp by mucus produced by glands in the skin. If, however, an earthworm is allowed to slip between the fingers it will prove to be very slightly rough, and if placed on a piece of paper one can hear a slight scratching sound as it moves.

In fact, each segment carries a few small bristles or chaetae and it is these that give the worm purchase as it moves through the earth.

In his book on earthworms published in 1881, Charles Darwin wrote 'It may be doubted whether there are many other animals which have played so important a part in the history of the world as have these lowly organized creatures'.

Earthworms are important because their burrows provide the soil with ventilation and drainage, and also because a they eat their way through the soil they mix the mineral components from the subsoil with the organic matter near the surface.

Earthworms only occur indoors a chance visitors. In certain cases they may appear in the lavatory pan, where they ar sometimes erroneously thought to be intestinal worms, but they can easily be distinguished by their possession of chaetae However, when they are seen in th sewage system they must have come i through a break, so their presence ther provides due warning that something i wrong.

Woodlice, Order Isopoda (Page 18)

The greyish, oval woodlice, somewha reminiscent of tiny armadillos, ar among the better known small crawlin invertebrates, and they have acquire many folk names. In Scotland, for instance, they are known as slaters.

Woodlice are the only crustacean which have become adapted to living exclusively on land. Other well-known crustaceans include lobsters, crabs, prawn and sandhoppers.

The relationship of woodlice to th other crustaceans is shown by the fac that the female carries her eggs aroun in a special brood pouch, and that the breathe by gills, which are in the forn of thin-skinned appendages on the legs.

Woodlice have to live in damp place for the gills can only function if they ar kept damp. The body does not have th waterproof, waxy outer cuticle charac teristic of an insect, and if a woodlous wanders into a dry room it will becom desiccated within a few hours.

Woodlice can gnaw wood that has been softened by fungal attack (Elvig Hansen photo)

These small crustaceans feed mainly on plant matter, but may also gnaw dead animals. Those that are seen in houses and cellars usually belong to the species *Oniscus asellus* and *Porcellio scaber*.

When large numbers of woodlice are seen indoors it means that the atmosphere is too damp. Sometimes several of them may find their way into a room or cellar, and these will usually be newly hatched individuals from a pile of old straw or withered leaves, or other garden refuse. They occasionally cause damage by gnawing fruit and vegetables stored in a damp cellar.

Centipedes, *Class Chilopoda*

These are predatory invertebrates which hide away by day and come out at night to hunt smaller invertebrates which they kill with the help of the powerful poison claws positioned on the first segment of the body. None of the European species are dangerous to man, but their venom is very lethal to their natural prey.

Lithobius forficatus
(Page 18)

This very common centipede can reach a length of 3 cm. It is easily found by turning over stones in the garden or by searching under loose bark. It sometimes occurs in compost heaps and outhouses, or in piles of dried leaves, and occasionally one comes indoors during its nocturnal hunt for prey.

Centipedes are very sensitive to desiccation so they do not survive long indoors, except in damp cellars.

Geophilus carpophagus
(Page 18)

With its long, thin, flexible body this centipede is well adapted for living in tunnels and holes in the soil. Now and again it may enter houses, probably during the night when hunting for prey.

These centipedes are seen particularly in the spring and autumn and their ap-

The centipede Geophilus carpophagus *on a damp floorcloth*

pearance may possibly be due to heavy rainstorms having driven them out of the ground.

They will soon become desiccated in a completely dry house, but in old properties, where they can find suitable damp hiding-places, they may survive for a long time and become a nuisance. They are sometimes seen in houses with thatched roofs, where they may possibly establish themselves in moss cushions on the roof or in the thatch itself.

These centipedes cause no damage in the house, they do not gnaw timber or anything else, but are naturally rather unpleasant when they occur in large numbers.

This centipede sometimes produces a luminescent secretion, whose origin is not fully understood. In the dark this secretion appears as a luminescent track.

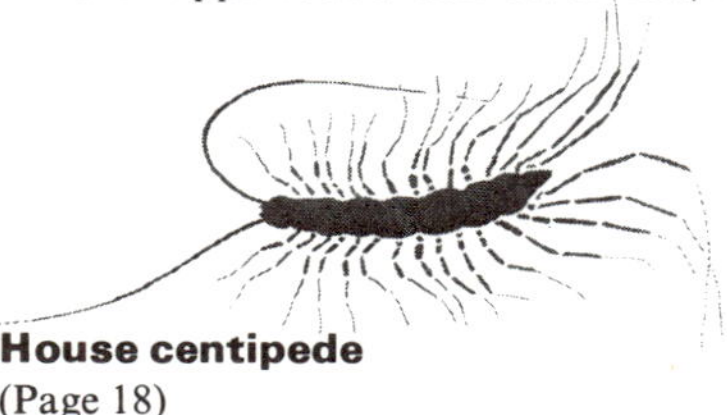

House centipede
(Page 18)

This animal has extremely long legs which are used as a kind of capture net when hunting insects and other invertebrates. It occurs naturally in central and southern Europe where it is frequently seen indoors, but is only found very occasionally in northern Europe, having been brought in from further south (see also p. 34).

Millipedes, Class Diplopoda
(Page 18)

Millipedes differ from centipedes in having a greater number of segments and in having two pairs of legs on each segment. In addition, they are peaceful vegetarians which are found, often in large numbers, in the soil, under stones and in similar dark, damp places.

There is no doubt that, like earthworms, they play a part in the breakdown of fallen leaves, and in mixing and aerating the soil.

Normally millipedes are not much noticed owing to their nocturnal habits but now and again they appear in large numbers, and sometimes stray into houses.

One of the species frequently seen indoors is *Ommatoiulus sabulosus* which reaches a length of 4–5 cm. It is dark and shiny with two yellowish longitudinal stripes down the back.

Millipedes cause no damage in houses or other buildings.

Bryobia praetiosa
(Page 20)

These are very tiny mites which sometimes occur in large numbers on the walls and windows of houses with gardens, particularly if the lawn comes close up to the walls. Their red colour often gives rise to the idea that they suck blood, but in fact they live by sucking the juices of green

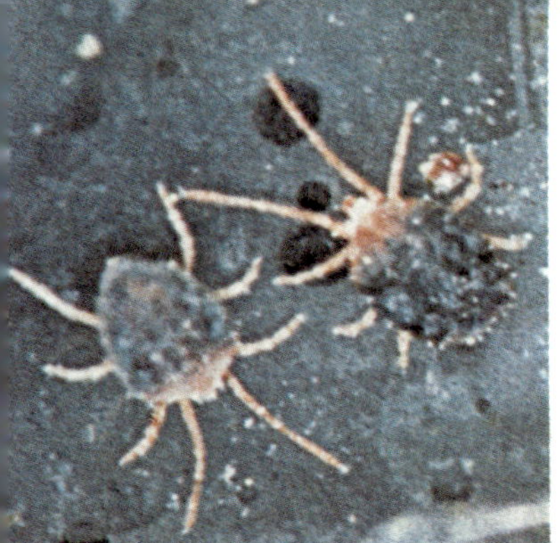

Mites (Bryobia praetiosa) *on a window-pane*

plants. During the course of their life they wander back and forth between the plants and suitable retreats on trees, rock or walls, where they lay eggs, moult and also spend the winter.

Normally they overwinter as eggs, and show no activity until the spring when the temperature rises about 7° C and the eggs start to hatch. They do not become really active until the temperature is considerably higher, and are often seen on walls facing south or west.

When the eggs hatch the young mites immediately move down to the grass to feed, but return to their hiding-place on the wall to moult after their first feeding period. This process is repeated three times, until the mites have become adult. The adult females also migrate, their feeding periods alternating with egg-laying periods. In this way the mites are sometimes seen indoors in large numbers, particularly in the spring, entering through cracks and crevices, and especially through the windows.

Males are never seen so the species must breed parthogenetically.

These mites cause absolutely no damage in the house and they very quickly die in the dry climate. They are completely dependent upon the presence of plants on which they can feed. Normally they are only seen in houses where the lawn goes right up to the walls, so the most rational method of control is to create a break between lawn and wall. This can easily be done by having a strip of gravel or stone chips $\frac{1}{2}$–1 m wide.

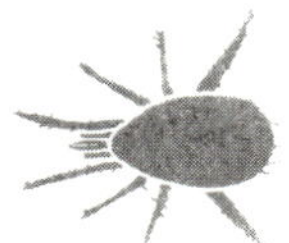

Gamasid mites
(Page 20)

These are very large, yellow-brown, active mites with long legs. Most of the species feed as predators on other mites and on small insects, but some, e.g. *Kleemannia plumigera*, feed on moulds. Now and again they occur in new houses that are still damp, or in lofts with damp hay or straw where they may multiply in large numbers, and find their way down into the house.

Springtails, Order Collembola
(Page 20)

In these tiny insects one of the abdominal segments has a forked appendage which can be jerked backwards, thus propelling the animal into the air.

They are usually greyish, but some species are bright green or black.

Springtails live in places with a high humidity and feed on decaying vegetation and on mosses, algae and moulds. Most of the species live in the surface layers of the soil where they may occur in populations of up to 2 millions per square metre. They can also be found in large numbers on dunghills and on the surface of lakes and pools. They often wander into houses for no apparent reason, either from compost, from decaying leaves in the gutters or from mossy roofs.

If they survive indoors in a house this suggests that it is too damp, as for example in some cellars. In rooms that are otherwise dry, springtails sometimes find suitable living conditions behind cupboards standing against damp external walls.

They cause no damage indoors but naturally they are annoying when present in large numbers. They do not bite humans, but they may produce an itching sensation when they walk about on the skin.

Thrips,
Order Thysanoptera
(Page 22)

These are very small, often dark insects, forming a quite distinct order. Each of the legs ends in a protrusible vesicle, and the two pairs of very narrow wings have hairy edges. In Denmark they are sometimes known as cholera flies. This is because they occurred in enormous numbers in Copenhagen during the cholera year 1853, and it was erroneously thought that they had some connexion with the disease.

Most thrips are associated with plants, where they feed on the sap.

They fly very well, but normally only take to the wing on warm, still days. They may then occur in enormous numbers and can be very irritating when they crawl around on the skin producing a tickling sensation, and because they have a tendency to creep beneath clothing and into ears, mouth and eyes. Although, as already mentioned, they are plant-suckers, their mouthparts can penetrate human skin.

Under certain circumstances thrips enter houses in large numbers. They have a special habit of creeping into narrow spaces and they are therefore found behind wallpaper and even behind the glass of pictures. However, they soon die in the dry climate of modern houses. The species usually seen is *Limnothrips cerealium*.

Earwig, *Forficula auricularia*
(Page 20)

Earwigs start to come into houses in late summer, seeking good hiding-places, for they are nocturnal animals which spend the day in sheltered places. These they find in abundance in the human environment, in the cracks and crevices of doors and windows, folded handkerchiefs, bath towels and so on.

By mid-September, however, they have mostly buried themselves in the ground where they spend the winter.

Earwigs mate in the autumn and the male and female often spend the winter together until early spring when the male is driven out. The female then prepares a brood chamber in the ground and lays *c*. 50 eggs in it.

The female earwig is very faithful and remains with her eggs, something which is very unsual in the insect world. She defends them valiantly against enemies, and keeps them clean. Without her care and attention they would be attacked by moulds and would soon die.

Even after the eggs have hatched the family remains together, but gradually the young move further and further away from the nest in their search for food. They become sexually mature during the course of the summer.

The common earwig is almost omnivorous, eating dead vegetable matter, live plants and carrion, and also catching small insects and mites. Earwigs may cause damage in gardens and nurseries for

The pincers of an earwig form a powerful weapon, but completely harmless to humans (Elvig Hansen photo)

they gnaw plants. On the other hand, they destroy many other plant pests, such as aphids.

Many people find earwigs repulsive, and one would need to delve into their subconscious to understand why. They have, of course, always played a part in folklore and in practically all European countries their popular name refers to their predilection for ears. 'The sweet innocence', says an earwig mother in one of Hans Andersen's stories about her son, 'His greatest ambition is to be able to creep into the ear of a priest. He is so touchingly childish, it gladdens a mother's heart'. The really gruesome stories tell how earwigs cut their way through the eardrum and lay their eggs in the brain. This is, of course, absolute nonsense, although it is true that an earwig may occasionally creep into an ear, as into any other dark corner.

The terminal forceps are used both for attack and defence, but mostly as a deterrent. Earwigs only nip humans when squeezed, as for example when one rolls over on them in bed. They may leave a tiny bruise, but the skin is not punctured.

The best method of avoiding a plague of earwigs is to deny them suitable living conditions close to the house. Luxuriant plant growth and compost heaps provide excellent quarters for them. The nuisance can be ameliorated by catching them in traps. Simply fill a flowerpot with peat or plant fibre and stand it with the bottom up. The earwigs will creep into the trap which can be emptied every morning.

Dusky cockroach

Ectobius lapponicus
(Page 21)

As already mentioned (p. 59) the cockroach species commonly found indoors come from warmer climates. On the other hand, the dusky cockroach occurs throughout Europe from Lapland to the Mediterranean. These small, active cockroaches live mainly in woodland and on heathland where they run around among vegetation on the ground; they also fly well. In Lapland they are very common 'domestic' animals in the tents and further south in Europe they may occasionally occur indoors. They are frequently seen in weekend cottages, mainly because these are often close to their natural habitat.

Cone bug, *Gastrodes ferrugineus* (Page 22)

This is an example of an insect which has nothing to do in a house, but which may be brought indoors from time to time. It is a bug that lives in coniferous forests where it can be found under the bark of trees. In winter large numbers of these bugs live in fallen spruce cones, and if a number of these are collected for decoration it is quite easy for the bugs to find their way into the house.

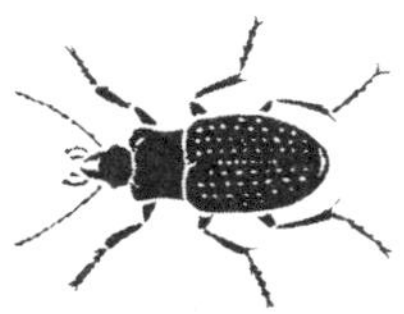

Carabus nemoralis (Page 25)

These are fast-moving, agile beetles with powerful legs and long antennae. The species normally seen indoors are 2–3 cm long and black or brownish. Only a few of them can fly, and in some species the elytra which cover the abdomen are fused together.

Most carabid beetles are predatory, feeding on worms, slugs and insects, and some species have been released in American forests to control injurious moth larvae. These beetles handle their prey in a characteristic manner, for much of the digestive process takes place outside the animal. They regurgitate dark brown digestive juices on to the prey, which is thus paralyzed. Its tissues gradually become liquefied and this liquid is then sucked up.

Carabids or ground beetles spend the day hidden among vegetation, under stones, behind loose bark or in similar places. Several species are very common in gardens and fields, and these may find their way into houses when they are running around at night in search of food. As they prefer damp places they are frequently seen in cellars.

Some species are partly vegetarian and in rare cases these may attack vegetables and fruit, and very rarely they have been known to gnaw textiles, but by and large carabids can be regarded as quite harmless visitors.

If it feels threatened a carabid may regurgitate on to a finger, and they also have another form of chemical warfare. If one is seized it will often produce a secretion with a sharp, sourish smell, which remains on the fingers for a long time. The secretion is produced by certain glands at the rear end of the abdomen; it contains various organic acids, and probably serves as a means of defence against attackers. Some mammals which normally eat insects are very sensitive to strong smells.

Devil's coach-horse, *Staphylinus olens* (Page 25)

This large predatory beetle is common in woodland, but is also found in gardens and sometimes enters houses when hunting for prey, usually small insects, slugs and worms.

It is easily recognizable by its size (up to 3 cm long) and by its dark colour. As is typical of the staphylinid beetles the elytra are very short, and in fact they only cover the foremost part of the segmented abdomen, while the remainder is therefore free and very mobile – somewhat resembling the abdomen of an earwig.

When threatened this beetle assumes a posture with the abdomen bent upwards rather like a scorpion. This is, however, an empty threat for the beetle can neither sting nor bite with its abdomen. What then is the function of this behaviour pattern? It is, indeed, a fact that some people are frightened by it, and it is quite likely that the beetle's natural enemies, insectivorous birds and mammals, are also scared by it.

When seized a staphylinid will naturally try to bite with its powerful mandibles, but they are not powerful enough to pierce skin, so from the human viewpoint this is a completely harmless insect.

Black vine-weevil,
Otiorrhynchus sulcatus
(Page 28)

This is one of the larger weevils. It moves around in a characteristic slow manner, and like all weevils it is vegetarian. The larvae live in the soil and feed on the underground parts of plants.

The adults avoid the light and hide themselves during the day, often in the surface soil at the base of a plant, but they emerge at night to feed. They attack many different kinds of plant and may cause considerable damage to fruit trees and bushes.

These beetles are sometimes brought indoors, usually with pot plants. If only a few are seen there is no need for concern. They cannot damage textiles or timber, nor do they bite or sting humans.

Cis boleti
(Page 26)

A great number of different animals may be brought into the house with cut flowers and other garden produce, and there is

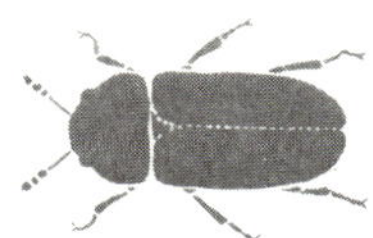

seldom any doubt about where they come from. It is however particularly annoying when a house or flat is suddenly found to be teeming with these small, dark beetles.

The larvae live in fungi of the type that grows on stumps and fallen trees, and that may be taken home for decorative purposes. The beetles emerge from the fungi through round holes, often long after the decoration has been put aside and forgotten, and one wonders where they have come from.

Some of the fungi which attack building timber have fruiting bodies (comparable to toadstools) which these beetles could live in, so if there is no more feasible explanation for their appearance, it may be advisable to have the house examined for fungus.

Hoverfly, *Syrphus ribesii*
(Page 31)

During the late summer of some years the house may be swarming with enormous numbers of rather attractive insects, re-

Hoverflies belong outdoors, but occasionally enter houses, where they are mistaken for small wasps

sembling small wasps. These are hoverflies which on a sunny day can be seen hovering almost motionless in the air, and suddenly darting off so quickly that it is very difficult to follow them with the eye.

Like all the true flies they have only one pair of wings, whereas the wasps with which they may be confused have two pairs of wings.

Their resemblance to wasps provides a good example of the phenomenon known as mimicry, in which a peaceful, harmless species may closely resemble another species which is dangerous or aggressive. Wasps can be said to be dangerous, and of course not just to man, and they advertise the fact by having a striking pattern of yellow and black which serves as warning coloration.

Over a period of perhaps millions of years certain hoverflies have developed a pattern of warning colours similar to that of the wasps. This has not been a conscious effort on the part of the hoverflies but is the result of natural selection over a long period of time, based on the principle that those hoverflies which resemble the model best will be less likely to be eaten. These will be the hoverflies that survive to pass their mimicking coloration to their descendants.

Hoverflies are sometimes seen perched on flowers, particularly umbellifers, for they feed on the flower nectar and pollen, and play an important role in pollination.

Their larvae are very effective consumers of aphids (greenfly), so in addition to being attractive hoverflies are also extremely beneficial, and with them in mind it may sometimes pay not to spray the garden with an insecticide.

When hoverflies come indoors it is simply because the house, with open doors and windows, acts as a large trap, from which they have difficulty in finding their way out.

Dronefly larva, *Eristalis tenax*
(Pages 31 and 105)

This is the larva of a hoverfly (Family Syrphidae), and it is not very well known, perhaps because it lives in drainage channels, in pools receiving water from dunghills and similar places with water that is grossly polluted with organic matter.

At its rear end this larva has a breathing tube which can be extended like a telescope to a length of up to 15 cm. With this organ it is able to reach the surface of oxygen-deficient water and breathe air.

When fully grown and ready to pupate the larva, often known as a rat-tail larva, creeps out on to the land and seeks a suitable dry place in which to pupate. In so doing it may enter porches or cellars. The

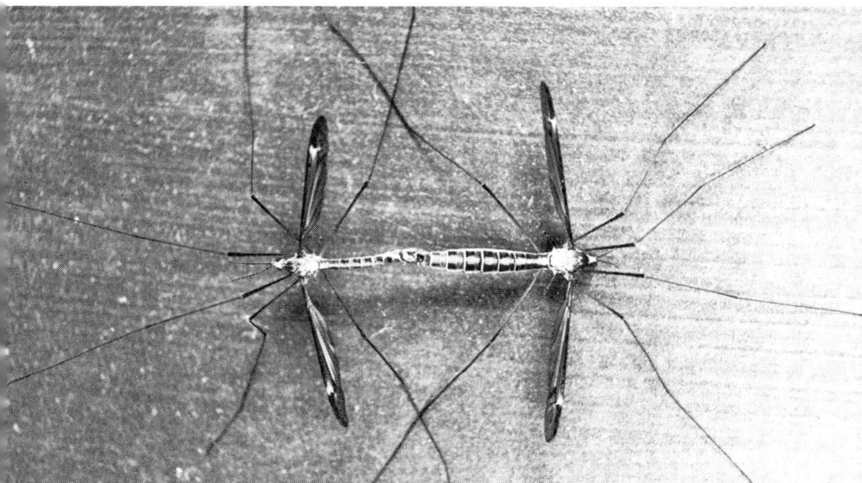

Craneflies mating on an internal wall form a decorative pattern

pupae are 10–12 mm long, grey-brown, almost oval, but they retain the long 'tail' and look somewhat like tiny grey mice.

From the pupa emerges a hoverfly, but unlike those already mentioned, this species is remarkably like a honey bee (see p. 31).

Some hoverfly larvae can live in carrion and these have given rise to the very old story that bees can come forth from the rotting carcase of an ox. The myth appears to have been old in the time of the ancient Egyptians where both the bull and the bee were sacred animals, and in somewhat altered form it found its way to the Bible where Samson, after having killed a lion, finds both bees and honey in the mouth of the rotting carcase. There are also numerous references to this phenomenon in Greek and Roman literature. The myth continued right up to modern times and the final explanation, namely that it referred to hoverflies, not bees, did not come until the 1880s.

The rat-tail larvae that find their way into the house are quite harmless, and the best thing is just to take them out again. If they continue to appear and start to become a nuisance, it would be a good idea to find out where they have come from and then drain the source, so that the adult hoverflies can find no stagnant polluted water in the immediate vicinity of the house in which to lay their eggs.

Cranefly, *Tipula paludosa*
(Pages 30 and 105)

Craneflies are among the animals which can cause panic in the bedroom when – attracted by the light – then fly in from outside and flap against the lampshades.

Craneflies are merely large flies. They do not feed as adults, nor do they bite or sting. The female lays eggs in the ground, where the larvae feed on vegetation, sometimes causing damage by gnawing the roots of plants.

As mentioned on p. 159, some craneflies can live in old thatch.

Faeces

It is not uncommon for the faeces or droppings of animals to be found before the animals themselves are seen. In some cases it will be possible to identify the species that has produced the faeces from their shape, colour and size, and from the conditions under which they were found.

Spider faeces are greyish-white and liquid when deposited, and they occasionally contain the remains of the prey's integument. They are found particularly under the webs, for example as spots on a window pane or as greyish stripes on walls. The faeces of spiders that live in houses are sometimes found behind pictures and cupboards, that is in places where there may also be bed bug faeces, but the latter will be darker.

Bed bugs deposit their black, blood-containing faeces in sheltered places (p. 44). They dry out to round spots which sometimes have a small 'tail' (see opposite page). They are extremely resistant and therefore very useful as signs to show whether bed bugs are or have been present in a house.

Fleas deposit their faeces as drops of more or less digested blood. They normally produce several such drops while they are sucking, thus leaving small red spots on the skin, clothing or sheets. Flea faeces can be found on the skin of dogs and cats as dark coagulated particles, about the size of a pin's head.

Louse faeces are firmer than those of fleas and are not absorbed by cloth. They are usually deposited as dark, roundish particles.

Fly faeces are similar in shape and size to those of bed bugs, but usually somewhat paler. Blood-sucking flies may, however, produce faeces that are almost black. Flies usually deposit their faeces out in the open and often on objects hanging from the ceiling.

Clothes moth larvae produce faeces which can be found together with their silken threads in the places where they have been feeding. They are almost spherical, and have the same colour as the material on which the larvae have been feeding.

The wood-eating larvae of furniture beetles, house longhorns, etc., deposit their faeces in the tunnels as what is known as frass. The appearance of this material may be a help in identifying the species which has been attacking the timber, but in many cases a microscope will be required to make an accurate identification on the basis of the shape of the faeces.

Wood dust of the common furniture beetle

Examples of faeces.
Top left: common house spider.
Top right: bed bug.
Bottom left: flies.
Bottom right: clothes moth larva.

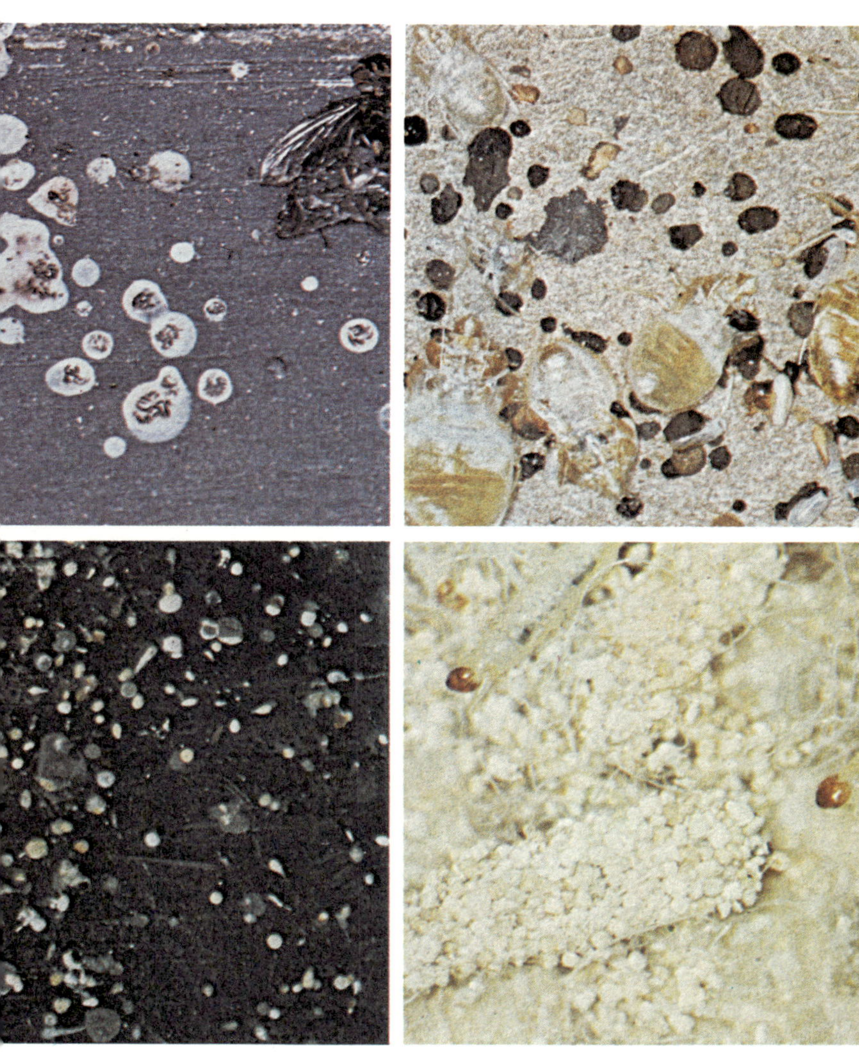

Cockroach faeces may, in the case of the rge species, easily be confused with ıouse droppings, although they are sually somewhat smaller. They can be istinguished by the fact that they are ıarked by longitudinal ridges and their ıds are more truncated.

House mouse droppings are cylindrical, ıd usually *c.* 6 mm long and 2.0–2.5 mm :ross.

Yellow-necked mouse faeces are rela-vely short and thick in comparison ith those of the house mouse.

Brown rat droppings are cylindrical, sually with blunt ends, and they are 17 mm long and 6 mm across, but the ze varies considerably according to the ge of animal. Brown rats have a ndency to use special latrine sites but ıe droppings may also be found else-here, frequently in a small pile.

Black rat droppings are shorter and ıinner than those of the brown rat, 10 mm long and 2–3 mm across, and 'ten slightly curved and pointed at the ıds. It is characteristic of black rats liv-g in a loft that their droppings will be attered over the whole floor, whereas ıder the same conditions brown rats ave their droppings in corners or along e walls.

Bat droppings may be rather like those mice, but they are much more porous, they consist exclusively of finely vided insect remains. The colour is rk brown to black, and the size varies cording to the species. These drop-ngs are often found in large heaps mediately below the animals' roosts lofts and cellars.

Beech marten faeces are normally 8–10 cm long and 1.2 cm across, cylindrical and usually twisted and drawn out to a point. The colour is dark grey or black (see p. 208). The contents include fur, feathers and bones. These droppings have a strong smell and the animals frequently establish special latrine sites on boxes or similar places, where large amounts of faeces may accumulate.

Bird droppings can be recognized by the conspicuous white urine which is deposited together with the faeces.

'amples of faeces.
p left: cockroach
p right: house mouse
ttom left: rat
ttom right: beech marten

Footprints

The tracing of footprints is primarily an outdoor pursuit, but even indoors it is occasionally possible to learn something from the track left by some unknown animal.

In mills and other establishments where there is always a certain amount of dust lying around tracks will often provide evidence of the presence of pests even though it may not always be possible to identify them with any degree of accuracy.

Insect tracks are a difficult problem, mainly because an insect has six legs and there is really no chance of identifying one from its tracks alone. The most that could be deduced would be an idea of its size, and whether it left distinct tracks as it ran around or merely a few signs of creepin, such as would be left by a larva.

Mice and rats have four well-develope toes on each fore-foot, while the con siderably larger hind-feet have five toes. I is not possible to differentiate the variou mouse species from their tracks, but mic and rats can be distinguished by their size

Beech marten tracks are oblong, an nearly always show the imprint of th claws. They can be easily distinguishe from the round tracks of a domestic cat which is the only largish mammal wit which they are likely to be confused. Se p. 188 for further information on beec martens.

Mouse *Rat* *Cat* *Beech marten*

Footprints of black rats on the floor of a grain store. The curving double lines are beetle tracks.

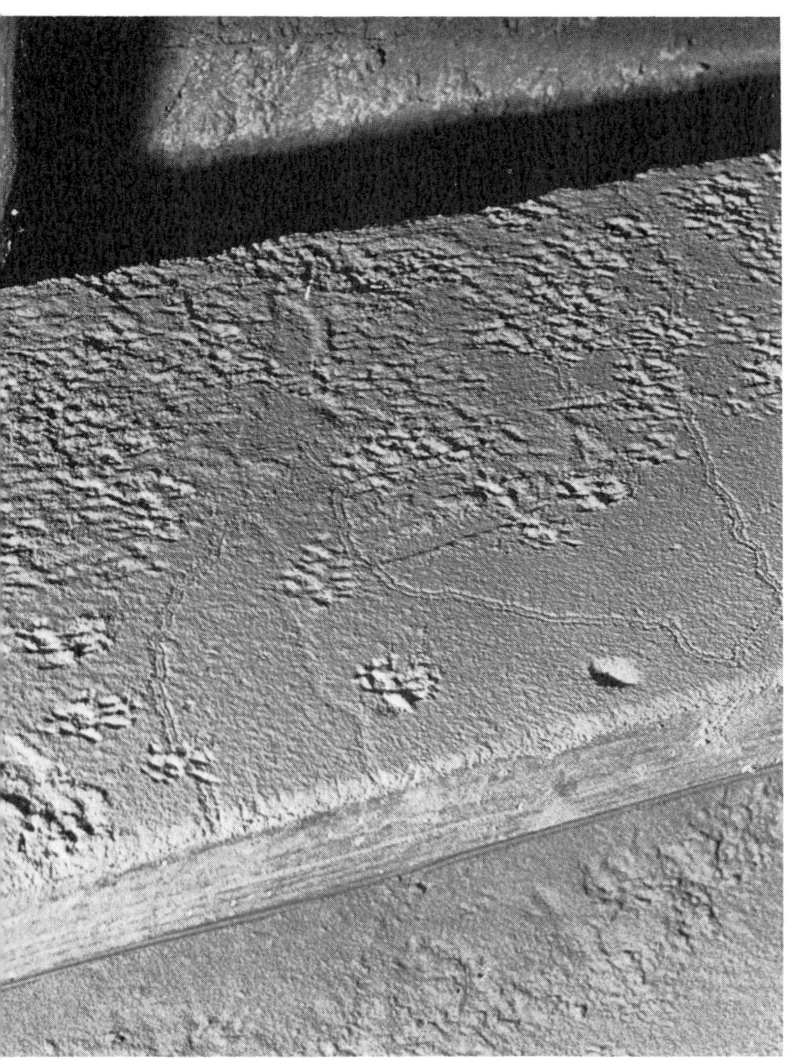

Scent

The sense of smell is not nearly so well developed in man as it is in most other mammals, but there are occasions when even man's olfactory apparatus is of some use to him.

This applies particularly in the case of foodstuffs. We are, for instance, very sensitive to the smell of decomposing food, but certain live animals also leave traces of scent.

Flour mites in flour or grain impart a sweetish, sickly smell to these foodstuffs, while the beetle *Tribolium destructor* produces a substance with a smell like lysol, and this will be particularly noticeable when infested goods have been kept in tight-fitting containers.

Cockroaches have a characteristic sweetish smell, but there have to be several of them before this becomes apparent, and normally they will already have betrayed their presence in some other way.

Most bugs produce a rather unpleasant smell. This comes from a secretion produced by special stink glands on the underside of the thorax, and a room housing several bed bugs will often have a close, sickly smell.

The jet black ant *(Acanthomyops fuliginosus)* which frequently builds nests in timber produces a not unpleasant, pungent aromatic smell, which sometimes enables one to find the nest by scent. Otherwise the insect pests of timber do not appear to have any characteristic smell, but the close, stuffy smell of mould in a house is an indication of damp.

Many carnivores produce an acrid smell and this will have been apparent to anyone who has crossed the tracks of a fox. In some parts of Europe the beech marten is a not uncommon visitor to the lofts of houses in the country and these produce a secretion from glands at the base of the tail, which has a typical carnivore smell. The marten produces this secretion when frightened, in exactly the same way as a skunk, and it serves as a scent marking, for these animals communicate with each other by scent.

It is a curious fact that the rank carnivore smell in a house has in some cases been found to come from lamp fittings made of bakelite, which owing to a fault in the manufacture give off a sharp smell when the fitting becomes warm.

Scent marking can also be carried out by urine and faeces, which in many animals have a characteristic smell. This happens, for example, in the case of rats and mice.

The smell of decomposition in a house can nearly always be traced to a dead mouse or rat underneath the floor, and this often occurs after poison has been laid down.

Sounds

Normally the presence of animals in a house will be confirmed either by directly seeing them or by finding their tracks. Sometimes, however, we can use our sense of hearing, as well as of smell.

The sounds made by animals are very varied and naturally these come mainly from the larger species. Most of us will have suffered insomnia due to a persistent mouse trying to gnaw its way through the skirting-board, or will have heard it playing hide-and-seek with its mates up in the loft.

On account of their size rats tend to make even more noise. They have a very disturbing habit of dragging large objects around at night, which has given rise to stories of poltergeists. The fact that rats are involved is betrayed by the shrieks and squeals which accompany their petty squabbles.

Beech martens in a loft also make noises, particularly if there is a female with a litter of large, playful young.

Bats can often be heard during the day as they move around in their roosts and disturb each other. In the evening they also make a certain amount of noise when they wake up and prepare to fly out.

In addition to these relatively large animals, some of the much smaller ones also betray their presence by the sounds they make. One has only to think of the irritating hum of a gnat in a darkened room, or of blowflies and wasps which are usually heard before they are seen.

The nests of wasps, bumble bees and feral honey bees produce a continuous humming sound throughout the day and night, and this sometimes sounds like the snoring of a large mammal. The sound

increases in volume when the insects are disturbed by vibration.

The noisiest sound made by an insect indoors is undoubtedly the singing of a house cricket. The males will perform for hours at a time from their favourite corner, and unfortunately mostly at night. However, the song has the advantage that it betrays their position, so that one can deal with the matter.

The larvae of many pests of timber can also be heard as they gnaw the wood. This has been likened to the sound of a nail being scraped across a piece of rough timber.

The larvae of wood wasps sometimes gnaw so loudly as to sound like a mouse.

Among the cerambycid beetles the larvae of *Callidium violaceum* and *Phymatodes testaceus* can often be heard gnawing beneath the bark. *Callidium* is particularly common in the bark edges of, for example, roof timber made of softwood, while *Phymatodes* occurs in fire logs of birch and beech. The larvae of the house longhorn can also be heard from time to time, particularly on warm summer days when they are most active and their appetite reaches a peak. Normally a larva will feed for 5–10 minutes in each hour and rest for the remainder of the time. The sounds of gnawing may be a great help in confirming that an attack is still active, for this is often very difficult to detect visually. Special apparatus, comparable to a stethoscope, can also be used for this purpose.

Many of the furniture beetles that live in timber also make their presence known by special sounds. These are the ticking sounds heard at night when the house is at rest. They are made, for instance, by death-watch beetles. The sound is produced by the adult beetle striking its thorax, in rapid succession, against the substrate. Both males and females make use of these sound signals, which probably serve to lead them to one another.

Some of the species of booklice that live indoors can produce tapping sounds, and this applies particularly to the winged booklice. Here again both sexes are calling to one another, and they produce the sound by tapping the abdomen against the substrate. They often appear to favour a position, such as an area of loose wallpaper, where the substrate is resonant, so that the sound produced is louder.

There may be a multitude of different sounds to be heard in most houses, and these can usually be traced quite quickly. Sometimes, however, these occur with such regularity that one is convinced that they must be made by some animal. Naturally the sound may emanate from one of the animals mentioned above, but in many cases it may be due to strains or tension set up by temperature changes in the central heating system or to the creaking of timber in furniture or elsewhere caused by periodic fluctuations in temperature and humidity.

On Animal Pests in general

One might get the impression that all the world's invertebrate animals are wholly bent on making life difficult for us, but in fact only a tiny proportion of them can be regarded as pests.

The insects are, of course, by far the largest group in the animal kingdom, and they also include the largest number of pests. It is estimated that about a million different insect species have been described, but far fewer than one in a thousand of these can be accused of causing damage or injury of one kind or another to man. And of course some insects are beneficial to man.

It is difficult to define exactly what an animal pest is. There are certain species which are exclusively adapted for plaguing us, and the body louse is a good example, but there are not many to which the term pest can reasonably be applied. It may be sufficient to say that some species under certain conditions may become so numerous as to encroach on some of man's interests, and must therefore be regarded as pests. This does not preclude the possibility that under different conditions they may be harmless, or possibly even beneficial.

In modern agriculture and forestry the aim of pest control is normally not to exterminate the pest animals concerned. In the majority of cases it will be a much sounder principle to reduce them to a level where the damage they cause can be tolerated, the actual level depending upon economic considerations.

It is rather more difficult to decide how many invertebrates can be tolerated in a home. Most people will not be concerned if there are a few flies buzzing around the lights or the odd spider in a corner of the garden shed, but it must be recognized that for some people the presence of a single invertebrate in the house is a traumatic experience.

Rat catching in the 16th century, a contemporary woodcut

Prevention

It is obviously not possible to exclude animals completely from a house. In most cases the most sensible course will be to hinder the entry of animals and, subject to technical and aesthetic considerations, to deny them suitable living conditions if they do succeed in gaining entrance. Fortunately, such measures will usually also promote general domestic hygiene.

Details on preventive measures have already been discussed in the individual sections of this book, but in general it can be said that all kinds of cracks, crevices and inaccessible spaces are highly undesirable, particularly in kitchens and canteens, for they allow the accumulation of dirt and the multiplication of pests where they will be most difficult to control.

Although the complete exclusion of all animals from a house is virtually impossible, certain simple measures such as fitting netting over doors and windows may be effective in keeping out flies, mosquitoes and wasps.

On a more technical level, insects can b excluded by a so-called air curtain. Thi involves setting up a current of air throug which the insects cannot pass.

Practically speaking, all insects an mites thrive best in places with a hig humidity and relatively high temperature Dry, cool storage of foodstuffs and clean ing without the excessive use of water ar therefore indicated.

Methods of treatment

Vacuum-cleaners. There is no doubt tha the daily use of a vacuum-cleaner is th most important method of keeping pest under control, and this applies both t private houses and to industrial concerns Many invertebrates are immediately kille and removed by vacuum-cleaning. As al ready mentioned, some pests thrive best i places where there is a deposit of dust.

Fly swats can be a useful weapon when only a few gnats or flies have to be dealt with.

Heat. Insects are sensitive to high temperatures and will be killed in half an hour at 60° C; this applies to eggs, larvae and adults. Thus, heating clothing will kill all vermin in it, and heating foodstuffs or wooden objects may also prove a rational method of treatment.

Cold. At temperatures below 10° C most insects stop moving and developing and they cease to lay eggs. However, even lower temperatures are required to kill them, and there is considerable difference in the tolerance of the different species. Insects that are adapted to a temperate climate tolerate much lower temperatures in winter than those from the tropics (see p. 189). It is perhaps fortunate for man that a large number of household and foodstuff pests have come from warmer parts of the world. These cannot survive the winter in an unheated room, and they will, of course, be killed by deep-freezing.

Light traps. Many insects move towards the light and most of them are particularly attracted by light with a wavelength in the ultraviolet part of the spectrum. This light is invisible to us and is sometimes known colloquially as black light.

Entomologists have for a long time used light traps for collecting moths and other insects, and in more recent years there has been an increasing interest in using this type of apparatus for insect control. Light traps operate in different ways. The light may come from electric bulbs or from tubes, and the capture mechanism may involve either sucking the insects into a container by means of an air current, or attracting them to an electrically charged grille which kills them by electrocution. The dead insects then fall into a collection tray.

It has been shown that light traps are very effective against wasps. When correctly positioned they can keep bakeries

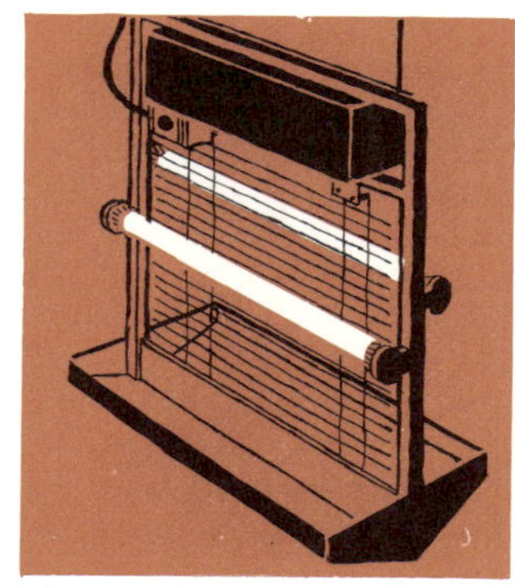

Light trap with grille

and fruit shops practically free of these insects. Blowflies and many smaller flies and gnats are also caught, but in most cases it has been found that such traps are not very effective in dealing with common houseflies.

Light traps are not suitable for catching mosquitoes and other irritating insects on verandas, in vegetable gardens, etc. A light trap set up in the garden will certainly kill a large number of insects but it will attract still more to the area, and of those killed the majority will be harmless.

Other traps. For rats and mice traps will usually be the most effective method of control (see p. 87). The old-fashioned sticky flypapers can still be obtained in some places, but nowadays most people would find them rather ugly. Cockroach traps appear at intervals on the market but hitherto they have not proved very effective.

Fly trap.
The flies are enticed below the trap by sugar or a similar sweet substance. When they fly up they are caught in the container and soon drown in the liquid.

Radio-active irradiation. Broadly speaking such irradiation can affect insects in three ways. A relatively weak dose will increase the rate of mutation, a somewhat higher dose will sterilize the insects, and a really high dose will kill them. Insect populations have been successfully controlled by releasing sterilized males in such large numbers that all the females mated with them and subsequently laid infertile eggs. This method would not, however, be suitable for insects in the house. Radioactive irradiation has been used in some places for controlling pests in cereals, but the method is seldom economically viable, partly because the amount of irradiation required to kill an insect is very large, in fact about 500 times more than a human can tolerate.

Biological control. The release of predators, parasites or pathogenic microorganisms, which keep down the numbers of pests, can be a very effective method of controlling agricultural pests. Domestic pests also have their natural enemies (see, e.g., p. 150) and possibly these could be used more effectively than they are at the moment. However, the problem is that in a house the need is for rapid and complete eradication, whereas natural enemies would normally only be able to keep the pest populations down to a certain level.

Chemical methods. When modern insecticides came into use at the beginning of the 1940s – DDT was the first – there was great optimism. These substances were effective against mosquitoes, flies, lice and fleas which spread disease, and against a wide range of plant pests, so that the earth's total production of food could start to increase.

These insecticides are still very important weapons in the fight against hunger and disease, and many of them are extremely effective when used indoors. It has, however, been shown that their use is not so free from problems as was at first thought. In part this involves the much discussed poisoning and pollution of the environment (see p. 220) and in addition

*'Biological control', one of the oldest known woodcuts (*c. *1420)*

it was soon shown that some animals can develop a resistance to the poisons (p. 220).

Insecticides are obtainable in a variety of formulations. Powders, for example, are very suitable for treating cracks and crevices. Sprays are used when it is not practical to have powder lying about. In spite of their high cost aerosol sprays have become very widely used during recent years for household purposes. The contents usually consist of varying solutions of insecticide together with a propellant which pushes the solution out in the form of a fine spray. Insecticidal lacquers are used, for example, against cockroaches and ants. Their active principles are very dangerous poisons but their formulation has been so designed that the poison cannot spread but remains where the lacquer has been applied, usually in strips along walls and floors. Furthermore, the poison does not all come to the surface of the lacquer strips at the same time, but comes out little by little, so that a single application may be effective for several months.

In view of the many other efficient methods of treatment the use of poison gas is now fairly restricted. Thus, gas can be used against insect infestations in cereals, foodstuffs, tobacco and various groceries, and also in mills where it is used as a matter of routine to get rid of flour moths. Gas is also used in ships to kill rats, in order to prevent the spread of disease.

Timber, furs and hides can also be fumigated with gas.

The commonly used insecticides can be subdivided into four main groups, according to their origin: 1) the so-called natural poisons derived from plants, 2) the chlorinated poisons, 3) the organic phosphorous compounds and 4) inorganic substances.

The most important plant poison is pyrethrum which is derived from a plant of the chrysanthemum group. It is not very poisonous to warm-blooded animals, but acts very rapidly on insects. Pyrethrum breaks down quickly when exposed to light and air, and it is sometimes incorporated in the insecticides that are used indoors, as it does not constitute a hazard to foodstuffs.

Pyrethrum, a relative of the chrysanthemum

Rotenone or derris, obtained from various tropical plants, is used particularly against vermin.

The chlorinated insecticides, such as DDT and lindane, are not particularly poisonous to warm-blooded animals, but the objections to their use depend on the fact that they break down very slowly. This, coupled with the fact that they are fat-soluble, means that they have a tendency to accumulate in the fatty tissues of animals. Chlorinated insecticides are incorporated in various ant powders and in certain timber preservatives where durability is required. Dieldrin is considerably more poisonous than the substances mentioned above, and its use is now mainly restricted to insecticidal lacquers and to some timber preservatives.

The organic phosphorus compounds include parathion which is extremely poisonous and must not therefore be used indoors. On the other hand, the substances in this group break down relatively quickly in nature and do not therefore present a serious pollution problem.

The inorganic substances used in powder form against insects include boric acid and kieselguhr.

Some insecticides have to be eaten by the insect before they are effective. These can be incorporated in the food, as for example when woollen goods are impregnated against clothes moths or timber against wood-boring insects, or they can be put in food supplied as a bait. Some insecticidal powders also act on the alimentary tract and the insects acquire these when cleaning themselves with their mouthparts.

Other insecticides work through the skin, as contact poisons. In fact, most of the modern synthetic insecticides (sprays, powders, lacquers) act in this way.

Gases work on the insects' respiratory system.

This division into categories is not completely sharp. Some of the alimentary poisons have a slight action as contact poisons, and most of the contact poisons are also effective when they reach the stomach.

RISKS OF USING POISONS

During recent years there has been much discussion about the risks involved in using these poisonous substances. In order to avoid misunderstanding it is important to differentiate between three main kinds of hazard. There is, first, the risk of acute poisoning. A substance may just be so poisonous that a small dose taken by mistake or as an oversight may prove dangerous. Secondly, there is the risk of chronic poisoning. Some substances are not particularly poisonous in small doses but are only broken down or excreted very slowly, so that a small daily dose may accumulate in the organism and eventually reach a level where it becomes injurious.

Thirdly, the excessive use of substances which break down slowly has given rise to fears that they may accumulate in the soil and in water and have an injurious effect on animal and plant life. Fortunately this problem is not serious in the case of pest control in the home.

The danger of acute poisoning is very small with the substances supplied for indoor use. However with insecticides being used in farm buildings, silos and grain stores, in the food manufacturing industry and in private households there is always a risk that small daily doses will add up to a dangerous level.

On Resistance

One of the weak points in using poisons is that some animals can apparently develop a resistance to them. This is not a question of a single individual becoming resistant during its lifetime. Within a large number of individuals, such as a population of flies, there will be numerous different combinations of hereditary material, and among these there will be some individuals with a genetic constitution that confers a greater degree of resistance to a given poison. There will be a tendency for such individuals to survive and to pass on this resistance to their offspring.

This ability to resist does not, however mean that the animals are in other respects superior to the 'old' types. On the contrary, it has been shown that dieldrin resistant cockroaches, for example, have a reduced breeding capacity compared with that of the originally sensitive cockroach population.

Resistance is normally developed only to the particular poison that has been used, or to poisons of the same type, e.g. the chlorinated poisons. In such cases it should be possible to find a substance with a different composition which will prove effective.

There is no doubt that the resistance of certain pests to poisons is a serious problem, but in many cases of unsuccessful treatment it has been shown that this was due to the use of incorrect methods. Sometimes a treatment is thought to have been unsuccessful because insects have been seen to crawl away apparently unharmed by the poison. This frequently happens and it is due to the fact that synthetic insect poisons act very slowly, and it may be several hours before the animals die.

WHERE TO GO FOR FURTHER GUIDANCE

Pests in houses and stores
The Environmental Health Department of the Local Authority should be able to advise on choosing one of the many firms specialising in pest control; some Local Authorities may carry out de-infestation themselves.

Fungal diseases
An estate agent/chartered surveyor or the local telephone directory will have the names and addresses of the many firms specialising in the treatment of woodworm, wet rot, dry rot and other fungal diseases.

Pollution of foodstuffs
Private individuals or retailers should consult the Environmental Health Department of the Local Authority. Manufacturers, wholesalers, farmers etc should consult the Pests Officer of the nearest region of the Ministry of Agriculture, Fisheries and Food.

Plant Diseases
The Plant Pathology Laboratory, Ministry of Agriculture, Fisheries and Food, Harpenden, Herts.

Index

BIBLIOGRAPHY

BUSVINE, J. R. *Insects and Hygiene*. The biology and control of insect pests of medical and domestic importance. Methuen, London. 1966.

JAWES, M. T. & HARWOOD, R. F. *Herms's Medical Entomology*. 1969.

MALLIS, A. *Handbook of Pest Control*. New York. 1960.

MATHESON, R. *Medical Entomology*. Constable, London; Comstock, Ithaca, N.Y. 1950.

MUNRO, J. W. *Pests of Stored Products*. Hutchinson, London. 1960.

SMITH, K. G. V. (ed.). *Insects and other Arthropods of Medical Importance*. British Museum (Natural History), London. 1973.